VOLUME 480 JULY 1985

THE ANNALS

of The American Academy *of* Political *and* Social Science

RICHARD D. LAMBERT, *Editor*
ALAN W. HESTON, *Associate Editor*

RELIGION IN AMERICA TODAY

Special Editor of this Volume

WADE CLARK ROOF
Department of Sociology
University of Massachusetts
Amherst

Ⓢ SAGE PUBLICATIONS   *BEVERLY HILLS   LONDON   NEW DELHI*

THE ANNALS

© 1985 *by* The American Academy *of* Political *and* Social Science

ERICA GINSBURG, *Assistant Editor*

Editorial Office: 3937 Chestnut Street, Philadelphia, Pennsylvania 19104.

For information about membership* (individuals only) and subscriptions (institutions), address:

SAGE PUBLICATIONS, INC.
275 South Beverly Drive
Beverly Hills, CA 90212 USA

From India and South Asia,
write to:
SAGE PUBLICATIONS INDIA Pvt. Ltd.
P.O. Box 4215
New Delhi 110 048
INDIA

From the UK, Europe, the Middle
East and Africa, write to:
SAGE PUBLICATIONS LTD
28 Banner Street
London EC1Y 8QE
ENGLAND

* Please note that members of The Academy receive THE ANNALS with their membership.

Library of Congress Catalog Card Number 85-050644
International Standard Serial Number ISSN 0002-7162
International Standard Book Number ISBN 0-8039-2482-8 (Vol. 480, 1985 paper)
International Standard Book Number ISBN 0-8039-2481-X (Vol. 480, 1985 cloth)
Manufactured in the United States of America. First printing, July 1985.

The articles appearing in THE ANNALS are indexed in *Book Review Index; Public Affairs Information Service Bulletin; Social Sciences Index; Monthly Periodical Index; Current Contents; Behavioral, Social Management Sciences;* and *Combined Retrospective Index Sets.* They are also abstracted and indexed in *ABC Pol Sci, Historical Abstracts, Human Resources Abstracts, Social Sciences Citation Index, United States Political Science Documents, Social Work Research & Abstracts, Peace Research Reviews, Sage Urban Studies Abstracts, International Political Science Abstracts,* and/or *America: History and Life.*

Information about membership rates, institutional subscriptions, and back issue prices may be found on the facing page.

Advertising. Current rates and specifications may be obtained by writing to THE ANNALS Advertising and Promotion Manager at the Beverly Hills office (address above).

Claims. Claims for undelivered copies must be made no later than three months following month of publication. The publisher will supply missing copies when losses have been sustained in transit and when the reserve stock will permit.

Change of Address. Six weeks' advance notice must be given when notifying of change of address to insure proper identification. Please specify name of journal. POSTMASTER: Send change of address to: THE ANNALS, c/o Sage Publications, Inc., 275 South Beverly Drive, Beverly Hills, CA 90212.

Origin and Purpose. The Academy was organized December 14, 1889, to promote the progress of political and social science, especially through publications and meetings. The Academy does not take sides in controverted questions, but seeks to gather and present reliable information to assist the public in forming an intelligent and accurate judgment.

Meetings. The Academy holds an annual meeting in the spring extending over two days.

Publications. THE ANNALS is the bimonthly publication of The Academy. Each issue contains articles on some prominent social or political problem, written at the invitation of the editors. Also, monographs are published from time to time, numbers of which are distributed to pertinent professional organizations. These volumes constitute important reference works on the topics with which they deal, and they are extensively cited by authorities through-out the United States and abroad. The papers presented at the meetings of The Academy are included in THE ANNALS.

Membership. Each member of The Academy receives THE ANNALS and may attend the meetings of The Academy. Membership is open only to individuals. Annual dues: $26.00 for the regular paperbound edition (clothbound, $39.00). Add $9.00 per year for membership outside the U.S.A. Members may also purchase single issues of THE ANNALS for $6.95 each (clothbound, $10.00).

Subscriptions. THE ANNALS (ISSN 0002-7162) is published six times annually—in January, March, May, July, September, and November. Institutions may subscribe to THE ANNALS at the annual rate: $45.00 (clothbound, $60.00). Add $9.00 per year for subscriptions outside the U.S.A. Institutional rates for single issues: $10.00 each (clothbound, $15.00).

Second class postage paid at Philadelphia, Pennsylvania, and at additional mailing offices.

Single issues of THE ANNALS may be obtained by individuals who are not members of The Academy for $7.95 each (clothbound, $15.00). Single issues of THE ANNALS have proven to be excellent supplementary texts for classroom use. Direct inquiries regarding adoptions to THE ANNALS c/o Sage Publications (address below).

All correspondence concerning membership in The Academy, dues renewals, inquiries about membership status, and/or purchase of single issues of THE ANNALS should be sent to THE ANNALS c/o Sage Publications, Inc., 275 South Beverly Drive, Beverly Hills, CA 90212. *Please note that orders under $20 must be prepaid.* Sage affiliates in London and India will assist institutional subscribers abroad with regard to orders, claims, and inquiries for both subscriptions and single issues.

THE ANNALS

of The American Academy *of* Political
and Social Science

RICHARD D. LAMBERT, *Editor*
ALAN W. HESTON, *Associate Editor*

——————— FORTHCOMING ———————

SOVIET FOREIGN POLICY IN AN UNCERTAIN WORLD
Special Editor: John J. Stremlau

Volume 481   September 1985

CHANGING PATTERNS OF POWER IN
THE MIDDLE EAST
Special Editors: Marvin E. Wolfgang and Thomas Naff

Volume 482   November 1985

RELIGION AND THE STATE:
THE STRUGGLE FOR LEGITIMACY AND POWER
Special Editor: Robert J. Myers

Volume 483   January 1986

See page 3 for information on Academy membership and
purchase of single volumes of **The Annals.**

CONTENTS

BOOK DEPARTMENT CONTENTS

SOCIOLOGY

ECONOMICS

PREFACE

To assemble a collection of articles on the present state of American religion is at once challenging and frustrating. For sure, it is challenging considering the renewed interest in religion in the 1980s and the controversies now surrounding its role in American public life; yet it is frustrating because of the vast number of themes and topics that should, but cannot, be covered in such a volume. The present collection does not attempt comprehensive coverage, but rather is limited to looking at the major religious traditions, and recent developments within them, that broadly affect the beliefs, practices, and outlook of millions of Americans. Hence we look primarily at the religious establishment today and not at its fringes, at the mainline churches and synagogues rather than cults and sects or other more privatized expressions of religious and spiritual ferment.

This more limited focus is justified. The vast majority of Americans claim some loyalty to the historic Protestant, Catholic, and Jewish traditions. Persons of virtually every persuasion—religious or otherwise—are influenced in one way or another by these majority religious cultures. Historically they have played a great role in shaping the values and norms, the life-styles and attitudes of the American people. So much a part of the nation's history, religious themes have molded the character of collective life and set the terms for public moral discourse. But some dramatic shifts in these historic patterns have occurred in recent times. There is good reason to believe that the decade of the 1960s was a watershed in American life, and that changes stemming from that time may have substantially altered long-standing relations between religion and culture. The late 1960s is remembered as the age of Aquarius and a time of countercultural new religions, and the mid- to late 1970s witnessed an evangelical, conservative religious resurgence. Consequently, by the 1980s the currents of change had rocked virtually all the mainline religious institutions, forcing them to adjust to new social realities, to grapple with unprecedented moral challenges, and to seek realignments of power and influence.

The articles assembled here address these currents of change, both within the religious traditions and in the relationship between religion and culture. The articles are organized around several major themes.

One theme is that of regrouping and reposturing. Martin E. Marty's lead piece on transpositions addresses the recent shifts in religious groupings, some of which would hardly have been anticipated even a decade ago. As his discussion suggests, the religious scene in America today is a whole new game—the same players but in quite new positions. Wade Clark Roof and William McKinney, concentrating particularly on denominational subcultures, examine the changing religious landscape since the 1950s. Both articles focus on broad changes in the nation's religious pluralism that cause the situation in the mid-1980s to be strikingly different, somewhat tense and unpredictable, yet also very interesting and full of possibilities.

A second set of articles looks at changes within the major religious traditions. Benton Johnson explores the loss of energy and influence within liberal Protestantism over much of this century. He attaches a good deal of significance to the legacy of Reinhold Niebuhr's thought and the attacks upon popular middle-class

9

religiosity in the 1950s as contributing to the current plight of liberal Protestantism. Phillip E. Hammond charts the curious path of conservative Protestantism, and especially the events of the 1960s as they play into its resurgence; moral and cultural issues figure significantly in its rebirth as a religious and political movement. Patrick H. McNamara focuses on two crucial aspects of change within American Catholicism—the erosion of authority and the current controversies surrounding the new activism on the part of bishops and church leaders. Throughout the discussions on liberal Protestantism, conservative Protestantism, and Catholicism, a common theme is that of modernity and religion's responses—accommodation or resistance—to it. With Jews and blacks, in contrast, the theme is that of group interests. Steven M. Cohen and Leonard J. Fein argue that there was a shift in American Judaism from integration to survivalism, pointing out that generational changes, liberal disillusionment, and international events have all led to new group concerns since the late 1960s. James Melvin Washington analyzes Jesse Jackson's 1984 bid for the presidency, examining the symbolic politics of black Christendom, its historic roots, and the heritage of ambivalence toward the dominant culture.

The next three articles concern aspects of religious change and continuity that transcend and cut across the various traditions. Robert Wuthnow inquires into the many reform movements emerging in recent times and emphasizes their role and significance in mobilizing commitment to popular religious causes. Barbara Hargrove, Jean Miller Schmidt, and Sheila Greeve Davaney look at changing roles of women and the implications, both social and ideological, for religious organizations. Both articles stress external cultural change and its impact upon religion. In a somewhat different vein, Samuel S. Hill looks at the religious regions of the country and finds, contrary to much thinking, that the religious distinctiveness of the regions persists in the face of much geographic mobility and mass cultural trends. Continuity in regional religious life is a welcome counterpoint to the usual emphasis on change.

A final set of articles addresses the public presence of religion in contemporary America. Peggy L. Shriver reflects upon the 1984 presidential election and the role of religion in providing a vision of the public good. N. J. Demerath III and Rhys H. Williams argue that the nation's civil-religious heritage, once a source of such vision, has lost coherence and is now a source of much discord and division. Unresolved national issues of religion and politics, civil faith and morality, pluralism and consensus all loom large in the discussions. In the closing article, George Gallup, Jr., reviews recent survey indicators on public and private faith and offers his comments upon the American religious situation at present. His data reveal strengths as well as startling inconsistencies in popular piety.

I would like to extend my appreciation to all the contributors for their superb cooperation in making this project possible.

WADE CLARK ROOF

ANNALS, *AAPSS*, **480**, July 1985

Transpositions: American Religion in the 1980s

By MARTIN E. MARTY

ABSTRACT: American religious forces and movements have been undergoing significant repositioning for decades. By the middle of the 1980s, however, public awareness of these transpositions has become widespread. The major religious event of the decade has been a transposition of forces, exemplified by the following: (1) secularists are in disarray, religionists have regrouped; (2) Protestant evangelical-moralism has become aggressive and culture affirming; (3) Roman Catholic leadership has interchanged position with mainline Protestantism with respect to the articulation of a social vision to its constituency and the public; (4) black religionists and Jews have interchanged position with respect to predictable public and partisan stands; (5) civil or public religion has been shifted to conservative and nationalist contexts; and (6) extraordinary religion has acquired an ordinary cast. Implications of these transpositions are appraised for the future.

Martin E. Marty, Fairfax M. Cone Distinguished Service Professor at the University of Chicago, is the author of numerous books including, most recently, Pilgrims in Their Own Land, *a history of American religion through 500 years. He is presently completing volume one of a four-volume work on twentieth-century American religion.*

RELIGIOUS forces are positioned. Spiritually, West complements East. Spatially, Islam abuts Christendom. Maps locate Southern Baptists 'and Canadian Anglicans, while Utah is a Mormon domain. Displaced European Jews repositioned their Judaism in Israel or in urban America. Religious movements are also positioned with respect to their status and roles. Many are privileged while others are treated as outsiders. Some support the political establishment; others are in positions of dissent.

American religious forces and movements have been undergoing significant repositioning for decades. Of course there are continuities: about the same percentage of the population believes in God, belongs to and attends church, and cherishes chosen denominations as it did at midcentury.[1] By the middle of the 1980s, however, public awareness of discontinuities due to shifts in place among the movements is widespread. It is possible to take advantage of this awareness by putting less energy into documenting the details of the changes and more into interpreting the moves. Seen in this context, the major religious event of the decade has been the transposition of forces.

CHANGING PLACES

To transpose, the Oxford English Dictionary reminds us, is "to alter the position of [a set or series of things]; to

1. The best depiction of American religious positioning is Edwin Scott Gaustad, Historical Atlas of Religions in America, rev. ed. (New York: Harper & Row, 1976); see esp. an attached colored map. For updating, see Jackson W. Carroll, Douglas W. Johnson, and Martin E. Marty, Religion in America: 1950 to the Present (New York: Harper & Row, 1979).

put each of (two or more things) in the place of the other or others, to interchange." Here are six examples.

Secularists and religionists

Secularists are in disarray, while religionists have regrouped. Of course, it would be wildly inaccurate to say that the secular dimensions of national society have diminished. The media, the academy, and most centers of power reveal an unreflective secularity to be in control. What has changed is the character of rationales. In colloquial terms, religions around the world have gotten their acts together. Whether in resentment or out of reasoned positive commitment, they have often become aggressive. Theologian Langdon Gilkey celebrated the two-century-old myth of progress with its promotion of democracy, science, and technology. He saw that it had functioned in American "social existence 'religiously,'" that is, as the ultimate formative and authoritative symbolic structure of our commonality."

Now, he went on, "the disintegration of this *secular* myth—not that of the traditional Christian mythos— . . . constitutes the present religious crisis of American Society."[2] Public philosophy, even where plausibly expounded, gains little hearing. Religion, from Iran through India and Ireland to Israel and Washington, bids stridently for attention and power.[3] The religious ratio-

2. Langdon Gilkey, Society and the Sacred: Toward a Theology of Culture in Decline (New York: Crossroad, 1981), pp. 23-24; see also the collection of 25 essays in Gabriel A. Almond, Marvin Chodorow, and Roy Harvey Pearce, Progress and Its Discontents (Berkeley: University of California Press, 1982).

3. Regarding aggressiveness, even of a lethal sort, on the part of religion in cultural complexes, see Harold R. Isaacs, Idols of the Tribe: Group

nales may all be wrong; indeed, being mutually contradictory, they cannot all be right. Yet they speak afresh to the passional sides of life, while the dispossessed keepers of the secular myth settle for relations chiefly with life's operative sides, by which I mean the practical running of things in spheres such as science, commerce, government, and daily affairs. Two two-century-long trajectories have begun to trade courses.

Protestantism: mainline versus evangelical-moralist

The privileged Protestant mainline has become passive or dissenting, while Protestant evangelical-moralism has become aggressive and culture affirming. During recent decades the heirs of colonial establishment—the Congregational, Presbyterian, and Episcopal denominations; of frontier achievement—the Northern Baptist, Methodist, and Disciples of Christ denominations; and of continental immigration—the Lutheran and Reformed denominations—ironically came to be called "mainline" at precisely the moment when their place was being challenged. They had long been custodians of the cultural lore, had had access to power all the way to the White House, and had occupied a privileged status in the national ethos, although not in law. They remained centers of experiment; for example, in these mainline churches feminist causes and agents keep getting their best religious hearing. But as early as 1972, with the publication of *Why Conservative Churches Are Growing*, National Council of Churches leader Dean M. Kelley was documenting mainline stasis or de-

cline. Exactly 10 years later, in the essay "Mainline Religion in Transition," Wade Clark Roof could take for granted such documentation and suggest how the mainline might find and meet new challenges in the future.[4]

Beneficiaries of the transposition, along with Mormons and several other latter-day American religions among the conservative churches of which Kelley wrote, were those Protestants who had often been regarded as culturally and societally marginal, despite their millions of adherents. Their earlier marginalization had been ironic, too, for they were heirs of another side of the very traditions to which the mainline Protestants also appealed. Though seen as old-time religion in the mid-twentieth century, these churches had often been experimenters and creators of novelty. Their ancestors were revivalists and innovators who challenged settled establishment and privilege as far back as the 1730s. Their parties were often called or devoted to the New Side, New Light, New School, or New Measures.[5]

Historians should not have been surprised at the recovery of this lineage,

4. Dean M. Kelley, *Why Conservative Churches Are Growing* (New York: Harper & Row, 1972); Wade Clark Roof, "America's Voluntary Establishment: Mainline Religion in Transition," *Daedalus*, 111(1):165-84 (Winter 1982). The best accounting for change is a collection, Dean R. Hoge and David A. Roozen, eds., *Understanding Church Growth and Decline, 1950-1978* (Boston: Pilgrim Press, 1979).

5. A succinct, if controversial, history of these movements in respect to their revivalist roots is William G. McLoughlin, *Revivals, Awakenings, and Reform* (Chicago: University of Chicago Press, 1978), esp. pp. 5-24. See also McLoughlin's suggestion, depending upon an insight of Anthony F. C. Wallace's, that what we are seeing today may be only an early "nativist or traditionalist" stage in revitalization. Ibid., p. 14. I believe we are seeing a longer-term global trend.

Identity and Political Change (New York: Harper & Row, 1975).

because after the 1730s the mainline was almost always in retreat, always being overtaken by new competing forces. Yet after the Fundamentalist-Modernist battles around 1925 or the time of briefly renewed mainliners' visibility just before 1965, few predicted that by 1985 the "evangelical-moralist" subculture—Daniel Bell's term[6]—would match active Catholicism and mainline Protestantism in size and outdo them in scope. Although self-portrayed and perceived as critical of some aspects of society—witness their attacks on legalized abortion and pervasive pornography—the evangelical-moralists have moved into positions of privilege. They have had the ear of or a voice in the White House during the presidencies of Ford, Carter, and Reagan. All of the Protestant celebrities now come from this camp. By 1984 it had come from apparently nowhere to hold the most visible and assertive political position in American religion.

Catholicism's public voice

Roman Catholic leadership interchanged position with mainline Protestantism with respect to the articulation of a social vision to its constituency and the public. Mainline Protestantism did not slink from the scene; however, it was being chastened by a realism acquired during social activist forays two decades earlier, preoccupied with regrouping, beset by backlashers all the way from its own pews to *Reader's Digest* and CBS television, and suffering reaction to bureaucratization. It had become virtually silent as a concentrated political force by the 1984 presidential campaign. Far

6. Daniel Bell, "The Return of the Sacred: The Argument about the Future of Religion," in *Progress and Its Discontents*, Almond, Chodorow, and Pearce, pp. 501-23, esp. pp. 518-20.

from acquiescing to the terms of the present culture, it was seeking new symbols, vocabulary, and outlets, chiefly by a new responsiveness to local social justice concerns. Whereas in 1964 the mainline would have acted through pronouncements of world or national councils or denominational task forces and conventions, by 1984 it more readily dealt with issues of housing, aging, or sanctuary on local scenes even while its members became more aware of Third World need.

Roman Catholic leadership meanwhile began to interchange positions with the mainline through a series of public advocacies culminating in May 1983 in "The Challenge of Peace"—a pastoral letter on nuclear weaponry—some intervention in the 1984 presidential campaign over the issue of abortion, and, immediately thereafter, a draft of a pastoral letter on the economy. Here was another major transposition in American religion. While the general social justice posture was not new, as the hierarchy drew on papal social documents from as far back as 1891 and on American bishops' programs dating from 1919, their leadership previously had always needed to be cautious and defensive about its role in national politics. Before the election of Catholic John F. Kennedy to the presidency in 1960 and the passage of the Declaration on Religious Liberty at the Second Vatican Council in 1965, the bishops had been wary of being accused of disrupting American civil life with the claims of Roman, and hence foreign, dogma and control.

Those cautions seemed gone in 1984 when New York's Archbishop John O'Connor and many other bishops and leaders all but implied that Catholics should not vote for candidates who did not work openly for legislation agreeing with the bishops' teachings against abortion. Yet most hierarchical representatives were still extremely careful to make distinctions regarding claims and audiences. Thus "The Challenge of Peace" began with the reminder that the letter on nuclear war was "an exercise of our teaching ministry . . . addressed principally to the Catholic community," yet, like the later letter on the economy, it was also to be "a contribution to the wider public debate in our country." The letter was "therefore both an invitation and a challenge to Catholics in the United States to join with others in shaping the conscious choices and deliberate policies required."[7] The once-suspect Catholic leadership had changed places in the public eye with mainline Protestants. It also challenged the ascendancy of evangelical-moralist New Right Protestantism as speaker to and, more ambiguously, for its own constituency in the context of the pluralist civil order.

Internal unity of
blacks and Jews

Black religionists and Jews interchanged with respect to predictable public and partisan stands concerning their own interests. Ever since American blacks, usually under pastoral and local church leadership, shifted allegiance from the Republican to the Democratic party between 1932 and 1936, most of them represented both black and national interest through support of Democratic partisan and social causes. Therefore, their posture in the mid-eighties

7. Jim Castelli, *The Bishops and the Bomb: Waging Peace in a Nuclear Age: With the Text of the Bishops' 1983 Pastoral Letter* (Garden City, NY: Doubleday, 1983), pp. 195-96.

should have been seen as anything but new.

What was new was public perception and the organization of black religionists. Through the years of the civil rights struggle the black churches were seen chiefly as instruments of nurturing piety among blacks and defending blacks' self-interest. This perception began to change in the mid-sixties when Martin Luther King, Jr., began to enlarge the scope of his work to include efforts that would lead the United States to disengage from the war in Vietnam, not a specifically black issue. Over the next two decades blacks, again with a base in the churches and the precincts that they dominated or ministered to, became mayors of a large number of metropolises. By 1984 on the national level—with the presidential primary candidacy and later campaign involvement of the Reverend Jesse Jackson, and the support of the Democratic ticket by nearly 90 percent of blacks—it had become clear that these churches and their secular black counterparts held an inclusive vision and program for national and international life. They were massively united in support of it, if not of a specific leader.

Jews, meanwhile, despite their century-old identification with liberal movements and their half-century instinct for alliances with mainline Protestants and Catholics in support of interfaith and social causes, were perceived to be deeply divided and ambiguous over new causes and alliances. Much of the neoconservative movement, typified by the American Jewish Committee-sponsored *Commentary* magazine, was under lay Jewish leadership. Many more or less theological justifications for laissez-faire capitalism were being encouraged by these neoconservatives, who were clearly the most visible Jewish leaders in the media. Through a decade and more they have moved or were moving into conservative Republican policy camps. More astonishing, Jews were finding new alliance with the New Right evangelical-moralist leadership, thanks to the vocal and unwavering support of Israel by these Protestant ultras. One says "astonishing" because in public perception these Protestant conservatives had been anti-Semitic when it came to relations with domestic Jews, and Jews had known only urban mainline Protestants and Catholics.

In the 1980s, Israeli and American Jewish leaders were giving and receiving honors in the sanctuaries of Protestant theological intransigents and self-proclaimed political Far Right evangelists. Many of these evangelical-moralists were Christian Zionists who, to fulfill their understanding of biblical prophecy, saw the restoration of Israel as a modern political state to be a necessary prerequisite of the Second Coming of Christ.[8] *Commentary*'s Irving Kristol urged Jews to acquire a taste for association with Protestant Fundamentalists. These advocated a strong anti-Soviet defense policy, were more reliable partisans of Israel than were mainline Protestants and Catholics, and were staunch defenders of capitalism.

Other Jews, however, in the course of 1984 began to be suspect of the Fundamentalist support of Israel, as the Fundamentalist view of the final act of history both rewrote the script of Jewish expectations and, sometimes through efforts at evangelizing Jews, called into question the integrity of Jewish faith. What is more, the evangelical-moralist calls and programs in support of a legally privileged theistic or Judeo-Christian culture and its traditional values were seen and heard to be an ever less covert and more overt call for a privileged Christian America, created on right-wing Protestant lines. Jews were in a new dilemma over political and religious alliances, and had become less partisanly predictable than blacks, less visibly organized around the specifically religious agencies of their people's lives.

A conservative civil religion

Civil or public religion has been transposed in public perception, from moderate and liberal contexts to conservative and nationalist ones. Much of twentieth-century public religion had had the secular cast of John Dewey's *Common Faith*, a nontheistic but still ritualized public philosophy. In the era of Dwight Eisenhower's piety along the Potomac, it was to be an expansive and nondescript, generally benign faith for all. When Robert N. Bellah wrote his famed esssay "Civil Religion in America," he was speaking out of a vision shaped during the liberal advocacies of Presidents Kennedy and Lyndon Johnson. Bellah revisited the theme after President Richard M. Nixon's more jingoistic second inaugural address. He then expressed second thoughts and, in *The Broken Covenant*, rued the direction the civil faith was taking.[9]

8. For historical background on Christian Zionism, see Timothy P. Weber, *Living in the Shadow of the Second Coming: American Premillennialism, 1875-1982*, enlarged ed. (Grand Rapids, MI: Zondervan Academie Books, 1983), chap. 6, pp. 128-57, and chap. 9, pp. 204-26. An early assessment of the Jewish vote in 1984 and a reference to Kristol's call is TRB, "Still Chosen," *New Republic*, 3 Dec. 1984, pp. 4, 42.

9. See John Dewey, *A Common Faith* (New Haven, CT: Yale University Press, 1934); at the

While moderates and liberals were as persistent as ever in claiming attachment to quasi-religious democratic values and symbols, the public media accurately chronicled the seizure of the symbols by un-self-critical fortress-America nationalists who would move against the evil empires of their enemies. This transposition need not be permanent, for public and civil religions are episodic, subject to revivals and reforms. Yet the American conservatives' identification with their God and their own national purposes was consistent with what seemed to be a long-term and widespread international trend.

Entering the mainstream

Extraordinary religion acquired an ordinary cast. Daniel Bell observed both traditional redemptive—read "mainline Protestant, Catholic, Reform and Conservative Jewish"—and evangelical-moralist faith complexes. He also saw a third complex, summarized by British sociologist Bryan Wilson as a "diffuse tendency to mythical and mystical thought, . . . a demand for colour in a world which has become drab," an effort to return to the sacred by routes seen as alternative or esoteric in the larger society. A generation earlier, as the old liberal synthesis was breaking up after the mid-sixties, this complex became more visible than ever before or since, both in respect to its promise and its threat. News magazines could write of occult explosions in astrology, cult formation, and support of Eastern religions. All of this looked extraordinary in Bell's grey-on-grey world.[10]

By the mid-1980s such extraordinary religion had established itself, although without essentially changing the map of American religion. Present in a number of thriving cults and persistent in holistic health movements, small-group therapies, and most of all in private spiritual pursuits, most of this religion had begun to fit quietly into the larger landscape. What the public called cults no longer made news as a harbinger of the spirit that might alter consciousness and national life, bringing in a new age. Instead they were seen as only slightly less conventional denominations among the denominations, study accents among other Great Book interests, or, most of all, as merely self-preservative groups constantly fighting for legal rights and privilege—and often thus winning support of both mainline and evangelical-moralist partisans. In other words, they made news on the familiar and ordinary church-state legal front, not on the horizon of extraordinary spiritual promise. Majority America had settled back into drab or chose to recolor only slightly its traditional and evangelical-moralist faiths.

One could point to any of a number of other transpositions, such as the dominance of the southern world over the northern.[11] Thus Christians were

---

end of the Eisenhower era there was an assessment of the civil religion of that era and a reference to the literature in Martin E. Marty, *The New Shape of American Religion* (New York: Harper & Row, 1959). The literature on civil religion is assessed typically in Russell E. Richey and Donald G. Jones, *American Civil Religion* (New York: Harper & Row, 1974), which reprints Bellah's original essay of 1967 (pp. 21-44) and his revisionist probings of 1974 (pp. 255-72). The introduction and bibliographies are noteworthy.

10. For the paraphrases of Bell and argument with him, see Bryan R. Wilson, "The Return of the Sacred," *Journal of the Scientific Study of Religion*, 18(3):268-80 (Sept. 1979).

11. For statistics on Christianity, see David B. Barrett, ed., *World Christian Encyclopedia: A*

becoming aware that in their decade the Christian majority was in the southern world—sub-Saharan Africa, Latin America, Indonesia, and the like—for the first time in two millennia. Domestically, Sun Belt religious norms, long overlooked or seen as eccentric by media, historians, social analysts, and the northern public, were becoming determinative in the Rust Belt. Demography was on the side of the once-conservative churches of the newly prosperous and fast-growing American South. In various trickle-up ways, the music, ritual, evangelical experience, and programmatic life of Southern Protestantism, beamed over television and made visible in the celebrity world, influenced the culture of the American North.

Yet to cite all such interchanges and transpositions would only further substantiate the main point: that long-term exchanges of position, privilege, role, and status were seen to be, if not a final new resolution, still a clearly established and probably long-term situation in America. After a period of such consolidation, interpretation of many sorts is in order.

OPPORTUNITY FOR APPRAISAL

Transposition allows for appraisal. When people are uprooted and change their position on the landscape, they tell us something special about their values and their landscape as they migrate, are exiled, conquer, or replace each other. When schism and disruption occur in history, scholars can gain special insight on what previous settlements and continuities have meant and what the new situation promises. When literary works

Comparative Survey of Churches and Religions in the Modern World, A.D. 1900-2000 (New York: Oxford University Press, 1982).

are teased or subjected to the leveler of deconstruction, when, in the fashionable language of the day, one can "disturb a poem along its own fault lines," there is a chance for new disclosures in a text.[12] In biblical parabolic terms, revelation can occur when there are reversals and transpositions: the last become first and the first last; the uninvited come to the banquet and the invited are outside; the smallest seed becomes the greatest tree; the righteous are scorned and the unrighteous are welcomed and honored. Then the hearer or reader stands the chance of being upset, dislocated enough to discern what is being disclosed.

Analogically, something similar goes on during the upheavals and interchanges in this time of fulfilled American transpositions. What might now be safely discerned? One must begin such an appraisal with a few observations about religion in the 1980s.

Religion's strong roles

In a secular and pluralist society, religion is playing and will play surprisingly strong private, spiritual, and public roles. In part this is simply an anthropological insight. It runs counter to a simpler secularization theory that predominated during the years when the myth of progress, with its faith in democracy, science, and technology, held sway. Around the world there is a larger quantity of passional expression and

12. A popular summary of literary disturbances through transposition is in Robert Alter, "Deconstruction in America," New Republic, 25 Apr. 1982, pp. 27-32. A reference to the ways uprooted and marginal people add insight to social process is in Hans Mol, Identity and the Sacred: A Sketch for a New Social-Scientific Theory of Religion (New York: Free Press, 1976), pp. 31-34.

spiritual resource than the rational academy assessed or foresaw. Anthropologists and other social scientists have contributed to broader understandings and definitions of religion. Therefore, far more than religious institutions—which may indeed be in decline in many places—is involved in the category of religion.

Recent worldwide and American trends, meanwhile, have upset the prediction that the religion that survived would chiefly be, as Thomas Luckmann called it, privatized or invisible in the urban-industrial world.[13] Much of the new religious energy is poured into aggressive social movements that are often coextensive with huge subcultures, if not—in more coercive contexts—with both totalitarian states or a privileged Christian America. British sociologist Bryan Wilson may be right in his claim that a society is secular unless all its constituencies are responsive to a single set of spiritual symbols. Hence his critique of Daniel Bell's notion that in a society like America's the sacral can impinge through, say, the large traditional, evangelical-moralist, and mystical subcultures.[14]

True, it is easy to overdefine as religious many worldwide movements among peoples named by religions—Sikh, Muslim, Protestant Fundamentalist, Irish Catholic, and others—for sometimes their religion is epiphenom-

enal, barnacled to secular economic and political vessels. Yet the force of religion is now more securely recognized. It is also possible to overestimate the power of the newly privileged or the weakness of recently upset religious movements in America—for example, by making too much of alignments in the political campaigns of 1980 and 1984. Yet politicians are less likely, through at least the rest of the 1980s, to underestimate the cohorts and caucuses of all sorts of religionists, including the New Right Protestants, black Protestants, Jews, at least two kinds of Catholics, regrouping mainline Protestants, and mystical advocates of their own rights. Church and state issues will be constant in the courts and polling places, and future decisions by judges and voters may not follow traditional lines.

This is not to say that the United States will join the new theocracies or, barring now-unforeseen social upheavals, turn coercively into Christian America and abolish the older terms of its pluralism. Instead, citizens are becoming aware of what we might call a multiplex consciousness to come to terms with what Robert N. Bellah and Benjamin R. Mariante have called a multiplex world and universe. Mariante described its focus well:

Now when the world of religious institutions becomes the focus of the individual's consciousness in terms of his everyday experience, he is going to live, respond and act in that world. And about 96% of Americans respond positively in that institutional context, when this is the focus of consciousness. ... Most individuals are willing to accept the religious institutional pattern in society as part of the real world, much as they accept the economic institution. Thus their responses will be to these institutions as separate, autonomous institutions, i.e., their

13. I have commented on this broadening of the definition of religion in Martin E. Marty, "Religion in America since Mid-century," *Daedalus*, 111(1):154-57. See Thomas Luckmann, *The Invisible Religion: The Problem of Religion in Modern Society* (New York: Macmillan, 1967), chap. 5, "Individual Religiosity," pp. 69-76.

14. Wilson, "Return of the Sacred," p. 271; see the longer argument in Bryan Wilson, *Religion in a Secular Society* (New York: Penguin, 1966), pt. 1, pp. 21-108.

responses will be in the pluralistic frame-work. What has occurred is pluralization not secularization; people are religious when religion is at the center of conscious life, as on a questionnaire, "Do you believe in God?" They are economic when the econ-omy is at the center, as on a questionnaire, "What is the most important problem facing America today?"[15]

The disclosure of this unfolding multi-plex consciousness is a result of this moment of transposition in secular-religious realms.

The exploitation of
spiritual resources

How does one account for the trans-position of assertive Catholicism, in a time of many Catholic upheavals and setbacks, or of aggressive evangelical-moralist and New Right Protestantism and the recession of mainline Protes-tantism? And, further, what will be the role of that once-privileged and tradi-tional mainline, which remains almost as large as before the transposition, and which is institutionalized and cherished in many tens of thousands of congrega-tions and scores of denominations?

To respond to these questions I am going to make metaphoric and figura-tive use of two speculations or laws of cultural evolution. It is extremely im-portant that this endeavor not be mis-understood. First, historians tend to be mistrustful of evolutionary models be-cause of the models' determinism and long scale. They tend to be comfortable with evolution only or chiefly with re-spect to very general observations that everything develops and changes. Sec-ond, in the eyes of most historians,

cultural evolution has normally been seen as progressive, though in the more recent vision of its most noted American advocates, Leslie White and his stu-dents, it could as well be linked to nonprogressive and even devolutionary understandings. It should be clear that the present article is not built on pro-gressivist assumptions! Third, cultural evolution and ecology represent one challenged, perhaps ephemeral, episode or school in anthropology, questioned even by some scholars who earlier iden-tified with it. Given those cautions, it should be clear that a metaphoric ver-sion is here being used for the task of teasing, creating leverage, disrupting texts, and understanding a spiritual landscape.

The first of the two laws comes in the context of an argument proposed by Marshall D. Sahlins and Elman R. Service in 1960.[16] This Law of Cultural Dominance says that "that cultural sys-tem which more effectively exploits the energy resources of a given environment will tend to spread in that environment at the expense of less effective systems." Sahlins and Service talked about the ecology of an actual physical landscape as environment. Metaphorically, one must insert the word "spiritual" before "energy resources" to gain leverage for insight. In these terms it now seems incontrovertible that mainline Protes-tantism misread three such spiritual energy resources in recent America. These were a passionate hunger for personal experience, a resort to author-ity in the face of a relativism and chaos, and the pull toward institutions and

15. Benjamin R. Mariante, *Pluralistic Soci-ety, Pluralistic Church* (Washington, DC: Uni-versity Press of America, 1981), pp. 82-84.

16. Marshall D. Sahlins and Elman R. Ser-vice, eds., *Evolution and Culture* (Ann Arbor: University of Michigan Press, 1960), p. 75.

movements that provide personal identity and social location.

Mainline Protestantism, protean Catholicism, and Reform Judaism, as three examples, do of course offer kinds of cherished religious experience, but these rarely have the competitive potency of the born-again or charismatic sort. They all do care about authority, but they see it in the context of reasoned inquiry, of critical approaches to texts and institutions, and of sophisticated interpretation theory. They are thus no match for the evangelists who assert a variety of contradictory messages but always under the banner of "the Bible says" and "thus saith the Lord." Similarly they are no match for Pope John Paul II asserting traditional papal authority or for Orthodox Jews. They do provide identities: an Anglican is as easy to spot as a Pentecostal, a Methodist as a Mormon or Muslim. Yet Pentecostals, Mormons, and Muslims are quite precise about personal and communal boundaries and walls; they are constrictive about the range of possibilities for expressing identity. Mainline Protestantism, Catholicism, and liberal Judaisms would work to create and nurture core personalities and coherent centers of social existence but with less sense of constriction and boundary. They thus are outdone by competitors who "more effectively [exploit] the [spiritual] energy resources of a given environment."

While this transposition exposes to view the ecological niches of this spiritual landscape, one hastens to note also that in many respects the evangelical-moralist and other putatively conservative religious subcultures have changed more than has the environment. Bell was right to think of the mainline as traditional, for its once-privileged people do reach back to symbols long

identified with the culture for their *ressourcement*, their renewal. The old-time religion, in turn, after its selective critique of secular humanism, liberalism, and their effects, turns out to be the most world affirming of the competitors, even if the symbols of heaven, hell, and afterlife remain in its cognitive repertory.

A whole school of critics from within evangelicalism has effectively shown that evangelical-moralism, in its hypernationalism, materialism, success-mindedness, offering of more abundant life, identification with heroes and entertainers and athletes, and support of competitive capitalism, is probably the most worldly of the large options. Jon Johnston has written on a popular level, as have scholars on other levels, scoring evangelicalism for accommodation, hedonism, narcissism, materialism, faddism, "celebrityism," "youthism," and "technologism." Carol Flake speaks of the whole complex as "redemptorama" and demonstrates the this-worldliness of the movement.[17] Once upon a time, it was the liberal and mainline in Protestantism that overidentified with the success culture. In the neoorthodox and critical-realist period in the middle third of the century, under the impetus of theologians like brothers Reinhold and H. Richard Niebuhr, this form of Protestant leadership began to adopt dissenting, critical, and prophetic stances,

17. Jon Johnston, *Will Evangelicalism Survive Its Own Popularity?* (Grand Rapids, MI: Zondervan, 1980); Carol Flake, *Redemptorama: Culture, Politics, and the New Evangelicalism* (Garden City, NY: Doubleday, 1984); James Davison Hunter, *American Evangelicalism: Conservative Religion and the Quandary of Modernity* (New Brunswick, NJ: Rutgers University Press, 1983); Robert Booth Fowler, *A New Engagement: Evangelical Political Thought, 1966-76* (Grand Rapids, MI: Eerdmans, 1982).

offering henceforth less uncritical support to citizens in their spiritual strivings.

To face this transposition, the second law, the Law of Evolutionary Potential, argues that "the more specialized and adapted a form in a given evolutionary stage, the smaller is its potential for passing to the next stage." Again used figuratively, this law refers not to the physical landscape but to an ecology that is at least partly spiritual, though adaptation to past given evolutionary stages in American life was even less figuratively the fate of the mainline, hence its smaller potential for adapting and passing to the new stage. The cultural evolutionists quote Thorstein Veblen and Leon Trotsky. Veblen spoke of "the merits of borrowing" and "the penalty of taking the lead" and Trotsky of "the privilege of historic backwardness." They all meant that underdeveloped complexes have certain potentials that advanced and adapted ones lack. Later comers are permitted or compelled to adopt "whatever is ready in advance of any specified date, skipping a whole series of intermediate stages."[18]

The mainline religionists, the early advocates of progressivism and modernism, later became wary of the dehumanization and depersonalization or technical reason and technological artifact. They carry the burden of identification with the earlier stages, and they are self-critical about that. The innovators and adapters of today, the advocates of old-time religion, in turn are thoroughly at home with the technology of electronic media and computers, less critical—with some very notable exceptions—of technical reason and capitalist rationalism. They plunge into politics with more

self-assurance and less ambiguity than did the old mainliners in their prime. God and the party and cause of their choice are easily identified with each other. The mainline suffers the penalty of taking the lead and meets rejections that go with its inner uncertainties, while the borrowers and leapfroggers advance.

After the transposition, is there a mission for the once-privileged mainline? H. Stuart Hughes thought that among nations, late-starting, leapfrogging America would be to Western Europe as Rome was to Greece, for the ways it "raised certain aspects of that civilization to new levels of efficiency and specialization." Hughes then saw the United States becoming more like the later Byzantium than Rome itself.[19] Extending this analogy now, one can picture that mainline Protestantism, Catholicism, and Judaism will look on the newly efficient exploiters of their environment's spiritual energy resources in similar aristocratic ways. They will not disappear, convert, or lose all sense of mission.

Like latter-day Hellenists in an efficient and specialized spiritual Rome— by analogy—they will have renewals of their own tradition and will freshly ritualize their own symbols. They are likely to serve a more modest but still important role as advocates of sorts of tolerance in an increasingly tribal world. They will be bewildered by the acceptability of the evangelical-moralist culture and stunned by its worldliness under the very symbols of transworldliness. Mainliners will generate scholars and interpret texts, minister to a very large subculture, and represent aspects of the larger culture, confident that their

18. Sahlins and Service, eds., *Evolution and Culture*, pp. 97, 99-100.

19. Ibid., p. 102, cites Hughes.

philosophy is nobler than the near bar- barianism of the newcomers. They are even likely to clarify their own views of experience, authority, and identity, and to minister to those who seek what they offer while also acquiring a new status as dissenters. The world of the late twen- tieth century is not arranged to promise that theirs can become a mass mission. Yet they will find articulators of selec- tive missions in the awesomely rich and complex American spiritual environ- ment. All the other movements will also be making adjustments after the trans- positions of their age.

ANNALS, *AAPSS*, **480**, July 1985

Denominational America and
the New Religious Pluralism

By WADE CLARK ROOF and WILLIAM McKINNEY

ABSTRACT: This article examines the changing character of religious pluralism in America since midcentury. Major changes bringing about a new climate include an expanding pluralism, declines of the liberal establishment, and a conservative religious and moral resurgence. As a result there have been broad shifts and realignments of religion and culture and a changing social and demographic basis of religion in the country. Patterns of religious switching point to a new voluntarism in identifying with the religious tradition of one's choice. The demographics suggest that in the future the liberal sector of Protestantism will continue to decline and that the divergence of conservative religious and secular cultures may intensify.

Wade Clark Roof is professor of sociology at the University of Massachusetts, Amherst, and recently completed a term as executive secretary for the Society for the Scientific Study of Religion. He is the author of numerous publications dealing with the sociology of religion, race relations, and American society.

William McKinney is research director for the United Church Board for Homeland Ministries and past president of the Religious Research Association. He is the author of Varieties of Religious Presence *and* Religion's Public Presence *and coeditor of a forthcoming book on congregational studies.*

NOTE: The authors are engaged in a larger study of denominational religious pluralism in America currently. Support for this research has come from the Spencer Foundation, the Lilly Endowment, Inc., and the United Church Board for Homeland Ministries, which is gratefully acknowledged.

24

I N a time when religious news is dominated by controversies over which candidate for public office is the better Christian, by popular television preachers and calls for restoring the nation's morality, and by esoteric cults and strange new religious movements, denominational religion receives little attention. The religious traditions that once shaped so much of America's way of life now seem distant—matters of individual concern, for sure, but of limited social significance. There is a vague awareness that Jimmy Carter is a born-again Southern Baptist, Marie Osmond a Mormon, and Michael Jackson a Jehovah's Witness, but these affirmations seem to be little more than personal idiosyncrasies, interesting raw material for *People* magazine feature articles.

Religion, after all, is personal, a matter of one's opinion, a private matter with which neither church nor state has the right to interfere. A Gallup poll finds that 81 percent of the American population feels "an individual should arrive at his or her own religious beliefs independent of any church or synagogue" and that 78 percent feels "a person can be a good Christian or Jew without attending a church or synagogue."[1] That trends have moved in the direction of greater religious privatism in this century is hardly disputable. Indeed, viewing the American religious scene circa 1985, one might well make the case for the triumph of what Ernst Troeltsch in 1911 called mysticism, that radically individualistic form of religion that, as he said, envisions "a new situation altogether, in which it will no longer become necessary to connect religion with the decaying churches." Troeltsch went on to say,

It creates no community, since it possesses neither the sense of solidarity nor the faith in authority which this requires, nor the no less necessary fanaticism and desire for uniformity. It lives in and on communities which have been brought into existence by other ruder energies; it tends to transform these groups from confessional unities into organizations for administration, offering a home to varying minds and energies. It is opposed to ecclesiastical spirit by its tolerance, its subjectivism and symbolism, its emphasis upon the ethical and religious inwardness of temper, its lack of stable norms and authorities.[2]

Yet for all the truth here, as a description of American religion this statement is flawed. Troeltsch's other seminal institutional types—church and sect—do not fully conform to the American environment, and neither does mysticism. Seeing only the individualistic strands, it ignores the communal and group character of religion in this country that continues to find expression in that unique socioreligious form, the denomination. Moreover, it attracts attention away from some of the more crucial aspects of religious change in America over the past three decades, which should not go unnoticed in any mapping of the current religious scene.

Three observations about the current scene seem irrefutable:

1. Americans continue to identify with the historic religious traditions. The same polls that suggest the strength of religious individualism in this country also reveal that 90 percent of the population expresses a religious preference and two-thirds are members of a local church or synagogue. Even the unchurched and those only nominally involved in orga-

1. The "Unchurched American" Study (Gallup Organization, Inc., 1978).

2. Ernst Troeltsch, The Social Teachings of the Christian Churches, trans. Olive Wyon (New York: Harper & Row, 1931), 2:796.

nized religion tend to a remarkable degree to profess loyalty to their religious tradition.

2. For Americans, religious groups continue to fulfill important quasi-ethnic functions providing millions with a sense of meaning and belonging. Even in a time when church religion may not be highly salient for many and connections between faith and life seem vague, such groups remain deeply embedded in American life as the major voluntary organizations. Like the family, the neighborhood, and other voluntary activities, religious groups are mediating structures, linking individuals and families to the larger social order; they are people-sized, face-to-face institutions where the things that matter most in personal and communal life can be dealt with.

3. Religious themes have taken on new significance in the public arena. A greater evangelical and fundamentalist religious presence plus the polarization along ideological lines have made Americans keenly aware of the differing religious traditions that make up the American religious mosaic. In a crystalized and very forceful way, religious developments of the past decade have forced to the forefront the question of religious America—if, and in what way, the country can be conceived of as a sacred enterprise.

As organization, as heritage, and as community, denominational religion is still very much a part, even if in the background, of the changing patterns of religion and culture. Denominationalism has seen its character altered because it is so deeply embedded in the structures of American life; the story of its persistence and change since midcentury is in fact the story of the nation itself. What, then, can be said about the character of religious life in America from the standpoint of the existing collectivities that give it shape and flavor?

EXPANDING PLURALISM

In the years since midcentury, the nation has become much more pluralistic in its religious life. Far from being the "triple melting-pot" of Protestants, Catholics, and Jews that Will Herberg envisioned in the 1950s, religious boundaries have developed in new and unanticipated ways.[3] Denominational identities did not dissolve as some—including Herberg—expected they would in the course of assimilation; there have been denominational unions—mainly reunions—but institutional attachments are as strong and maybe stronger today than they were three decades ago. Beneath the gloss of popular religious labels—for example, "born-again," "evangelical," "charismatic"—Americans still identify with specific subcommunities: "I am a Protestant, but more than that I'm a Baptist, and a born-again Southern Baptist at that," or "a post-Vatican II Catholic," or "a Jew and a member of the Lubavitcher movement," or maybe even "a Lake Wobegon Lutheran."

A broad profile of religious America currently is as follows: liberal Protestants—Congregationalists, Presbyterians, Episcopalians, and Unitarians—comprise 9 percent of the population; moderate Protestants—Methodists, Lutherans, American Baptists, Disciples, and Reformed—24 percent; conservative Protestants—Southern Baptists, Church of God, Pentecostals, Assemblies of God, and many others—15 percent;

3. Will Herberg, *Protestant, Catholic, Jew* (Garden City, NY: Doubleday, 1955).

black Protestants, 9 percent; Catholics, 25 percent; Jews, 2 percent; other faiths, 8 percent; and non-affiliates, 7 percent.[4] Over the years there have been gradual but significant changes in the relative sizes of the three great religious communities, Protestant, Catholic, and Jewish.

Most notable is the steady decline of the Protestant majority. Since 1952 Protestant preferences have declined from 67 percent of the population to 56 percent, or a proportional loss of 16 percent. These losses continue a larger pattern of Protestant decline throughout this century. But more than a matter of numbers, the erosion of Protestant strength is a matter of ethos. Historians date the beginnings of the Protestant establishment's decline early in the twentieth century, but the age of the white Anglo-Saxon Protestant (WASP) did not really end in the minds of Americans until the 1960s. The nation elected a Roman Catholic president, and two Supreme Court decisions mandating one man, one vote, and rendering public school prayer unconstitutional profoundly undercut Protestantism's hold on the culture. Even more so now than when he wrote it, Herberg's comment is true: "Protestantism in America today presents the anomaly of a strong majority group with a growing minority consciousness.[5]

In contrast, the Catholic community has steadily grown almost decade by decade. In the short space of 30 years

4. These figures are based on a composite sample of over 17,000 Americans from the General Social Surveys, from 1972 to 1984. These surveys are conducted by the National Opinion Research Center and provide a representative sampling of the adult population. Unless otherwise indicated, data reported in this article are taken from these surveys.

5. Herberg, p. 234.

Catholics increased from 22 percent to 26 percent of the population, or by 15 percent. Benefiting from a high birthrate and immigration, they have gained numbers in about the same proportion as Protestants have lost them. Of course, they have grown in social standing and cultural influence as well. In the postwar period, Catholics made spectacular gains in education, occupational status, and income, such that their overall status levels are now equal to those of Protestants. With upward mobility and assimilation, they have come to resemble Protestants in many respects: in social attitudes, political party affiliation, and in religious practices.

The Jewish population appears to have declined relative to the others. A low birthrate and high levels of intermarriage have worked to keep the size of this faith community relatively small. Because of the concentration of Jews in a few metropolitan areas, it is conceivable that their numbers are underestimated in the polls. Even so, they remain a distinctive and identifiable religious minority whose social standing and influence are disproportionate to their numbers.

All three religious communities are experiencing declines in religious participation. Throughout the period of public opinion polling, from the 1940s until the mid-1960s, roughly three-quarters of the American population consistently reported they were church or synagogue members. But polls in the 1970s and early 1980s began to show distinct declines, to a low 67 percent in 1982. Eighty percent of Catholics are church members, 73 percent of Protestants report the same, and 45 percent of Jews say they are members of a synagogue.[6] Of

6. *Religion in America, 1984,* Gallup Report, no. 222, pp. 54-55 (March 1984).

course, many Americans who say they are church members are effectively unchurched because of lack of involvement in religious institutions. Using a more rigorous definition that includes active religious involvement, a major study in 1978 identified 41 percent of the adult population in the country as unchurched.[7] The evidence suggests that the unchurched are overwhelmingly believers and quite religious in many respects, but choose to express their religiousness apart from churches and synagogues. Compared with the churched, they tend more to welcome social change, hold less to conventional values, and are less rooted in stable social networks in the communities in which they live. Although the cultural profiles for the two are not so distinct at present, should the downward trend in church membership continue, the differences quite possibly will become more pronounced in the years ahead.

The largest proportionate increase in religious preference has come in the categories of other religions or no religion. Now 4 percent of the population indicates a faith outside the three major traditions compared to about 1 percent in the early 1950s. Currently 9 percent identify as non-affiliates, which is 7 points higher than in the previous period. Of course, the percentage base for these categories is small, and hence the proportional changes should not be overdrawn. Still, the figures are striking. A heterogeneous grouping of non-Judeo-Christian faiths in this country now commands the loyalties of more Americans than Judaism does. This represents

7. The unchurched were those who reported not being a member of a church or synagogue, or had not attended a religious service in the past six months apart from weddings, funerals, or special holidays. See "Unchurched American."

a sizable number of followers and practitioners falling outside the more conventional faiths. And the fact that almost 10 percent of Americans choose to identify as non-affiliates is revealing on several counts: it points to a growing non-affiliated sector and to the greater ease for Americans now to reject a religious affiliation. It is interesting that the decline in religious membership since the early 1970s—7 or 8 percent—about equals the current percentage expressing no religious preference. Their numbers suggest the possibility of a widening secular constituency, perhaps more irreligious than anti-religious, but in any case a force of growing cultural importance in a pluralistic society.

No one expected the rise of the so-called new religions and the religious counterculture of the late 1960s. Many middle-class youth dropped out of the churches and experimented with alternative religions that promised new modes of meaning and belonging. Beneath the superficial quality of much of the counterculture, there was a deeply based spiritual ferment that took the form of rejecting the establishment and of searching for new realities. It was a time of turning inward and exploring the self with new spiritual technologies, as expressed in the language of "getting into" a range of experiential frames, from astrology to Zen. Ironically, just at the time when Protestant, Catholic, and Jewish mainliners had begun to blur boundaries, many others were seeking them. The conventional, luke-warm religiosity of the established churches paled in the face of newer, more esoteric alternatives that seemed more capable of linking belief and behavior, or how one thinks and what one does.

LIBERAL DECLINES

The dislocations and tensions of the period were felt more acutely in liberal Protestantism than in any other religious sector. Beginning in about the mid-1960s, the historic mainline churches began reporting significant membership losses. Protestant churches with long-standing records of sustained growth and prosperity, some dating to colonial times, experienced their first major downturns. There had been a religious depression—perhaps more accurately a recession—in the 1930s, but what was later to come was of greater magnitude. To cite some examples, the Episcopal church, the Presbyterian denominations, the United Methodist Church, the Christian Church (Disciples of Christ), and the United Church of Christ, all of which had enjoyed considerable prosperity in the 1950s, experienced sizable losses in the 1960s and 1970s. The losses in the 1970-80 period were staggering: the United Presbyterian Church, down 19 percent; Disciples, 17 percent; the Episcopalians, 15 percent; United Church of Christ, 11 percent; and the United Methodist Church, more than 9 percent.[8]

The declines were fairly abrupt, hitting all the churches at about the same time. Across the board, the liberal churches were suffering. In general, the losses resulted more from decreasing numbers of new members than increases in dropouts. Proportionately fewer persons were joining after the mid 1960s, and among those joining fewer were becoming active participants. Younger

8. The data come from the *Yearbook of American and Canadian Churches, 1984* (Nashville, TN: Abingdon Press); see also Dean R. Hoge and David A. Roozen, eds., *Understanding Church Growth and Decline, 1950-1978* (New York: Pilgrim Press, 1979).

adults were conspicuously absent, raising speculation about a lost generation in these churches.

Trends in religious participation and support were the same. Institutional support was high in the 1950s, but attendance at services declined steadily during the 1960s and into the early 1970s. Among Protestants the declines were greatest for the moderate to liberal bodies—in particular for Methodists, Presbyterians, and Episcopalians. Religious giving—in relation to inflation—declined as well. Thus numerous institutional indicators pointed to a religious decline of considerable proportions.

To a lesser extent, Catholicism experienced some of the same reverberations. Membership continued to increase, but at a declining rate. Declines in religious participation were striking, from 74 percent of Catholics attending mass weekly in 1958 to 51 percent in 1982.[9] The declines were most evident for young, upwardly mobile communicants. Rising socioeconomic levels and rapid assimilation into the culture in the years after World War II led Catholics to discard much of the old immigrant heritage. In addition, Vatican II brought about a new climate of lay involvement and voluntarism. As they joined the ranks of the mainline, they took on both the privileges and the burdens of the establishment.

CONSERVATIVE RESURGENCE

Virtually all the churches that continued to grow after World War II were conservative—particularly Protestant evangelical and fundamentalist bodies—with membership increases often exceeding the nation's population growth

9. *Religion in America, 1984.*

rate. Among these bodies were the Seventh-Day Adventists, the Church of the Nazarene, Assemblies of God, the Salvation Army, and various small pentecostal and holiness groups. In both the 1960s and 1970s these churches grew at phenomenal rates, some as much as 60 to 70 percent each decade. The Southern Baptists also grew, becoming in 1967 the largest Protestant denomination. Indicators other than membership suggested an upswing in religious conservatism: church school enrollments, missionary support, book publishing, the founding of Christian schools. This marked growth in the conservative faiths along with the liberal declines indicated, as Martin Marty noted, a "seismic shift" in the nation's religious landscape.[10]

Nor was the shift limited to conservative Protestantism. Within Catholicism there was reaction to the liturgical and modernizing trends set in motion by Vatican II. While some sought to adapt to new ways, others called for a return to traditional Catholic values and authority. Pope John Paul II's opposition to abandoning priestly celibacy and ordaining women confirmed for many that the church would remain a bedrock of stability and continuity, despite the changes underway. Within American Judaism there was a discernible shift in mood as well. Orthodox Judaism grew more rapidly than did either the Reform or Conservative branches in the 1970s. Rejecting what many regarded as the lax observance and permissiveness of the latter, growing numbers of Jews turned to the more traditional faith in search of a distinct religious identity and prescribed way of life.[11] This turnabout in trends is noteworthy, considering that for years there had been a continual movement of Jews from Orthodoxy toward more liberal faith or non-affiliation.

In many sectors, then, conservative religious currents were flowing. A dominant secular culture provoked deep reactions—anti-pluralist and antimodern. In religion, as in other realms, a back-to-basics mood prevailed. Evangelical and fundamentalist faiths flourished as the cultural and religious center seemed to collapse. Rigid and demanding beliefs, traditional values, certainty, absolutist moral teachings—all seemed to fill the needs of the times. By drawing cognitive and behavioral boundaries and adhering generally to a non-accommodating stance toward modernity, they offered a clear alternative to secular and diffusely religious points of view.

A MORAL CRUSADE

Nowhere was the rising tide of religious conservatism more visible than in the growing confrontation over moral issues. By the late 1970s, supporters of the conservative ideologies of the religious Right clashed on one issue after another with ideologies they unceasingly labeled "secular humanism." Views came to be most polarized around two basic social institutions: the family and the school. At the center of controversy were family and gender-role issues such as abortion, the Equal Rights Amendment, and gay

10. See Marty's introduction to Hoge and Roozen, *Understanding Church Growth and Decline.*

11. See Natalie Gittelson, "American Jews Rediscover Orthodoxy," *New York Times Magazine,* 30 Sept. 1984; see also Harold S. Himmelfarb and R. Michael Loar, "National Trends in Jewish Ethnicity: A Test of the Polarization Hypothesis," *Journal for the Scientific Study of Religion,* 23: 140-54 (June 1984).

rights. Pro-family leaders crusaded for a return to traditional roles for men and women and actively opposed equal legal protection for women and homosexuals. The polls show that evangelicals and fundamentalists are far more inclined than mainliners to favor a ban on abortion, to oppose the Equal Rights Amendment, and to be against the hiring of homosexuals as teachers in public schools; differences between evangelicals and non-evangelicals are often wider than those between Protestants and Catholics.

Like the family, public schools were viewed with great concern. Leaders in the pro-family movement accused the schools of eroding the morality of children by teaching evolution, by using humanist textbooks, and by not having mandatory school prayer. There is widespread support for a constitutional amendment permitting prayer in the schools, and the public seems to be about equally divided on whether evolution or creationism should be taught in the classroom.[12]

The New Christian Right emerged as a visible force, partly as a result of the electronic church and its vast network of religious programming and popular television preachers. Using the most sophisticated of media technology, televangelists such as Jerry Falwell, Pat Robertson, and Jim Bakker are effective in mobilizing support for religious and moral causes. But the change is more than just an increase in media exposure: there is a new tone of political involvement. Long known for their more private faith and suspicion of involvement in politics,

they have become more involved in voter registration; in speaking out on issues such as school prayer, abortion, pornography, and national defense; and in openly endorsing or denouncing candidates for public office on the basis of their voting records or positions on issues. President Reagan's landslide second-term victory reflects to some extent this new activism.[13] The Moral Majority and Religious Roundtable have thrust the religious Right into the public arena in an effort to reshape American public life, calling for traditional moral values and a return to Christian America. Focusing on moral, and not simply religious, concerns, evangelical and fundamentalist leaders have been able to forge an alliance with others also disturbed by these issues—religionists as diverse as Mormons, traditional Catholics, and some Jews.

THE CHANGING SOCIAL AND DEMOGRAPHIC PROFILE

As the face of the religious establishment has changed, so has its underlying social and demographic basis. Three aspects of the changing social location of religion are especially important: the age structure, regional distribution, and class composition.

Poll data reveal striking age differentials among Protestant groups. The denominations that constitute the Protestant mainline have aging constituencies. With the losses of many youth in the 1960s, the average age is noticeably high in the liberal churches: 42 percent of Disciples of Christ, 41 percent of Meth-

12. *Emerging Trends,* a newsletter published by the Princeton Religion Research Center and the Gallup Organization, regularly provides data on these trends. See, for example, vol. 6, no. 4 (Apr. 1984).

13. According to a *New York Times*/CBS News poll, 81 percent of white born-again Protestants voted for the Reagan-Bush ticket in 1984, as compared to 58 percent of white Catholics, 69 percent of other white Protestants, and 32 percent of Jews. See *New York Times,* 25 Nov. 1984.

odists, and 43 percent of the United Church of Christ are age 55 or older. None of the conservative Protestant groups has as many as 40 percent over 55 years of age; indeed, fewer than one-third of the Jehovah's Witnesses, Pentecostals, and Assemblies of God constituencies are of this age.

Young adults, on the other hand, account for only 26 percent of the members in the Reformed Church, 21 percent of the United Church of Christ, and 28 percent of the Methodists. The significance of these figures becomes apparent when one considers that almost 40 percent of the nation's adult population belongs to the 18-to-34 age category. Young adults are far better represented in the conservative churches: more than 50 percent of Jehovah's Witnesses belong to this younger category. Compared with moderate and liberal churches, conservative Protestants are more successful in holding on to their young members.

Regional profiles for the mid-1920s and early 1980s suggest that most denominations have remained in their traditional areas of concentration: Catholics in the Northeast, liberal and moderate Protestants in the Northeast and Midwest; conservative Protestants in the South. But there have been changes. Episcopalians, Presbyterians, and the United Church of Christ—all branches of Anglo-Protestantism—are not as concentrated in the Northeast as they once were. Although the Northeast was at one time a stronghold of WASP power and influence, shifts to the Sun Belt have undercut the numerical base of those denominations in this region. Conservative Protestants are increasingly finding members outside their regions of strength. Southern Baptists are growing in all regions today but more in the

Northeast and West than elsewhere. Now found in the West are 33 percent of Jehovah's Witnesses, 27 percent of Assembly of God members, and 30 percent of Adventists; 29 percent of all Mormons are found outside the West. Those without a religious preference are well represented in all the regions, but more so in the West.

Finally, there are the changes in class composition since mid-century. Jews and the old WASP establishment—Episcopalians, Presbyterians, United Church of Christ, and Unitarian—continue to hold their elite positions, yet there have been far-reaching changes in the status hierarchy. Status differences between many groups have declined, and some groups have noticeably moved upward in their standing. Catholics have moved upward: increases in their income levels lag somewhat behind gains in education and occupations, but they are now a solidly middle-class constituency. Evangelical Protestants in the 1960s and 1970s benefited from expanding education and job opportunities. Whereas in 1960 only 7 percent of members in evangelical and fundamentalist denominations had attended some college, by the mid-1970s that figure was 23 percent—a rate of increase that far exceeds the increase of any other group, including Catholics.[14] These gains stand out against those of mainline Protestants, whose educational base hardly changed at all during this period. Increasingly represented in the lower-middle eschelons of American life, the conservative Protestant community has taken on a new style and presence as it accommodates the mainstream culture.

14. John S. Hendricks, "Religious and Political Fundamentalism" (Ph.D. diss., University of Michigan, 1977).

Profiles for non-affiliates have changed perhaps most of all. Once an uneducated, highly alienated, and marginal group, those fitting the secularist image today are young, single, urban, and highly professional. They are called yuppies and are much less alienated—in fact, they are firmly a part of the mainstream. In many respects, they are at the opposite end of the social and demographic spectrum from the evangelicals: more secure in their standing and more at the center of modernizing, secular trends. This more distinctly secular constituency is sometimes linked to the rise of the so-called new class, a new stratum deriving its livelihood from the production and distribution of knowledge in modern society, distinguished from the old bourgeoisie, or entrepreneurial class.[15] Being more secular, more rational, and more cosmopolitan, the knowledge class espouses values and an outlook that differ sharply with bourgeois morality and life-styles; indeed, abortion, the Equal Rights Amendment, gay rights, and various environmental and consumer issues have taken on symbolic significance in a confrontation of class interests. Religion in America—especially in the mainline churches that have solidly middle-class constituencies and large bureaucratic staffs—is itself caught up in this struggle between old and emerging classes.

THE NEW VOLUNTARISM

The traditional ascriptive loyalties that once shaped America's religious communities have lost much of their hold on the contemporary setting. The lines of class, race, ethnicity, and region—the "social sources of denominationalism" identified by H. Richard Niebuhr[16] a half century ago—are not as clearly drawn today as they were in an earlier time. Niebuhr wrote of a time when the country was in its formative stages and the religious communities were taking shape around the evolving caste and class cleavages of the period. Since then social and demographic shifts have significantly altered the social basis of religious life and have leveled many of the historical differences in doctrine and piety. These trends, combined with the greater confrontation between religious and secular forces, now place the denominational scene in flux and are bringing about new relationships between religion and culture.

Modernity creates a situation in which faith becomes a highly individualized, privatized matter. In this respect Troeltsch is absolutely correct. Less and less bound to an inherited faith, the present-day believer is able to shop around in a consumer market of religious alternatives and pick and choose among aspects of belief and practice. As Peter L. Berger points out, the modern pluralistic world forces upon individuals a "heretical imperative"—the necessity to choose among alternative interpretations and select those elements within a single heritage that are illuminating from those that are not.[17] That is to say, in the tradition of religious voluntarism, the individual is given a great deal of autonomy as well as responsibility in arriving at a religious

15. There is little unanimity on what precisely the new class is or how to define it. See Irving Horowitz, "On the Expansion of New Theories and the Withering Away of Old Classes," *Society*, 16 (2): 55-62.

16. H. Richard Niebuhr, *The Social Sources of Denominationalism* (New York: Meridian Books, 1929).

17. Peter L. Berger, *The Heretical Imperative* (Garden City, NY: Doubleday, 1980).

frame of reference. Religious pluralism of course encourages the privatization of faith, as it forces a denominational preference, and trends of the modern period have further accentuated this tendency. Greater opportunity to exercise choice on the part of the believer is simply the logical extension of religious voluntarism, or as Parsons says, "the individual is bound only by responsible personal commitment, not by any factor of ascription."[18]

Trends toward religious privatism are evident in all the major faiths. Liberal Protestantism especially is vulnerable. Because the liberal churches have historically encouraged freedom of choice among their members, institutional loyalties often suffer. Consequently, some members in these churches can be thought of as believers but not belongers in the conventional sense. But even in the conservative churches, where group loyalties are stronger, there is great emphasis on individual salvation and personal responsibility. Evangelism thrives on individuals who make their own decisions; first comes the decision to believe, and then comes voluntary membership in the church. Perhaps the appeal of the electronic church to so many evangelical, fundamentalist Americans is that it particularizes and renders private religious experience and choice.

Even within the tradition with the greatest heritage of ecclesiastical authority—American Catholicism—there are ample signs of a growing religious individualism. Vatican II unleashed enormous energies in this direction. In this country especially, with its heritage of religious voluntarism, the relaxation of institutional standards led to what Andrew M. Greeley describes as selective Catholicism—with emphasis on participation as a matter of individual conscience and on drawing on the tradition as one chooses.[19] Over the past decade many young Catholics have opted for religious styles that allow for greater individuality in matters of belief and practice, and with this choice has come less respect for the authority of the church, especially in matters of sexual morality and personal life-style.

Yet it would be easy to overstate the case for a growing religious individualism. With the possible exception of liberal Protestants, group-based institutional attachments remain fairly strong for conservative Protestants, blacks, Jews, and many Catholics. Quasi-ethnic communal ties are not diminishing in any significant way. The declines in church attendance appear to have bottomed out in the late 1970s, which may portend a more stable period of institutional religious attachments for the future. And even those who are highly privatized in their faith tend not to lose their religious identities. For example, many who have drifted away from regular mass still think of themselves as Catholics. Today there are growing numbers of communal Catholics—that is, young well-educated persons not so much involved in the institutional church yet self-consciously, and at times even militantly, Catholic in outlook. Even liberal Protestants have their alumni associations; such Protestants are no longer very active but on occasion they rise to defend their religion's causes.

---

18. Talcott Parsons, "Christianity and Modern Industrial Society," in his *Sociological Theory and Modern Society* (New York: Free Press, 1967), p. 413.

19. See his "Selective Catholicism: How They Get Away with It," *America,* 30 Apr. 1983.

PATTERNS OF RELIGIOUS SWITCHING

The new voluntarism is apparent in patterns of switching among the faiths. Switching from one faith to another is common in the United States: one-third of all Americans no longer belong with the tradition in which they were born; fully 40 percent of today's Protestants have changed affiliation at one time or another in their lives.

Switching from conservative to liberal Protestant churches has long been observed as accompanying upward mobility. As people's socioeconomic status has improved, they often have changed religious affiliations. Theologically liberal and higher-status churches are deemed to be in keeping with advances in educational and occupational attainment. Over the years the liberal churches have benefited from this movement. In the past Episcopalians especially, but also Presbyterians and Congregationalists, enjoyed net gains from switching at the expense of moderate and conservative religious bodies. Today there is still some shifting of this kind but to a lesser extent. Since the 1960s switching has become more diverse and has taken on symbolic qualities peculiar to the cultural climate of the times.

Today there are three distinct streams of religious movement. Two amount to a circulation of the saints among Protestant churches, and a third involves a secular drift out of organized religion.

The liberal movement is one of the streams. Those shifting into liberal churches are older, more educated, and have high-level occupations; they are less active religiously than those they leave behind in other churches; they tend to be liberal on moral issues. The liberal churches enjoy net gains in the switching process, almost wholly accounted for by older switchers. Many of these in-switchers are only nominally religious as church members.

The second stream is the conservative movement. Those switching to the conservative churches tend to be somewhat younger and have lower status levels. They are more active in the churches, and they are more conservative on issues such as abortion, the Equal Rights Amendment, and civil liberties.

Liberal churches enjoy somewhat larger net gains from switching, but conservative churches pick up better converts in the sense of institutional belonging and commitment. Those switching have characteristics similar to the traditions to which they switch, and thereby contribute to the maintenance of existing life-style and institutional differences among the faiths. The big losers in the switching directions are the large moderate denominations—Methodists, Lutherans, American Baptists, and Disciples of Christ.

The third stream, qualitatively different, is the switching to no religious preference, or the growth of the secular constituency. In all the sifting and sorting in the recent period, this group has become the main beneficiary. For every person raised without religion who adopts a church, over three people forsake the churches for no organized religion. All religious groups lose people to this category, but losses are greatest among liberal and moderate Protestants, Catholics, and Jews. Those becoming non-affiliates are young, predominantly male, well educated, committed to the new morality, and oriented generally to an ethic of personal fulfillment.

Greater diversity in switching patterns, however, does not mean that institutional religious attachments are crumbling. The opposite may actually be the case. A new religious order appears to be in the making in which life-style choice and moral values play a bigger part in selecting a religious affiliation. With the erosion of traditional group loyalties, individually based choices can now operate more freely; people can affiliate on the basis of genuine religious preference. Individuals sharing a common outlook or behavioral style are likely to cluster around those institutions identified, officially or unofficially, with a preferred constellation of beliefs and moral values. To the extent that this happens, the religious communities could take on clearer social and religious identities as they become ideologically more homogeneous.

THE FUTURE

It would be risky, of course, to predict the religious future on the basis of current patterns of switching. Trends such as these change, and often rather abruptly and in unanticipated directions. Of greater long-term importance in shaping the religious composition of the country are the demographics: declining birthrates, migration, and birth-cohort changes over time. These factors virtually assure that trends now set in motion will continue throughout this century and into the next.

The Catholic population is growing, and will continue to do so, because of its birthrates and immigration. In the post-Vatican II era, American Catholicism suffers from being pulled in conflicting directions—toward greater personal religious freedom, on the one hand, but also toward traditional stands in matters of faith and morality, on the other. Last year's presidential election brought these tensions to the fore in exchanges be-

tween vice-presidential nominee Geraldine Ferraro and Archbishop John J. O'Connor over abortion. The growing activism of the bishops on matters such as nuclear warfare and the economy signal a dramatic shift toward greater public involvement. American Catholicism is at a crucial moment in its cultural and institutional alignments and is now in a position to exercise considerable influence in shaping public life. Much depends on the vision that is articulated and on the church's success in resolving issues of personal faith and morality without alienating large sectors of its constituency.

Already we observed age discrepancies for Protestant groups, which translate, of course, into fertility differentials. Conservative Protestants have far higher birthrates than liberal and moderate Protestants. Rates are highest for Nazarenes, Pentecostals, Mormons, Church of God members, and black Southern Baptists.[20] For younger women in liberal and moderate churches, the average number of children is well below the replacement level. Not only are there fewer young women, but even those that remain have fewer children. The birthrates are partly due to class patterns of fertility, but the demographics today also reflect the heavy losses of young adults from the liberal churches in the 1960s. Even the net gains that the liberal churches enjoy from switching are not sufficient to offset this lack of natural growth.

Even more telling are the figures pertaining to birth cohorts. Throughout

20. See William McKinney and Wade Clark Roof, "A Social Profile of American Religious Groups," *Yearbook of American and Canadian Churches, 1982* (Nashville, TN: Abingdon Press), pp. 267-73.

this century there has been a gradual erosion of the liberal Protestant community. Most of the moderate to liberal groups have lost ground, almost decade by decade; defectors include those born in the post-World War II period in particular. Methodists, for example— often cited as the most representative American religious group—made up 16 percent of all Americans born around the turn of the century but only 7.7 percent of those born between 1958 and 1965.[21] Similar declines are observed for Lutherans, Presbyterians, Episcopalians, Jews, the United Church of Christ, and Unitarians. Overall the evidence is unmistakably clear: the liberal sector of Protestantism as well as of the total religious community in this country is shrinking and will continue to do so for the foreseeable future.

Gradually, and at times almost imperceptibly, numbers have increased over the decades at the extremes of the religious distribution—for conservative Protestants as well as for non-affiliates. In the aftermath of the Scopes trial fundamentalists lost ground, but actually their numbers have grown in the years since World War I. They made up 11.8 percent of the generation born at the turn of the century, dropped to 7.8 percent for the 1907-23 cohort, but have risen ever since, reaching a record high of 12 percent for the 1958-65 cohort. This pattern, extending over three-quarters of the century, combined with the shrinkage in the liberal camp, suggests that the size of the conservative Protestant community will be propor-

21. See Tom W. Smith, "America's Religious Mosaic," *American Demographics,* pp. 19-23 (June 1984). Also using the General Social Surveys, Smith looks at five birth cohorts since the early 1900s.

tionately larger at the end of the century than it was in 1900. Whatever their power or influence in the culture in the future, the numbers favor the conservative side.

The non-affiliates have also increased, especially in the baby-boom years following World War II. They accounted for about 3 percent of those born around the turn of the century; about 11 percent of those born between 1941 and 1957; and 13 percent of the 1958-65 birth cohort. The number of Americans growing up outside the religious traditions is increasing. The fact that this growing sector differs from the religious conservatives on so many issues—civil liberties, life-styles, child rearing, and family values—portends the possibility of diverging separate cultures and ever-sharper confrontation over issues of great public significance. As older cohorts die and the more recent cohorts come to make up a larger share of the population, there is a good chance of heightened conflict between the two sectors. Quite possibly, religiously grounded values will be at the center of much debate for the future, maybe even the basis for struggles over the public posture of American life and who will exercise decisive influence over it.

But even this scenario is a tentative one, for much depends on what happens in the religious middle. Despite the plight of the liberal Protestant mainline currently, the moderate Protestant faiths may recover a new middle ground. By virtue of their size and heritage, moderate to liberal groups are in a position and have the resources to forge a broadly based synthesis of belief and culture. These groups are at the center religiously at a time when there is no center. The temptation is to move either to the left or to the right—or fluctuate in one direction or the other depending on the issue—but neither extreme is really natural for these groups. Yet to remain in the middle requires creating a new vital synthesis, a prospect that at present is not apparent but may yet evolve. If this happens it will likely occur by engaging other groups—most notably, conservative Protestants and Catholics—in debate and compromise on specific issues bearing upon public faith, and by generating a social vision capable of broadly encompassing middle America.

Today the lack of a public religious presence is lamented. Richard Neuhaus speaks of the "naked public square" and observes that various groups are now contending to become culture-defining forces in American life.[22] It is noteworthy that the religious voices now attempting to articulate a public vision—Catholics, conservative Protestants, and, to a lesser extent, black Protestants—all have and draw upon a strong group or ethnic experience. Those faiths most capable of galvanizing a new cultural center are those deeply rooted in the life of the people. In the debate over religion and its role in public life that will certainly continue, no doubt new religious and cultural configurations will yet emerge, but it is hardly imaginable that this will happen without the historic religious traditions as major players.

22. Richard J. Neuhaus, *The Naked Public Square* (Grand Rapids, MI: Eerdmans, 1984).

ANNALS, *AAPSS*, **480**, July 1985

Liberal Protestantism:
End of the Road?

By BENTON JOHNSON

ABSTRACT: The liberal Protestant denominations, long the most influential of America's mainline religious bodies, have suffered serious membership losses since the late 1960s. The principal sources of the losses are in the failure of the children of members to remain affiliated; this failure has been traced to a value shift that began among college-educated youth in the 1960s. Although this shift caught the liberal churches by surprise, their leaders contributed to the intellectual climate that made it possible. This climate was created in the 1930s by Reinhold Niebuhr in his critique of the optimistic religious liberalism of his day as the self-serving ideology of the bourgeoisie. As an alternative he urged theology to recover a sense of the sinful and tragic side of life and urged Christians to support the struggles of oppressed peoples. Although these themes profoundly affected liberal Protestant leaders, they failed to attract most lay people. In the 1950s Protestant intellectuals began mounting a frontal assault on the popular piety of the laity. This assault, which eventually extended even to theistic belief itself, was thematically similar to secular intellectuals' critiques of American culture and institutions, which were later embodied in an exaggerated form in the youth rebellions of the 1960s. If the liberal churches are to recover their strength and cultural influence they will have to make liberal Christianity more relevant and compelling to its own constituency.

Benton Johnson, Ph.D., is professor of sociology at the University of Oregon in Eugene. He is the coeditor of American Mosaic *(1971) and the author of numerous articles on American religion.*

TWENTY-FIVE years ago the late historian and Protestant churchman, Sydney E. Ahlstrom, wrote an article for *The Annals* on the current state of American religion. Its tone was positive and optimistic. Like most contemporary observers, he noted that the Protestant churches had recovered from the decline that had begun in the mid-1920s and that the nation as a whole was enjoying a revival of interest in religion. Although he had misgivings about some aspects of the new popular piety, he was enthusiastic about the renewal of theological activity, a renewal largely set in motion by the works of Reinhold Niebuhr. It was, he declared, a "renaissance unparalleled since the age of the Reformation."[1]

A mere decade later everything had changed. Ahlstrom's 1970 *Annals* article contained a radically different assessment of the state of American religion. The totally unpredicted cultural revolution of the 1960s had profoundly reshaped the religious landscape. The revival following World War II was only a memory; the institutional church was under attack as irrelevant; conventional moral codes were being overturned; and the "WASP [white Anglo-Saxon Protestant] ascendancy" in national life was being challenged by radical students and black militants. As for the theological renaissance, that, too, was history. Theology had turned critical and destructive and was undermining the very foundations of the Christian faith.[2]

It soon became apparent that the liberal Protestant churches and to some extent the Roman Catholic church were among the major casualties of the revolutionary ferment of the sixties. By the early seventies, it was clear that all the liberal denominations were losing members. By the middle of the decade the losses numbered in the millions.

Now, 10 years later, the decline has slowed and some denominations are even reporting modest gains, but there is no evidence that a genuine turnaround has begun. The liberal Protestant community remains mired in depression, a depression far deeper and more long-lasting than it suffered earlier in the century. Moreover, this time the conservative, or evangelical, wing of Protestantism has been spared from decline. It escaped serious damage in the sixties and has continued to grow at rates at least equal to the growth of the population as a whole. As the liberal wing lost numbers and influence, the conservative wing achieved high public visibility and made greater strides toward claiming the leadership of the Protestant community than anyone would have thought possible even 15 years ago. Meanwhile, no Reinhold Niebuhr has come forward with new theological resources to energize the liberal wing. No wonder a note of sadness and defeat has recently crept into the writings of many liberal Protestant intellectuals. No wonder many of them have little hope that their community can regain its former preeminence in American religion.

What went wrong? Why did this once mighty and still large religious community begin to decline? What are the prospects of recovery? These are the questions we will address.

1. Sydney E. Ahlstrom, "Theology and the Present-Day Revival," *The Annals* of the American Academy of Political and Social Science, 332:30 (Nov. 1960).

2. Sydney E. Ahlstrom, "The Radical Turn in Theology and Ethics: Why It Occurred in the 1960's," *The Annals* of the American Academy of Political and Social Science, 387:1-13 (Jan. 1970).

KELLEY'S THESIS

The first serious attempt to come to grips with these questions—indeed the first serious attempt to face up squarely to the existence of the decline itself—was made by Dean M. Kelley in his widely read book of 1972, *Why Conservative Churches Are Growing.*[3] Kelley, a liberal Protestant with a record of involvement in the civil rights movement, argued that the reason the liberal churches were declining was that they failed to provide their members with a clear-cut vision of the meaning of life and with a moral code to govern their conduct. People are attracted to religion, he asserted, because they need an overall sense of meaning and purpose in their lives. Churches that satisfy these needs and have high expectations for their members' behavior are churches that succeed in recruiting people and holding on to them. In Kelley's opinion, the reason liberal churches were losing members was that they were theologically unsure of themselves. They did not proclaim with confidence a distinctive outlook on life, they did not actively seek members, and they did not require their members to observe a common moral code. They spoke with uncertain and diverse voices and demanded very little of anyone. Some of them substituted social action programs for the real business of religion. As a consequence, many of their members drifted away and few new ones were found.

Kelley's thesis had a ring of plausibility. Liberal Protestant churches were indeed uncertain about theological issues, were reluctant to sell themselves, and had long ago given up any formal

effort to oversee their members' moral conduct. Moreover, Kelley's observation that social action is no substitute for religion in church life seemed to pinpoint the really decisive factor in the decline of the liberal denominations. All the other conditions in Kelley's thesis had existed in these denominations for decades and could therefore not explain why the losses began so recently. Only a condition operating in the short term could do that, and that condition was the decision most of these church bodies made in the early 1960s to concentrate much more heavily on social action programs than they had in the past.

WHAT SURVEYS SHOW

As Kelley presented no conclusive empirical evidence for his thesis, it remained for others to discover the factors actually at work in the decline of the liberal denominations. By the end of the 1970s a number of well-designed studies, many based on national survey data, had provided a clear view of what some of these factors were. The only support that Kelley's thesis received was Dean R. Hoge's finding that a number of Kelley's factors were highly correlated with denominational growth rates in the 20-year period beginning in 1955.[4] Even during the 1950s, when all denominations were growing, relatively strict, self-confident bodies such as the Assemblies of God had higher growth rates than more permissive and timid bodies such as the Congregationalists. On the other hand, no evidence has been found that Kelley's decisive factor—namely,

3. Dean M. Kelley, *Why Conservative Churches Are Growing* (New York: Harper & Row, 1972).

4. Dean R. Hoge, "A Test of Theories of Denominational Growth and Decline," in *Understanding Church Growth and Decline, 1950-1978,* ed. Dean R. Hoge and David R. Roozen (New York: Pilgrim Press, 1979), pp. 179-97.

an emphasis on social action—had anything to do with the decline.

It is now firmly established that the prime source of membership losses sustained by the liberal denominations is the failure of the offspring of their members to affiliate with a liberal religious body. There has been no mass exodus of those who were already affiliated. Even the older, more conservative members who grumbled about social action projects and political preaching have tended to stay put. On the other hand, the evangelical churches have done a far better job of holding on to their youth. This fact and the fact that evangelical women have higher birthrates than liberal Protestant women are largely responsible for the growth advantages that these churches enjoy. Although they have been able to proselytize some of the young people who were brought up in liberal churches, the great bulk of these youth have ended up neither as evangelicals nor as members of such new religious movements as Rajneeshism or the Unification church. They have simply remained without religious affiliation.

The decline of the liberal churches has been exacerbated by their relatively low birthrates and by an apparent falloff in what was probably an important source of their growth during the 1950s: a pattern of membership transfer first documented by Rodney Stark and Charles Y. Glock with data collected in the 1960s.[5] That pattern involved a change of membership from a relatively low-status to a relatively high-status denomination. As lower-status denominations tend to be conservative and higher-status denominations tend to be liberal, the result was an augmentation of the strength of the liberal churches. Recent data suggest that this pattern of upward switching is less common now than it was a generation ago.

Finally, as the result of all these trends, the liberal churches have acquired a lopsided age composition. Compared to the conservative churches as well as to the population at large, they are disproportionately made up of people over the age of 50.[6] As a consequence, their death rates are relatively high and will become higher still unless they are able to recruit a large number of young people, especially young people with small children.

THE VALUE SHIFT

What is responsible for the primary cause of the membership losses of the liberal churches—namely, the failure of young people to become affiliated? On this question, too, the research findings are clear-cut, at least up to a point. A shift of value commitments, centered among white college-educated youth, seems to be the major precipitating factor in the losses. Because the constituency of the liberal denominations is largely of middle-class status, the shift has affected these denominations far more severely than it has affected the conservative denominations.

5. Rodney Stark and Charles Y. Glock, *American Piety* (Berkeley: University of California Press, 1968), pp. 183-203.

6. For an excellent summary and interpretation of these findings, see Wade Clark Roof, "America's Voluntary Establishment: Mainline Religion in Transition," *Daedalus,* 111:169-84 (Winter 1982). My interpretation differs from Roof's only in the influence it attributes to certain factors within the liberal denominations themselves to which he and most other observers have given little attention. See also Frank Newport, "The Religious Switcher in the United States," *American Sociological Review,* 44:528-52 (Aug. 1979).

This value shift was spearheaded by the large baby-boom cohort, which began reaching maturity in the mid-1960s, and was expressed in its most visible and extreme form in the great countercultural revolution that swept across elite college campuses and adjacent communities at the end of that decade. It was characterized by a rejection of traditional moral standards, especially in the areas of sexuality, family values, and personal life-styles, and by an affirmation of personal autonomy and tolerance for individual differences. It was also associated to some extent with a distrust of established institutions, ideologies, and systems of authority. Ironically enough, although many counterculture youth identified with the oppressed peoples who were served by the social action programs of the liberal churches, they rejected these churches because they seemed to stand for established authority and for traditional life-styles and moral standards.[7]

What was the source of the value shift of the 1960s? Why did it have such a profound impact on the liberal churches? To a very large extent the first question remains enshrouded in mystery. No one predicted it in advance and most attempts to explain it after the fact have been both sketchy and speculative. No doubt the existence of an unusually large cohort of youth in close contact with one another in college communities facilitated its articulation in the form of an alternative culture. No doubt the Vietnam war gave many young men a personal stake in committing themselves to

this value shift. But neither of these facts can explain the form the value shift assumed or why it occurred when it did. For one thing, young Americans have gone to war in the past without protest. For another, it is difficult to understand how the sheer size of the baby-boom cohort could have altered so profoundly the campus culture of the preceding decade. Moreover, in retrospect it is clear that signs of the value shift began appearing before the baby-boom generation entered college or the antiwar movement began. For example, among educated young people both church attendance and birthrates began dropping in the late 1950s.

At first glance, the question of why the value shift had such a profound effect on the liberal Protestant denominations seems less of a mystery. As the shift was led by white educated youth, a segment of the population that is disproportionately of liberal Protestant background, its impact was bound to be greatest on those denominations. The prevailing view is that whatever the causes of the shift might have been, they were secular in character, and that the shift struck the churches as a meteor might strike the earth. As Hoge and Roozen put it, the shift "has hit the churches from the outside."[8] Dean Kelley concurs. In his view, the liberal churches have become such weak organizations that they are unable to resist the intrusion of environmental forces. "In those churches," he argues, *"religion has become a dependent variable."*[9]

7. Hoge and Roozen, *Understanding Church Growth and Decline,* pp. 21-68, 94-143, 179-97, 315-33; see also Robert Wuthnow, "Recent Patterns of Secularization: A Problem of Generations?" *American Sociological Review,* 41:850-67 (Oct. 1976).

8. Dean R. Hoge and David A. Roozen, "Some Sociological Conclusions about Church Trends," in *Understanding Church Growth and Decline,* ed. Hoge and Roozen, p. 328.

9. Dean M. Kelley, "Is Religion a Dependent Variable?" in *Understanding Church Growth and Decline,* ed. Hoge and Roozen, p. 338, italics in original.

It is one thing to acknowledge that the value shift caught the liberal churches off guard and damaged them badly and quite another to assume that they played no part in it themselves, that they were and are the victims of influences having their origin in other institutions or in the dynamics of economic or political processes. The image of the liberal religious community as object rather than subject has pervaded the intellectual community for decades. Hoge and Kelley did not originate it; they merely drew on it as a convenient resource for making a theoretical judgment.

Yet one does not have to deny Kelley's thesis about the relative weakness of liberal religious bodies to recognize that this image is to some extent contrary to fact. If the liberal churches simply react to the pressures of their immediate environment—for example, the class-based perspectives of their most prominent members—why did they support the civil rights movement so strongly in the 1960s? Why did so many of their leaders later become involved in the antiwar movement? Now that public opinion has shifted to the right on a number of issues, why are they not advocating a stronger military posture or the return of prayer to the public schools? If they simply react, they evidently do so selectively, succumbing to some pressures willingly and resisting others.

It is closer to the truth to consider the liberal denominations as value-carrying communities that not only respond to environmental influences but seek some measure of autonomy and influence within their environment. Like most communities, they are periodically faced with threats and challenges from the outside to which they respond in varying ways; they are faced as well with ten-

sions and conflicting tendencies from within their own ranks. If we are to achieve a more complete understanding of why the liberal churches have declined, as well as an informed basis for assessing their prospects for recovery, this perspective will prove far more fruitful than the simpler view that the liberal churches are the passive victims of circumstance. It will also be able to throw light on the origin of the value shift and why these churches were among its principal casualties.

THE TWO EPOCHS OF LIBERALISM

The epoch in which the liberal Protestant churches are now living—and which, in my opinion, must come to a close if they are to recover—began in the depths of the Great Depression of the 1930s. Its identifying characteristics are a set of very general ideas, each evidenced in many concrete expressions, which have guided much of the intellectual activity and policy formation of these churches' leaders. If any single event ushered in the current epoch it was the publication in 1932 of Reinhold Niebuhr's *Moral Man and Immoral Society*,[10] a work that had a truly monumental impact on both clergy and laity and helped, among other things, to stimulate the great revival of theological activity that so impressed Sydney Ahlstrom in 1960.

Classical liberalism

In order to appreciate how important a break with the past Niebuhr's thinking represented, it is necessary to understand the dominant attitudes of the

10. Reinhold Niebuhr, *Moral Man and Immoral Society* (New York: Scribner's, 1932).

preceding epoch as well as the predicament that the Protestant community faced in 1932. The preceding epoch was the classical, or formative, period of liberal Protestantism as a major presence on the American scene. Unlike the current epoch, it did not begin abruptly. It originated as a set of tendencies among religious intellectuals and other spokesmen affiliated with high-status denominations having significant strength among the educated, affluent, largely WASP strata of the urban areas of the eastern and north-central states. By the 1880s these tendencies had made great headway in the major seminaries of these regions as well as in all the denominations currently considered liberal.

Broadly speaking, liberalism was an effort to assimilate the new intellectual climate of science, history, and philosophy while maintaining a distinctively Christian posture as well as the position of cultural leadership that these strata and their denominations had long enjoyed. In the process, the liberals gave up traditional Protestant views of the Bible and greatly modified their conception of human nature as sinful and in need of supernatural redemption. On the other hand, they retained and emphasized the older American Protestant expectation that history, under the leadership of the American nation and the Protestant churches, was moving toward a culminating stage, the millennial Kingdom of God that would be characterized by happiness, justice, and peace throughout the world. Theirs was an optimistic world view in which vibrant, self-fulfilled Christians would, by social reform and the example of their own lives, bring history to a triumphant climax. As for self-fulfillment, "it is good news," wrote William Ernest Garrison in 1928, "that we are not condemned by any power outside ourselves to live on the low levels where we have our dwelling and within the narrow limits that hedge us in."[11] As for social reform, wrote Walter Rauschenbusch in 1907, Christians should be "the masters of politics by creating the issues which parties will have to espouse."[12]

The golden age of classical liberalism occurred just prior to World War I. But hard times soon set in. The war itself called the hope of peace and progress into question. The largely middle-class constituency of the liberal churches proved reluctant to support the increasingly radical political programs of those liberal leaders who were dedicated to social reform. The fundamentalist movement shattered the liberals' hope of winning the allegiance of all Protestants. To make matters worse, during the 1920s secular intellectuals, many of them popular writers, began ridiculing the traditional values and life-styles of the Protestant community. As Robert T. Handy has shown, by the mid-1920s the major churches were showing signs of decline and sagging morale.[13] The economic depression that followed a few years later dealt a severe blow to the prestige of the elite class at the core of the liberal Protestant constituency.

The Niebuhr epoch

Niebuhr's stunning message was delivered in the midst of this predicament. At its core was a radical critique of classical liberalism, which he interpreted in Marx-

11. Winfred Ernest Garrison, *Affirmative Religion* (New York: Harper, 1928), p. 273.

12. Walter Rauschenbusch, *Christianity and the Social Crisis* (New York: Macmillan, 1907), p. 363.

13. Robert T. Handy, *American Religious Depression, 1925-1935* (New York: Fortress Press, 1968).

ist fashion as the self-serving ideology of the capitalist class. That ideology, which "thinks the Kingdom of God is around the corner," merely reflects the "sentimentalities and illusions of the comfortable."[14] It screens from view the realities of injustice and inequality, the important role that force and violence play in society, and the historical truth that justice can be achieved only through the political struggle of oppressed people.

Niebuhr's attack on what he considered the utopian illusions of the dominant classes of the Western capitalist nations was both sharp and unrelenting. Even in 1940, when his Marxism had become muted and he was urging the United States to resist Hitler, he wrote that "this culture does not understand historical reality clearly enough to deserve to survive. It has a right to survive only because the alternative is too horrible to contemplate."[15] And later, when he became something of a cold-war liberal, he never celebrated the virtues of American culture or religion in terms remotely resembling the sermons of the period of classical liberalism.

A very closely related theme of Niebuhr's was the need for the churches to recover the biblical sense of sin that had been discarded by liberals, who had imagined that human nature is perfectable and that social progress is automatic. Human beings, he argued, may be capable of self-transcendent love in intimate relationships, but group life produces collective egoism and greed that cannot be eradicated by moral preachment or the simple exercise of good will. Sin, especially social sin, will never be completely removed from human societies. Christians need, he wrote in 1934, "a more radical political orientation and more conservative religious convictions than are comprehended in the culture of our era."[16]

Despite its somber tones, Niebuhr's depression-era message fell on receptive ears. For one thing, it provided the radically new perspective on society and politics that many, even in the middle class, were desperately seeking in those crisis-plagued times. For another, although it dashed all hopes for a harmonious future under the cultural hegemony of the liberal churches, it did not undercut the social gospel; rather, Niebuhr's message gave the churches a new agenda and a new, tough-minded, realistic point of view. In fact, it held that a prime task for serious Christians—indeed the major point of Christian praxis—should be to assist oppressed peoples in their struggles for liberation. Finally, by calling theology away from its close alignment with bourgeois ideology and back to its neglected biblical roots, Niebuhr gave Christian thought a truly autonomous mission once again. Even in his most Marxist phase, Niebuhr never doubted that Marxism itself was deeply imbued with the spirit of nineteenth-century utopianism and needed to be tempered with insights from theology.

There can be little doubt that Niebuhr's basic message contributed to the revival of the morale and energy of the liberal Protestant community. It may well have been one factor in the quickening of popular interest in religion, especially among young educated adults, that got under way just before World War II. By the 1950s many intellectuals were showing interest in the issues that a

14. Niebuhr, *Moral Man and Immoral Society,* pp. 82, 80.

15. Reinhold Niebuhr, *Christianity and Power Politics* (New York: Scribner's, 1940), p. 174.

16. Reinhold Niebuhr, *Reflections on the End of an Era* (New York: Scribner's, 1934), p. ix.

host of new theologians were raising. By that time, too, Niebuhr's perspective on Christian praxis had convinced a new generation of church leaders to commit themselves to social action on behalf of the dispossessed.

TWO FLAWS

Although Niebuhr's reformulations had a stimulating effect on the liberal churches, they contained two serious flaws. It was only a matter of time until some development or other led to their becoming an active source of trouble for the liberal religious community.

The first flaw had to do with Niebuhr's plea for the renewal of theology as an intellectually autonomous activity. It consisted in the inability of the various systems that flourished in this country after 1932 to ground the theological enterprise in assumptions that would pass muster among critical intellectuals. These systems, sophisticated as some of them were, failed to address the issue of their truth claims either forthrightly or convincingly. All the various theological constructions of the so-called neoorthodox period were therefore highly vulnerable to intellectual assault. That assault came in the 1960s, revealing, as Ahlstrom lamented in 1970, that neoorthodoxy had, after all, only managed to place a "layer of dogmatic asphalt" over "the old claims of scientific and historical investigations."[17] Once this layer had cracked, theology went into a steep decline, thus depriving the liberal churches of any living roots for spiritual nourishment.

The second flaw consisted in the fact that the radical political praxis advo-cated by Niebuhr and strongly supported by many liberal church leaders who came after him was opposed to the class interests and the class ethos of the constituency of the liberal churches. Niebuhr himself was well aware of the problem this presented. As early as 1926 he conceded in his private journal that "it is a bit of unwarranted optimism" to expect that the churches will "make any serious contribution to the reorganization of society" because they are "on the whole thoroughly committed to the interests and prejudices of the middle classes."[18]

He was not, however, willing to write off altogether the churches' potential value as a constructive force in society. For all their faults, they played a valuable role in the formation of character and in mitigating the harshness of social conflict. Moreover, if they could be stripped of their rosy illusions and equipped with a new theological and political vision they might play a less dangerous role in society. Some of their members might actually contribute to the liberation of the captive peoples of the world.

If one or more of the theological perspectives that flourished in the wake of Niebuhr's writings had won the allegiance of the liberal laity and had also passed the rigorous examination of intellectuals, it is conceivable that Niebuhr's hopes would have been realized and that this second flaw would not have damaged the churches. But not only did these systems wither under critical scrutiny, they failed to generate much enthusiasm in the pews. And needless to say, the response of the laity to the call for social action was disappointing, even

17. Ahlstrom, "Radical Turn in Theology and Ethics," p. 7.

18. Reinhold Niebuhr, *Leaves from the Notebook of a Tamed Cynic* (Chicago: Willett, Clark, and Colby, 1929), p. 112.

though a large handful of lay people did become committed activitists.

THE ATTACK
ON POPULAR RELIGION

In my opinion, the single most important development that transformed both these latent problems into real sources of weakness and decline was the response of many religious leaders to the resurgence of popular piety that reached its height in the 1950s. Although the resurgence was good news for pastors, seminaries, and ecclesiastical officials, it was troubling to many religious opinion makers and intellectuals for it did not seem to reflect any serious theological or spiritual quest or any concern for social justice.

The most popular religious voices of the decade were not those of neoorthodox intellectuals or social activists but of writers and preachers, such as Norman Vincent Peale, who treated religious faith as a tool for achieving personal happiness and success, and Billy Graham, a product of a revitalized fundamentalism with its traditional emphasis on individual salvation. Much of the religious revival seemed motivated by a search for security and by a desire to enrich private life. Moreover, if the revival had any political content at all it was an affirmation of American values and institutions, and endorsement of the bourgeois state, albeit without the heady optimism and self-assurance of the epoch of classical liberalism. All in all, the hallmarks of the revival were conformity, security, and confident living. The response of religious intellectuals was to attack middle-class religiosity and middle-class biases with all the resources they could marshal.

The attack was carried out on a very broad front and became more radical as time went on. One of its earliest and mildest examples was Will Herberg's *Protestant-Catholic-Jew,*[19] first published in 1955, which argued that traditional confessional differences were being eroded and that a national religion was emerging whose basic object of veneration was not God but the American way of life. It was followed in 1958 by Roy Eckardt's *Surge of Piety in America,*[20] in 1959 by Martin E. Marty's *New Shape of American Religion,*[21] in 1961 by Peter Berger's *Noise of Solemn Assemblies*[22] and Gibson Winter's *Suburban Captivity of the Churches,*[23] in 1963 by John Robinson's *Honest to God,*[24] in 1965 by Pierre Berton's *Comfortable Pew*[25] and Harvey Cox's *Secular City,*[26] in 1966 by Ernest Harrison's *Church without God,*[27] and later by such titles as *The Last Years of the Church*[28] and *Never Trust a God over 30.*[29] And there were many others, including learned works on the death of God and the bankruptcy of legalistic ethics.

19. Will Herberg, *Protestant-Catholic-Jew* (Garden City, NY: Doubleday, 1955).
20. Roy Eckardt, *The Surge of Piety in America* (New York: Association Press, 1958).
21. Martin E. Marty, *The New Shape of American Religion* (New York: Harper & Row, 1959).
22. Peter Berger, *The Noise of Solemn Assemblies* (Garden City, NY: Doubleday, 1961).
23. Gibson Winter, *The Surburban Captivity of the Churches* (Garden City, NY: Doubleday, 1961).
24. John Robinson, *Honest to God* (Philadelphia: Westminster Press, 1963).
25. Pierre Berton, *The Comfortable Pew* (Toronto: McClelland and Stewart, 1965).
26. Harvey Cox, *The Secular City* (New York: Macmillan, 1965).
27. Ernest Harrison, *A Church without God* (Philadelphia: Lippincott, 1966).
28. David Poling, *The Last Years of the Church* (Garden City, NY: Doubleday, 1969).
29. Albert H. Friedlander, ed., *Never Trust a God over 30* (New York: McGraw-Hill, 1967).

Among the principal targets of attack were the laity's self-centeredness and preoccupation with the comforting aspects of religion; the lack of social concern among the laity and its insulation from contact with ethnic and racial minorities; its complicity in American militarism and imperialism; and its devotion to traditional familism and morality. After the early 1960s neither the parish church nor even God was spared. The idols of the laity were systematically smashed. The guiding concept was Niebuhrian but the targets were far more numerous than his.

The attack on the piety of middle-class Protestants ran roughly parallel to a larger movement of cultural analysis and criticism initiated by secular intellectuals in the early postwar years. Works like David Riesman's *Lonely Crowd,*[30] William H. Whyte's *Organization Man,*[31] and Paul Goodman's *Growing Up Absurd*[32] come immediately to mind. The critics were troubled by a variety of trends, among them the pressures for social conformity, the seeming loss of individuality, the preoccupation with security, and the general irrationality of much contemporary life.

As liberal Protestant and secular intellectuals share similar educational backgrounds, their perspectives on modern culture had much in common. But the Protestant intellectuals had a distinctive agenda that was framed along Niebuhrian lines. Moreover, it was they and not the secular intelligentsia who launched the assault on popular religion. With minor exceptions the latter paid little

attention to the subject. The loudest and most widely read critics of the church were themselves church people. The 1960s produced no H. L. Mencken. It was theologians and the new generation of activist clergy who killed God and pronounced the institutional church irrelevant.

The value shifts to which Hoge and Roozen attribute the recent decline of liberal church membership have sources that will be the subject of research and debate for years to come. But it seems likely that one of the sources was the intellectual climate of criticism that began in the 1950s and reached its peak in the late 1960s. For one thing, the shift was most pronounced among college-educated youth, the very segment of the population in closest touch with the intellectual community. For another, the themes that the shift embodied involved a rejection of conventional middle-class values and life-styles. To be sure, the shift, especially in its radical phases, had expressions and consequences that went far beyond what many critics had hoped for or could endorse. In this sense it caught most of the adult community by surprise and did hit the churches from the outside. But the liberal churches were not simply its passive victims. Their leaders, following a scenario made possible by the Niebuhrian legacy, furnished some of the resources that made it possible.

END OF THE ROAD?

Can the liberal churches recover from their current slump and resume their former position as senior partner among the nation's leading religious communities? A consideration of this question must begin with the frank acknowledgment that serious obstacles lie in the way

30. David Riesman, *The Lonely Crowd* (New Haven, CT: Yale University Press, 1950).
31. William H. Whyte, *The Organization Man* (New York: Simon & Schuster, 1956).
32. Paul Goodman, *Growing up Absurd* (New York: Random House, 1960).

of such a recovery. The most formidable obstacle is that many of the symbolic resources of the liberal churches have been depleted and cannot be renewed. The process of depletion began with the dawn of the epoch of classical liberalism, was carried further when the Niebuhr epoch began, and was carried further still when its project of theological renewal ran out of steam in the 1960s.

Classical liberalism destroyed the credibility of the orthodox conception of humanity as in need of redemption by the grace of a sovereign Lord. To orthodox believers of virtually all Christian confessions, the fear of hell and the hope of heaven were powerful emotions that preachers, teachers, and theologians nourished in their efforts to build strong churches whose members' lives conformed to a common moral code. As a substitute for this foundation of orthodox faith, classical liberalism emphasized the hope, already present in American Protestantism, of the millennial perfection of personality and society. Reinhold Niebuhr dealt this liberal hope a deadly blow by exposing it as the self-conceit of the bourgeoisie. In its place he offered a kind of penance in the form of a tough-minded praxis of service to the dispossessed. When this regimen failed to seize the imagination of the laity, the only strong resource left to Protestant opinion leaders was to play on the sense of guilt and duty implicit in Niebuhr's model. They could not threaten punishment in hell or divine judgment upon the nation, just as they could not offer the rosy hope of a world community of peace and happiness just around the corner. The best they could do was to scold.

In my opinion there is no ready remedy for liberal Protestantism's tired spiritual blood. A spiritual renewal on a really large scale would require a new theological perspective that is both intellectually sound and psychologically provocative. Such a renewal is not on the horizon. As far as theology is concerned, for the time being liberal Protestants would do well simply to conserve and appreciate the rich cultural legacy of their lineage and to draw from it insights and concepts that can be examined for their current validity and usefulness. They should practice a discriminating eclecticism.

There are some, however, who would consider pointless any efforts to rebuild liberal Protestantism. Harvey Cox has recently asserted that the "main stimulus for the renewal of Christianity will come from the bottom and from the edge, from the sectors of the world that are on the margins of the modern/liberal consensus." He believes that "the modern era itself is ending" and that liberation theology and the base communities of Latin America "are the germ cells of the next era of our culture."[33]

In my opinion Cox's prognostication is both naive and romantic, and it perpetuates a frame of mind that has the unintended effect of handing over the spiritual and political initiative of the American middle class to fundamentalists and right-wingers, for it assumes that the bourgeois enterprise is doomed and will be replaced by something that is both radically different and radically better. In one version or another this frame of mind has been common in recent decades among liberal intellectuals, both religious and secular. It is a legacy of Niebuhr's critique of bourgeois illusions, stripped, however, of his

33. Harvey Cox, *Religion in the Secular City: Toward a Postmodern Theology* (New York: Simon & Schuster, 1984), pp. 208, 268, 267.

critique of every form of utopian thought. It is actually the mirror opposite of the exuberant self-confidence of classical liberalism. It imagines that the United States, led by its white Christian bourgeoisie, is hopelessly reactionary and that liberation movements against it herald the beginning of a new age. This form of cultural self-hate dominated the thinking of white radicals during the 1960s. The Niebuhrian legacy made Protestant liberals particularly sensitive to criticism from allegedly progressive elements and particularly willing to think well of them and do their bidding.

If one assumes, as I do, that the American nation and its middle class will be around for some time to come as a major force in the world, then an effort to shore up the liberal wing of its historically most prominent and influential religious lineage is a sensible and responsible project. If it is currently impossible to correct the theological flaw in the Niebuhrian legacy, something can be done about correcting the other flaw, which is a tendency to define the Christian life in terms sharply opposed to the traditions and inclinations of its middle-class constituency. It is neither necessary nor possible to return to the celebratory themes of classical liberalism; but if the liberal churches are to recover their morale and influence in national life, their leaders will have to temper their criticisms with a frank appreciation of many of the values of the liberal bourgeoisie. They will have to tack in the direction of restoring to the middle class some way to articulate a respect for its own standards and its own historical accomplishments.

One way to begin the task of reengaging lay people is to pay close attention to their anxieties and hopes in a manner that will offer them moral guidance in their own lives. The traditional Christian practice of the cure of souls had that aim, but two tendencies at work during the Niebuhr epoch have made the cure of souls a lost art in liberal Protestantism. One tendency, which is present in Niebuhr's own work, simply overlooks private concerns, being preoccupied instead with larger social and political issues. It is also suspicious of the older liberal spirit that promises personal triumph and abundance while screening out the evil and tragic side of life. This tendency became pronounced in the 1950s and 1960s when liberal intellectuals began denouncing the laity for its privatism and infatuation with the self-help nostrums of Norman Vincent Peale.

The second tendency derives from secular psychotherapies, which have profoundly affected modern pastoral counseling. It derives, too, from the attack on middle-class conventions that was part of the social criticism of the 1960s. Although this second tendency has opened up choices to people that were unavailable to their parents, it has left them with little positive guidance other than their own impulses and the appealing but exceedingly vague value standard of love. The result has been an ethic of personal autonomy and moral relativism in private life and an ethic of moral absolutism in public affairs.[34] In liberal Protestantism the private and the public spheres have become so uncoupled that

34. One liberal Protestant writer has recently commented on the strange disjunction that has developed in the liberal Protestant community between the standards applied to issues perceived as social and the standards applied to issues perceived as private. "If it is not repressive," she asks, "to urge a lifestyle that diminishes world hunger, why is it necessarily repressive to urge a lifestyle that diminishes drug or sexual abuse?" See Peggy L. Shriver, *The Bible Vote: Religion and the New Right* (New York: Pilgrim Press, 1981), p. 100.

pastors are reluctant to offer moral guidance for the jungle of private life and are unable to mobilize personal energies for public service.

Finally, if liberal Protestantism is to avoid a slow death it must make an aggressive effort to hold and recapture the loyalty of younger adults. The older cohorts have by and large remained faithful; but unless they are replaced with new blood, the liberal Protestant community will face further declines in the years ahead. Perhaps another unanticipated value shift will bring young adults back into the churches in a few more years. Perhaps the children of cur-

rent members will prove more faithful than their predecessors have been. But the churches should not count on these possibilities. If they want to recover, they must do something to make recovery possible.

In the meantime, very little has changed. Although the strident self-criticism of the 1960s is heard less often and there are fewer specialized ministries for social action, the major themes seem much the same. Unless the liberal churches can fashion new ideas to launch a third epoch in their history, the end of their long road as a powerful presence in American culture will soon be in sight.

The Curious Path
of Conservative Protestantism

By PHILLIP E. HAMMOND

ABSTRACT: The effective origins of contemporary conservative Protestantism are found in the early nineteenth century, when an evangelicalism emerged and so influenced that century. This outlook, both theological
and moral, dominated until after the Civil War, when forces of immigration, urbanization, and education severely challenged at least the
theological domination. By early in the twentieth century, therefore,
Protestantism had split into two factions: a liberal wing that, by
accommodating theologically to those forces of modernity, remained
dominant, and a conservative wing that seemed, by the 1920s, to have
submerged from public life. To understand not only the resurgence of
conservative Protestantism but also its unusual political turn, therefore,
requires consideration of moral—not just theological—factors peculiar to
America since the 1960s.

---

*Phillip E. Hammond (Ph.D., Columbia, 1960) has taught at Yale, Wisconsin, Arizona,
and the University of California, Santa Barbara, where he is professor of religious studies and
sociology and currently chairman of religious studies. He is the author or coauthor of a
number of books in the sociology of religion, most recently—with Robert Bellah—*Varieties
of Civil Religion. *He is the editor of the recently published* Sacred in a Secular Age *and
coeditor, with David G. Bromley, of the forthcoming* Future of New Religious Movements.

NOTE: This article was written while the author was the recipient of a grant from the Lilly
Endowment, whose support is gratefully acknowledged.

WHETHER religion is judged to be conservative depends less on its doctrines than on its relationship to society. As conservative Protestantism in America in the 1980s was not always conservative, the task of this article—to trace its curious path—is really to track its transmutations. While we could start even earlier, we choose to begin this story in the first decades of the nineteenth century.

THE EARLY NINETEENTH CENTURY

For some years early in the nineteenth century, the American states and frontier were swept by a series of religious revivals generally labeled the Second Great Awakening. The major residue of these revivals was what we might call the voluntary church syndrome, a religious pattern we know variously as the separation of church and state, religious freedom, the competitiveness and commercialization of religious organizations, and the privatization of faith.

Although not uniquely Protestant, the voluntary church syndrome was felt first and most deeply in Protestantism. One reason was that this voluntary religious pattern had greater theological warrant in Protestantism than it did in Catholicism or Judaism. Catholic theology stressed the role of liturgy, priest, and church; Judaism, the role of community and ritual law. But Protestants were, so to speak, already theologically prepared to be told that salvation was their own responsibility, that internal spirituality was the measure of a Christian, and that inner light should shine out in the form of upright behavior.

The Second Great Awakening thus went far in enabling individualistic evangelicalism to become the dominant

religious perspective in America. Clergy and church gained in popularity even as they lost in power; formally, that is, religion declined, but informally its influence spread. Many features of organized life that we take now for granted—for example, hospitals, publishing firms, newspapers and magazines, and colleges—owe their origins to the religious enthusiasm of Protestant Christians intent on evangelizing society in the nineteenth century.

This evangelical Protestantism was hardly conservative—at least not religiously conservative—for it was in fact a new development, a departure from Puritan orthodoxy. It was a religion that capitalized on the growing sense of individualism even as it exalted social responsibility. A society in the throes of establishing democracy—of extending the vote and elevating the commoner, of demolishing hereditary privilege and holding out the promise of success for all, of broadening liberties while relying on self-control—such a society could hardly ask for a more compatible religion. Evangelicalism rather quickly became the dominant religious outlook, therefore, and not just among Protestants.

That this outlook had a strong reformist element is well known, abolition being its most visible early expression. Less dramatic but no doubt more widespread, however, was the element in evangelicalism that contributed to its subsequent conservatism: the "paradoxical combination of libertarianism and traditionalism."[1] Developing throughout the century along with the American nation, this element became as close to an established theology—with a parallel

1. Jerome L. Himmelstein, "The New Right," in *The New Christian Right*, ed. R. C. Liebman and R. Wuthnow (New York: Aldine, 1983), p. 22.

moral consensus—as America will ever know. In the nineteenth century it motivated missionaries to build schools and cover native breasts. It encouraged capitalists to build factories and hedge their investments with philanthropy. It exalted rural and small-town ideals, saturating America with the idea that people should be free to do pretty much as they like, as long as they look out for themselves—and, of course, behave. American evangelical Protestantism, it might be said, provided a creed that, even today, can stir Americans to action.

AT THE TURN OF
THE CENTURY

In due time, of course, social forces greatly challenged this creed; views that made sense in the context of farm, small town, and neighborhood were hard to sustain in the city, factory, and university. In these latter places the forces of modernity had to be confronted. Because persons differed in their closeness to modernity, however, they also differed in their responses to it.

Sometime after the Civil War, and for the next several decades, there developed within Protestantism two camps regarding this question of modernity—of just how to contend with it. As Peter Berger reminds us,[2] then as now there were basically two religious choices: accommodate religion to worldly circumstances, meeting changes with all available resources; or hold firm to the religious convictions, insisting that worldly changes do not alter supernatural truths. The first choice created liberals, the second conservatives.

2. *The Sacred Canopy* (Garden City, NY: Anchor/Doubleday, 1969).

The evangelicalism that had been mainline evangelicalism throughout most of the nineteenth century thus became conservative Protestantism by 1920, not so much because its tenets changed but because the surrounding world changed. Many Protestants not only did not change with it but also elaborated a theology that defended their decision not to change. About this time, indeed, there appeared a series of pamphlets proclaiming the fundamentals of Christian doctrine, from which came the label "Fundamentalist," a title used by friend and foe alike. Evangelicalism was still firmly entrenched in some sectors, but now it was defensive, locked in a struggle with its accommodative counterpart over control of Protestant institutions in America—local churches certainly, but more strategically the seminaries, church-related colleges, denominational headquarters, the church media, and thus the public face of Protestantism.

Conservatism lost that struggle, with the Scopes trial of 1925 being the publicized scene of surrender. The conservative troops did not dissolve and fade away, of course, but they were now weakened in leadership and infrastructure. Their established status had all but disappeared, to be taken over by the hated enemies they called, with justification, modernists.

What exactly was the battle about? The forces of modernity over which Protestantism split may be conveniently grouped into three areas: (1) immigration, especially of Roman Catholics, thus calling into question Protestant hegemony; (2) industrialization, especially in urban centers, thus revealing the need for new kinds of social ministries; and (3) education, especially in the form of Darwinism and biblical higher criticism, thus evoking new understanding of the Scriptures. Generally speaking, liberal Protestants saw the need to accommodate in all three of those areas; what had been conventional behavior and thought in the pulpit, seminary, and denominational office became, in little more than one generation, outmoded and disreputable—at least to the vast majority of Protestants occupying pulpits, seminaries, and denominational offices. As we shall see later, the change was by no means so swift or so widespread among Protestants in the pews.[3]

Theologically another difference intensified between the two camps: liberals became explicitly postmillennial in outlook, meaning that Christ's return awaits human effort and success in bringing about the Kingdom on earth. Many conservatives absorbed and upheld the opposing premillennial view—that things will get worse before Christ comes again to reign for a thousand years, and no human agency can influence the outcome; the most that persons can do is repent, get saved, and await the rapture.

Actually premillennialism was only one of several theological tributaries coming out of the past to make up the conservative Protestant stream. Two others of importance were Reformed or Calvinist orthodoxy and holiness teaching. As different as these three were from each other, however, they share the label "conservative" because all three, in Berger's words, "refused to accommodate themselves . . . and continued to profess the old objectivities as much as possible as if nothing had happened."[4]

FROM THE 1920s TO THE 1960s

The struggle over modernity was thus won by the liberal accommodationists, and they now controlled the so-called mainline churches. Evangelical Protestants—now conservative—either grew silent and disaffected in the pews of those mainline churches—and this was the case for many—or else they founded new, oftentimes nondenominational, churches. And not just churches but Bible schools, colleges, radio and then television ministries, publishing houses, and journals were established as well—in effect, new leadership and a new infrastructure developed. Conservative Protestants did not forgo the public arena altogether—for instance, between 1921 and 1929, 37 anti-evolution bills were introduced in 20 state legislatures[5]—but, having lost the theological war for control of the ecclesiastical mainstream, conservatives essentially submerged from public life and instead turned inward. Their earlier objections on theological grounds to Catholicism, Darwinism, and higher criticism did not exactly disappear, but neither did the warfare continue. Instead, they regrouped and, as it turns out, prepared behind the scenes for a new kind of battle.

Meanwhile, liberal Protestantism accommodated mightily. Optimistic in its adjustments to secular forces, it took as its goal the evangelization of the world in one generation. It was also prepared to

    3. Two excellent sources on this matter are George M. Marsden, *Fundamentalism and American Culture* (New York: Oxford University Press, 1980); and William R. Hutchison, *The Modernist Impulse in American Protestantism* (New York: Oxford University Press, 1976).

    4. Berger, *Sacred Canopy*, p. 153.
    5. Ernest Sandeen, *The Roots of Fundamentalism* (Chicago: University of Chicago Press, 1970), p. 226.

end all wars and solve all social problems. When warfare and economic depression interfered, a flirtation with neoorthodoxy ensued, but neoorthodoxy's impact was primarily to temper the optimism, not reverse liberalism's worldly accommodation.

When mainline denominations thus cooperated in waging World War II, followed by the ecclesiastical bull market of the late 1950s, the overlap of liberal Protestantism with modern, liberal culture was nearly complete. Churches absorbed the New Deal ethic along with the belief that government agencies are the proper way to address social problems. Ecumenism was espoused, denominational loyalty becoming simply a matter of stylistic preference. Civil rights, world peace, redistributed wealth, and control of nuclear arms became other planks in liberal Protestantism's agenda.

Of course, not everyone in the liberal denominations concurred with this agenda. Especially among many lay people, the churches' pursuit of social Christianity at the expense of the Gospel caused unhappiness. That is to say, even if some kind of theological peace had been achieved, the old "paradoxical combination of libertarianism and traditionalism" could generate unhappiness on moral grounds. People who may not really have cared about the turn-of-the-century theological battle lost by conservative Protestantism could nevertheless still care deeply about nineteenth-century moral formulations that were once expressed in those theological terms. Such people were, so to speak, political or cultural conservatives who had no political or cultural channels for expressing their unease. For them, conservative religion became their outlet.

THE CURRENT SCENE

We have in our midst, then, a sizable, visible, and vocal set of people—roughly identifiable as conservative Protestants—whose nineteenth-century pedigree is not conservative at all. Many are found in mainline denominations, but many more have long since gone elsewhere. They and their predecessors, having chosen not to engage in and address the forces of modern social life, retrenched through most of the twentieth century, only to burst now onto the national scene—via the media and the political arena—espousing a religious viewpoint that was common enough 100 years ago but was long ago judged naive by most literate Americans.

Theologically that viewpoint is still naive, as pathetic attempts to defend biblical literalism, especially creationism, illustrate.[6] It is not that such beliefs are no longer held by many; they clearly are and have been all along. But for more than half a century, people holding those beliefs kept silent in public, and now they are noisy. We can ask why the curious path of conservative Protestantism has taken this direction.

Actually that issue, as the discussion up to now would suggest, translates into two questions. Why has evangelical Protestantism surged in visible popularity since the 1970s? And why has it taken such a political turn? The remainder of this article will be devoted to these two questions, against the backdrop of the brief history just covered.

6. See, for example, the exchange regarding the teaching of evolution versus scientific creation in *Christianity Today*, 3 Feb. 1984. The several efforts to use courts in pursuit of their goals have led to utter legal defeat for creationists, although they have had some success terrifying textbook publishers and school districts.

THE CURRENT POPULARITY
OF CONSERVATIVE
PROTESTANTISM

The first thing to be said about conservative Protestantism's current popularity is that even more important than new membership in the movement is the new notoriety the movement has received in recent years. Conservative Protestants, in other words, did not disappear after 1920, only to reappear in the 1970s. Rather, social scientists and the mass media discovered them as they were showing renewed signs of strength[7] and even desiring public attention.

A second observation thus has to do with the facilities available to conservative Protestants since the 1970s that were not readily available before. Among these, television no doubt ranks supreme, for it was televangelists who first discovered the potential of slick broadcasting. Mainline denominations had long helped fill those public-service hours, on radio as well as television, but as a service, not in the aggressive, entrepreneurial manner of today's Robert Schuller, Jimmy Swaggart, and others.[8] Related is the investment of several decades of training new leaders, establishing networks of communication, and developing a unique public face. Billy Graham stands out here, of course, as no one can match his 30-plus years of spokesmanship at many levels, from personal crusade to television to book writing to counseling presidents. So when the time was ripe, conservative Protestantism was prepared through its many, many organizations to capitalize on its new opportunities.

7. The near-classic source remains Dean M. Kelley, *Why Conservative Churches Are Growing* (New York: Harper & Row, 1972).

8. J. K. Hadden and C. K. Swan, *Prime Time Preachers* (Reading, MA: Addison-Wesley, 1981).

But what made the time ripe? More specifically, what made evangelical Protestantism an attractive response to events in the 1970s? James Hunter, in his splendid analysis *American Evangelicals*, provides the single most important clue. It is true, he points out, that conservative Protestants lost the theological battle after 1920, but the moral viewpoint they shared at the time with most other Americans continued to be the dominant conventional viewpoint until the 1960s.[9] It was one thing to lose control of the major denominations, in other words, but it was quite another to see all of American culture threatening to deviate from the "paradoxical combination"—the conventionality inherited from the nineteenth century.

In effect, the Democratic party platform after 1932 must have seemed to many to advocate just that, but no doubt the counterculturists of the 1960s were bigger offenders. Similarly profound reverberations must have been brought on by the women's movement, and by affirmative action on behalf of blacks, homosexuals, unmarried mothers, and others. Upsetting also were court decisions declaring abortion to be right and school prayer wrong.[10] While the experience of moral crisis is not sufficient alone to explain the outpouring of evangelical fervor in the 1970s,

9. James D. Hunter, *American Evangelicalism* (New Brunswick, NJ: Rutgers University Press, 1983), p. 103.

10. The banality of the change—and thus its subtlety—is nicely illustrated by the comment of Dean Young, son of the creator of the "Blondie" comic strip and its present author-artist: "Some interviewer asked me if Blondie was in favor of abortion. I couldn't answer because I don't deal in controversy. I deal in fun. It's separate from reality." *Newsweek*, 1 Oct. 1984, p. 77. Much of the countercultural challenge existed before the 1960s, but not until then was it openly advocated.

then, certainly that sense of crisis, when directed by sophisticated leaders who are themselves interconnected and alert to the mass media, was a crucial element.

But even more can be said. Vietnam proved futile as military strategy but all too convincing as evidence that cold-war tensions are not amenable to simpleminded solutions. If conventional warfare is no longer feasible, and nuclear confrontation is indeed unthinkable, then the way is open to invent—or, in this case, reinvent—a scenario wherein at least good guys and bad guys can be identified. The premillennialist vision serves nicely in this regard.[11]

Another factor to be mentioned is a psychological change, purportedly widespread, but one on which conservative Protestantism could capitalize in a novel way. This has been to join evangelical religion with so-called new thought—putting together Billy Graham and Norman Vincent Peale, as Richard Quebedeaux so felicitously recounts it.[12] When the world seems out of control in almost every other respect, accepting Christ as one's personal savior may provide not only a certain comfort but also a warrant for not worrying about whether or not the world, too, is still redeemable.

11. Consider the shock given conservative Protestantism by Billy Graham's first visit to Russia, when he allowed that perhaps some religious freedom did exist in that society. To most thoughtful Americans, this admission on Graham's part was probably seen as a simple matter of fact, however lacking the USSR may otherwise be on this score. To his erstwhile friends, however, Graham was now a heretic, having relinquished the evil-empire view of Russia. This episode is but one in Graham's recent career indicating that he has finally discovered some of the forces of modernity that liberal Protestants have been confronting for decades.

12. *By What Authority?* (New York: Harper & Row, 1982), p. 82.

Yet another factor helping to explain why conservative Protestantism blossomed in popularity in the 1970s is the halt to economic growth, the retracting of an economy that had been chiefly expanding for decades. This factor had impact throughout the social structure, of course; but if government programs to enhance life had to be curtailed, if civil rights—of criminals, for example—were going to be restricted, then a certain comfort might be derived from seeing these not as failures of an idealistic agenda but as ideologically demanded. In a book that is otherwise curiously argued, Jeremy Rifkin does point out how compatible accommodative, optimistic Protestantism was with economic expansionism.[13] If, then, such expansion has ceased, if exploitation of the world's resources is leveling off, it is understandable that the seductive theology accompanying expansion would also experience difficulty. Where Rifkin errs is in seeing evangelicalism as a solution rather than a response to this no-growth situation, thus failing to note the reactionary character of evangelicalism. It is, after all, conservatives, not liberals, who defend nuclear power plants, off-shore oil drilling, the harvesting of redwoods, and acid rain, among other causes.

In sum, to a significant degree, conservative Protestantism has become a refuge for those Americans who, faced with a crisis brought on by a sharp escalation in the moral agonies associated with modern life, choose not to accommodate but persist in defining those agonies in once-common ways. Although for many these definitions are theological, the crisis evoking them is

13. Jeremy Rifkin with Ted Howard, *The Emerging Order* (New York: Ballantine Books, 1979).

not doctrinal so much as it is political or cultural. Evangelical language, so to speak, is but a convenient way to express one view of this crisis. As Hunter's analysis shows, the single strongest correlate of an evangelical outlook today is distance from modern social life, as indicated by, for instance, little education, rural residence, and occupations unrelated to high technology.[14]

THE POLITICAL INVOLVEMENT OF CONSERVATIVE PROTESTANTISM

If a surge in the popularity of conservative Protestantism can thus be explained by referring to the agonies associated with modern life, what explains its distinct—and, since the 1920s, unusual—political turn? After all, one of the strategies taken by evangelicals after their theological and ecclesiastical defeat early in this century was to reduce involvement socially—except for church—and politically. Other than a brief period during the McCarthy years, when such groups as the Church League of America and the Christian Anti-Communist Crusade gained attention, the disaffected religious Right remained relatively quiet. Indeed, for many, worldly involvement was specifically proscribed.

In tracking this feature of conservative Protestantism's curious path we might note first of all that the enemy has shifted significantly—from church and seminary to court and public school, for example. Similarly, therefore, the battleground has switched from ecclesiastical politics to community, state, and national politics. Nothing reflects this change so well as the fact that secular humanism has become conservative Protestants' new target.

14. Hunter, *American Evangelicalism*, pp. 59-60.

What agencies embody secular humanism? Surely not liberal churches. God is still their focus; the sacred is still present in their endeavors. It is rather agencies such as courts, public schools, hospitals, colleges, the mass media, and the entertainment industry that, by leaving God out altogether, raise the ire of conservative Protestants. It is the United Nations and, on occasion, the State Department. These are the agencies captured by secular humanism, in the conservative Protestant view.

The consequence has been a necessary shift of attention. For example, in the Pro-Family Forum's pamphlet "Is Humanism Molesting Your Child?" the platform of the "religion of secular humanism" is identified.[15] In only a few instances are its planks theological—for example, "denies the Biblical account of creation"—most being instead political and cultural—for example, "believes in sexual freedom" or "believes in control of the environment." It seems reasonable to suppose that the more political and cultural the objection, the more political the response must become. It is one thing to give up the fight if one's enemies do not believe correctly, but it is another when they behave improperly. Political involvement is almost required under these circumstances.

With this shift in mind, then, we can take note of a second feature of the present-day scene: the political right has sought out and joined forces with the religious right at least as much as the reverse. To put it simply—though accurately, even by its own testimony—the Moral Majority would exist with or without a Baptist clergyman at its helm,

15. "Is Humanism Molesting Your Child?" (Pamphlet, Pro-Family Forum, Fort Worth, TX, n.d.).

for it is not so much a theological as a moral organization.

The question remains, however, why conservative Protestants would join in political battle now when in the past they have been reluctant to do so. The conspiratorial answer is easy—they are being duped by the political right wing, an answer having some merit when one considers that Phyllis Schlafly and Richard Viguerie are Roman Catholic; Howard Phillips, Jewish; Paul Weyrich, Eastern Rite; and Orrin Hatch, Mormon. More benignly, one can assume that for some Protestant conservatives, some moral goals transcend their Protestant particularism.

Still, for many Protestant conservatives, political goals do not transcend religious particularism, meaning that nationally this religious constituency has been difficult to organize. Further, this means that there is little likelihood that the radical religious Right will capture either political party or make much of a dent if it begins its own. It also means that where conservative Protestantism has been effective politically, the effectiveness has been largely at the local level, on issues capable of generating a more homogeneous involvement—for example, the question of library books. In other words, the Christian Right can be stirred politically, but it is by no means of one mind with the agenda of the political Right.[16]

This last observation raises the final issue to be discussed here, What is the wider social meaning of conservative Protestantism's current status?

CONCLUSION

Recall the point made earlier that one factor helping to establish evangelical Protestantism as a national creed in the nineteenth century was its sanctioning of "libertarianism and traditionalism." This combination was called "paradoxical" because, as Tocqueville, for one, saw so clearly, ancient regimes exalted traditionalism but therefore discouraged libertarianism, suggesting that if a democracy encouraged libertarianism it would mean the end of tradition. That this did not happen in America puzzled Tocqueville, and he found the explanation primarily in evangelical religion, which encouraged what he called "self-interest rightly understood,"—that is, libertarianism tempered by traditionalism. In effect, Americans favored both change and continuity; they worshiped both capitalism and God. And this combination worked for nearly a century. It worked because the economy expanded, and it worked because consensus was largely maintained on what tradition—that is, God—meant.

But the forces of modernity broke the consensus. First to go was the theological consensus, initially by the inclusion of Catholics and Jews as first-class religious citizens—even yet not acknowledged in a few Protestant quarters—and second, within Protestantism, by the battle over the Bible, leading to the split at the turn of the century discussed earlier. There were other issues too, of course. If the disturbance had remained theological only, probably the camp identified as conservative Protestant after 1920 would have remained primarily nonpolitical. But as we saw, there

16. Two good collections of essays bearing on this issue, and containing empirical evidence in support of some of my assertions here, are R. C. Liebman and R. Wuthnow, eds., *The New Christian Right* (New York: Aldine, 1983); and D. G. Bromley and A. Shupe, eds., *New Christian Politics* (Macon, GA: Mercer University Press, 1984).

followed a disintegration also of the traditional moral consensus. This breakdown, it was suggested, reached symbolic culmination in the counterculture, and today is perhaps most sharply exemplified in the abortion issue.

To appreciate the reality—but also the profundity—of this breakdown, contrast the bumpers of two cars, one with stickers saying BPOE [Benevolent and Protective Order of Elks], National Rifle Association, and Buy American; the other with stickers saying ERA [Equal Rights Amendment], Greenpeace, and Get Out of El Slavador. One point is obvious; an observer can infer from the bumper stickers quite a bit of the moral philosophy of the two drivers. But what of their religion? Their party? If the drivers are religious and Protestant, the first probably leans toward theological conservatism, the second toward modernism. And, as research has shown, the first is probably a Republican, the second a Democrat. If, however, both drivers are secular, the first driver is just as likely to be a Democrat, the second a Republican, although neither will feel all that comfortable with his party's platform.

But change the circumstances slightly. Let the Republican party be led by a spokesman for moral traditionalism, who talks—although he need not act— like an economic libertarian. Suddenly evangelical Republicans find their historic creed being expressed, and Democratic traditionalists find warrant for switching their vote. Conservative Protestants thus seem to spring up all over the place, and the popular party becomes the Republican.

Something like this seems to have happened in America in the last decade. Jimmy Carter held out some theological hope for conservative Protestants in 1976 but quickly disqualified himself with his moral agenda. He was modern. In 1980, therefore, Ronald Reagan drew off sizable Democratic traditionalists on the basis of moral issues, and he managed to do so without losing many Republican modernists to the Democratic candidate. In 1984, this unbalanced switching seemed simply to have intensified.

Of course, political campaigns are vastly complicated things, and religious outlook is just one of the factors making independent impact on persons' votes. In the 1980s, nevertheless, evangelicalism has achieved a notoriety in the mass media it had not enjoyed since the 1920s, and this notoriety has been a result no doubt of its involvement in national politics. Its current resurgence thus cannot be understood as simply a theological phenomenon but must be understood as well as an event in America's national life. Such is the latest step on the curious path of conservative Protestantism.

ANNALS, *AAPSS*, **480**, July 1985

American Catholicism in the Mid-Eighties: Pluralism and Conflict in a Changing Church

By PATRICK H. McNAMARA

ABSTRACT: The decade of the 1970s saw continuing changes in American Catholicism as Catholics' religious beliefs and practices persisted in a decline that began in the mid-1960s. In the 1980s, issues of personal morality are salient among indicators of declining belief, particularly such issues as birth control, divorce with remarriage, and premarital sex. Yet there are signs of vitality in other respects: Catholic schools have grown in enrollment, charismatic and pentecostal groups have increased, and lay participation in liturgical functions is now a familiar feature of Catholic worship. The institutional church, as represented by the National Conference of Catholic Bishops, has adopted a critical stance toward American nuclear war strategy and recently toward the American economy for its neglect of the poor and unemployed. These stances occasion conflict both within the church, as Catholic groups organize to oppose them, and between the church, as represented by the bishops, and policies at the national level. A pluralistic model of the church in the 1980s would predict continuing individualism in religious beliefs and practice, and conflict on the institutional level, with considerable cost to the authority of the Catholic hierarchy.

Patrick H. McNamara, Ph.D., is associate professor of sociology at the University of New Mexico. He is past president of the Association for the Sociology of Religion and has published in various scholarly journals. He is the editor of Religion North American Style. *He has served as exchange professor at the National Autonomous University in Mexico City and maintains an interest in the sociology of the Hispanic community in the United States.*

FIFTEEN years ago, three articles explored post-Vatican II American Catholicism in *The Annals* issue for January 1970, *The Sixties: Radical Change in American Religion*. Eugene Bianchi wrote of "conservative-progressive tensions" in the American Catholic church: dissent from authority, a new "collegiality" manifested in priests' senates, revamped liturgies whose "democratic styles" of shared worship differed from the "hierarchical concepts of the recent past," a "new morality" that stressed "the internal determination of conscience over externally imposed edicts," and ecumenical initiatives in which Catholics, Protestants, and Jews were participating together in social movements for racial justice, peace, and an end to poverty.[1]

Jesuit sociologist Joseph Fichter noted the "manpower shrinkage" among Catholic priests, brothers, and sisters, and the sharp drop in numbers of seminarians after record high numbers in the late 1950s and early 1960s. Yet he saw signs of hope: pastoral renewal movements among the clergy and a sister formation movement indicated openings to "initiative, maturity, and creativity." Larger communities were breaking up into smaller pastoral teams stressing personal relationships and membership participation in decision making. Even as parochial schools closed—and fewer new ones were built—and religious orders withdrew from administration of colleges, hospitals, and social service agencies, the result might be a deeper renewal of spirit and a more "socially effective" ministry. Finally he noted the challenge to celibacy involved in the exodus of priests and religious order members, pointing out that the only concession thus far made was extension of the diaconate to married men—not women.[2]

Daniel Callahan pointed to the widening gap between actual lay practice of contraception and Pope Paul VI's resounding reaffirmation of traditional birth control prohibitions in the 1968 encyclical letter *Humanae Vitae*. He also chronicled the open dissent among some clergy and theologians regarding the issue and wondered, "If papal authority is allowed to be set aside on this occasion, its entire status is threatened—the implications are clear, also."[3] Callahan spelled them out:

At stake is nothing less than whether it will be possible, without destroying continuity with the past altogether, to accord a larger place to individual conscience as well as a larger place to democratic methods of decision-making within the church.[4]

Abortion caught his attention, too. Would the Catholic community gradually accept a more liberal stance on this issue? Considering an American public more accepting of abortion, Callahan wondered how long American Catholics could escape the impact of the larger culture.

A common theme running through these essays was an awareness that old forms were in disarray and new ones struggling to take their place. In the process traditional authority relation-

1. Eugene C. Bianchi, "John XXIII, Vatican II, and American Catholicism," *The Annals* of the American Academy of Political and Social Science, 387:38 (Jan. 1970).

2. Joseph P. Fichter, "Catholic Church Professionals," *The Annals* of the American Academy of Political and Social Science, 387:77-85 (Jan. 1970).

3. Daniel Callahan, "Contraception and Abortion: American Catholic Responses," *The Annals* of the American Academy of Political and Social Science, 387:114 (Jan. 1970).

4. Ibid.

ships were being badly shaken. Would they survive? Internal conflict, already evident, might well increase, causing Bianchi to speculate "whether American Catholicism is on the brink of schism or of a new kind of unification."[5]

A CONTEMPORARY SUMMARY

Fifteen years later, some of these developments seem to have run their course. The drop-off in priests, brothers, and sisters appears to have bottomed out. A modest increase in seminarians has occurred, although by no means at levels rivaling the green years of the mid-1950s and early 1960s. Liturgical experimentation causes little controversy as many parishes have introduced greater lay participation in the liturgy. Catholics wishing more unstructured and spontaneous worship can find innovative or floating communities. Lay persons, many trained in religious education programs sponsored by Catholic colleges, are found on parish staffs, in parochial schools, and in hospitals as chaplins. Abortion continues to meet strong opposition from Catholics, although abortion in cases of rape and incest gives them—like most people—serious pause.

Still excluded from the diaconate and priesthood are women; the prohibition extends to girls serving Mass, although individual pastors here and there defy the ban. Indeed, the role of women continues to be a subordinate one in terms of representation in the ranks of the clergy. As the conclusion of this article will indicate, this issue will very likely be an increasingly salient one over the next decade.

5. Bianchi, "John XXIII, Vatican II, and American Catholicism," p. 30.

Dissent has not abated, of course, and its present-day forms are explored in this article. Yet nothing like a schism has happened, if only because the institution itself has become more tolerant of dissent. Formerly effective means of moral coercion, such as excommunication, are no longer viable for many, if not most, Catholics, for whom the primacy of individual conscience stands above edicts of authority. The clergy, correspondingly, is also little inclined to impose or coerce.

Unanticipated almost completely by the *Annals* authors 15 years ago was the contemporary and conspicuous involvement of the institutional church in major social issues. Few foresaw bishops taking prophetic stands and replacing the Berrigan brothers and the marching clergy and sisters of two decades ago as challengers of the status quo.

This article, therefore, rather than attempting to catalogue all the changes and developments in American Catholicism over the last decade and a half, will focus on two areas deemed significant. One is the apparent continuation of profound shifts in Catholic religious belief and behavior. These mark a striking alteration of the monolithic image of Catholicism familiar to most Americans, and they move American Catholicism closer to the voluntary-membership model characteristic of Protestant denominations in this country. This trend shows little sign of abating in the future.

The second area, also containing deep implications for the future, is the current involvement of the Catholic church at its highest levels in controversial sociomoral issues: the nuclear arms race, the American economy, the status of women. As we shall see, while the bishops may appear to be shifting the official church from a more traditional culture-affirming stance to a critical one, a price paid is the creation of sharp conflict both within the American Catholic community itself and between the church and national social, political, and economic policies.

AUTHORITY AND
DISSENT

The indicators of decline in Catholic beliefs and practices are well documented and can be readily summarized. They derive from two sources: (1) yearly Gallup polls; and (2) National Opinion Research Center (NORC) special surveys of adult American Catholics conducted in 1963 and 1974, and a 1979 survey of American and Canadian Catholics, ages 14 to 29. The Gallup data show a decline in weekly attendance at mass among Catholic adults from a peak of 74 percent in 1958 to a low of 52 percent in 1973, a level virtually unchanged through 1983. Overall Protestant weekly church attendance, by comparison, has diminished from 44 percent

TABLE 1
AMERICAN CATHOLICS ADHERING TO CATHOLIC BELIEFS
AND PRACTICES, 1974 and 1979 (Percentage of Respondents)

Practice, Belief, or Norm	Age 30 and Over 1974	Under 30 1974	1979
Attend mass weekly	50	37	37
Pray once a day	60	52	32
Christ gave leadership of Church to Peter and his successors (certainly true)			
All Catholics	42	34	16
Weekly communicants only	60	45	27
The pope is infallible when he speaks as head of the church (certainly true)			
All Catholics	32	22	9
Premarital sex is morally wrong (strongly agree)			
All Catholics	35	35	17
Weekly communicants only	48	69	34
Divorce, if followed by remarriage, is wrong (strongly agree)			
All Catholics	25	17	11
Weekly communicants only	46	29	18
Artificial contraception is wrong (strongly agree)			
All Catholics	13	7	4
Weekly communicants only	24	24	13

SOURCES: Andrew M. Greeley, *The Religious Imagination* (Los Angeles: William H. Sadlier, 1981), pp. 204-5; Andrew M. Greeley, William C. McCready, and Kathleen McCourt, *Catholic Schools in a Declining Church* (Kansas City, KS: Sheed and Ward, 1976), pp. 35-36; Andrew M. Greeley, "Church Authority: Beyond the Problem," *National Catholic Reporter*, 26 Sept. 1980, pp. 7-8.

to 39 percent over the same time period.[6] The proportion of Catholics saying religion is "very important" in their lives dropped from 83 percent in 1952 to 56 percent in 1983; comparable Protestant figures are 76 percent and 61 percent, respectively.[7]

More detailed data come from the NORC surveys. Table 1 displays some trends in Catholic beliefs and practices. All adult Catholics in 1974 are compared to younger Catholics—under 30—at two dates: 1974 and five years later, in 1979. A striking finding is that the stronger declining trends among younger Catholics continue downward through 1979. A second notable result is that even among devout Catholics receiving Holy Communion weekly, orthodox Catholic doctrines and moral positions firmly held in former years are no longer invested with the same absolute certainty. Other traditional practices not listed have also suffered. In the 1974 adult survey, remarriage after divorce met with a 73 percent approval rate.[8] Almost a third of Catholic adults that same year "practically never" or "never" went to confession.[9] Five years later, three-quarters of Catholic teenagers age 14 to 17 reported going to confession once a year or less, and 56 percent of young adults 18 to 29 in the survey said they "never" went to confession.[10]

What is one to make of these trends? How significant are they? Interpretations vary. As senior study director of NORC, priest-sociologist Andrew Greeley has been a principal designer of these surveys and has written prolifically about them, often with colleagues as coauthors. Greeley's self-admitted hunch before analyzing results of the 1974 replication of the original 1963 study of adult Catholics was that the "confusion and uncertainty generated by the Second Vatican Council" was principally responsible for the decline phenomena.

Analysis of the 1974 results, however, convinced Greeley and his colleagues that the birth control encyclical, *Humanae Vitae*, was mainly responsible for Catholic falloff in practice and beliefs. American Catholics, the surveys showed, strongly endorsed changes in church worship stemming from the council such as the English liturgy's replacing the traditional Latin. In fact, even further changes would be favored by the laity, such as a married clergy. In any case, the declining trends could be accounted for, stated the authors, "almost entirely by a change in sexual attitudes and in attitudes toward the papacy among American Catholics."[11] The birth control encyclical "apparently seriously impaired the credibility and authority of the papacy, leading to a sharp decline in mass attendance and a sharp increase in apostasy in the years immediately after the encyclical."[12]

A variation on the erosion-of-authority interpretation is offered by Dean

6. *Religion in America, 1984*, Gallup Report no. 222, p. 57 (Mar. 1984).

7. Ibid., p. 32.

8. Andrew M. Greeley, William C. McCready, and Kathleen McCourt, *Catholic Schools in a Declining Church* (Kansas City, KS: Sheed and Ward, 1976), p. 35.

9. Ibid., p. 30.

10. Joan Fee et al., *Young Catholics in the United States and Canada* (Los Angeles: William H. Sadlier, 1981), p. 6.

11. Greeley, McCready, and McCourt, *Catholic Schools in a Declining Church*, p. 304. The 1963 survey is analyzed in Andrew M. Greeley and Peter H. Rossi, *The Education of Catholic Americans* (Chicago: Aldine, 1966).

12. Greeley, McCready, and McCourt, *Catholic Schools in a Declining Church*, p. 304.

Hoge in his study of Catholic dropouts and returnees.[13] Freedom-of-conscience-oriented young Catholics are little moved by exhortations couched as obligations under pain of sin. In fact, the value of personal autonomy in forming one's conscience is so deeply embedded in younger Catholics that formally stated doctrinal and moral imperatives have little or no impact on large numbers of younger Catholics. Catholic dropouts, Hoge indicates, discussed moral teachings, when interviewed, much more than doctrinal ones. Most salient in their minds were teachings concerning marriage and sexuality. Younger persons embracing a life-style associated with single young people found these teachings unacceptable and so experienced strong tension between themselves and the church in which they had been raised. Orthodox teachings are much more compatible with a mainline or straighter life-style characterized by marriage, child rearing, respectability, and acting as a responsible citizen. In this sense, as Hoge phrases it, the church is felt to be an ally of the straighter life-style, inimical to a more deviant one.[14]

Another explanatory framework developed by Greeley concerns the central importance of religious symbolism expressed in the imagination and in the emotions of Catholic believers. In a complex theory he has developed in *The Religious Imagination*, Greeley points out that Catholics who, in survey research, indicate that they have "warm imagery" of God, of Jesus, and of the Blessed Virgin—for example, describing them as "loving," "father," "moth-er," "warm," or "forgiving" rather than as "judge," "stern," or "distant"—are much less likely to be alienated in terms of adherence to both doctrinal and moral precepts. Moreover, they are much more likely to make it through crises of faith and even through marriage crises. Greeley therefore believes that emphasis upon sheer doctrinal and moral precepts as obligatory is misplaced in religious formation and is bound to result in alienation, given the serious erosion in authority for which he believes church officials are ultimately responsible.[15]

A further interpretation simply says that Catholics—especially younger ones—have merely taken seriously the Second Vatican Council's emphasis on greater freedom and responsibility and that they see no need for expressing their convictions in absolute terms such as "certainly true" and "always to be believed." After all, holds this viewpoint, if one combines "certainly true" responses with those simply saying "true" to survey items asking about doctrinal beliefs, a solid majority emerges anyway. As Dulles and Kelly put it, "A somewhat critical attitude toward church authority may be compatible with a strong Christian commitment and a keen sense of Catholic identity."[16] Furthermore, emphasis on trends of decline neglects strong Catholic support for parochial schools, the continuing Catholic support of right-to-life issues, and the large numbers of Catholics involved in a variety of renewal programs and move-

---

13. Dean R. Hoge, *Converts, Dropouts, Returnees: A Study of Religious Change among Catholics* (New York: Pilgrim Press, 1981).

14. Ibid., p. 170.

15. Andrew M. Greeley, *The Religious Imagination* (Los Angeles: William H. Sadlier, 1981), pp. 237-40.

16. Avery Dulles and James R. Kelly, "The Catholic Dilemma," *Britannica Book of the Year*, special supp. (Chicago: Encyclopedia Britannica, 1977), pp. 45-49.

ments from Cursillos to Marriage Encounter to charismatic and other prayer and bible-study groups. In this view, then, the indicators of decline hardly signal the end of Catholicism, but they may well presage a more personally thought-out and responsibly held religious belief and moral perspective.

INSTITUTIONAL CATHOLICISM

Perhaps nothing has been more surprising in the early 1980s than the emergence of the American bishops as a kind of collective conscience. Addressing themselves explicitly not only to Catholics but to all Americans, the bishops have jumped squarely into the central policy arenas of nuclear armament and the economy, and they will soon draft a statement on women's issues. How does one account for these stands, which seem unprecedented in a church that has, for the most part, been culture affirming in American society?

American bishops' speaking out on national issues is, of course, nothing new. Historian James Hennesey details the emergence of yearly bishops' statements going back to the year 1919. The newly formed National Catholic Welfare Conference, with its several committees, provided a new organizational base from which American bishops could, with the assistance of expert staff, issue annual letters on various topics. The first, in fact, was a document dealing with socioeconomic issues, the so-called "Bishops Program of Social Reconstruction." The ideas were those of Monsignor John A. Ryan, who had written extensively on labor issues; the ideas contained in the letter, as Hennesey makes clear, later became a substantial part of New Deal legislation under President Franklin D. Roosevelt.

Roman authorities, however—anxious to keep authority firmly in their hands—almost scotched the bishops' new body in the early 1920s. American bishops learned a lesson. For decades to come, the bishops looked to Rome for guidance, rarely, if ever, issuing annual pastoral messages that were anything but reaffirmations of Catholic teaching with applications to specific situtations. An example of this approach was the formation of the Legion of Decency as a response to morally offensive films issuing from Hollywood.[17]

But the Second Vatican Council again looms as a major catalyst of change. It set in motion shifts in the bishops' relationship to Rome as well as engaged them more directly with the world at large. The council encouraged collegiality; that is, it urged bishops to interact with one another on matters of collective concern, rather than act as "solitary monarchs," each isolated in his own diocese. In 1966, the American bishops formed the National Conference of Catholic Bishops to implement the decrees of the Second Vatican Council. The bishops also formed the United States Catholic Conference, closely paralleling the National Catholic Welfare Conference, which it replaced. Three departments constituted this body: education, communication, social development and world peace.

Important to note here is that a certain decentralization of authority was implicit in the ideal of collegiality. American bishops, as did other national and regional episcopal groups, began to look less to Rome for guidance, paying more attention to American problems

17. James Hennesey, *American Catholics: A History of the Roman Catholic Community in the United States* (New York: Oxford University Press, 1981), pp. 221-23.

and how they might collectively address them from their own experience as well as from the church's moral tradition. In 1968, the bishops urged a change in American law to allow for selective conscientious objection to war. In 1971 they issued a "Resolution on Southeast Asia," calling into question the basic justice of the war itself and asking for a "speedy end" to the conflict. This marked the first time in American history that Catholic bishops as a body had taken issue with a basic policy of the American government.[18] In 1972, they called for amnesty for deserters. The 1970s saw the bishops' issuing pastoral letters on a variety of social and economic topics, an effort reflected on by Kelly as follows:

The Catholic bishops, on a more regular basis, have used the United States Catholic Conference/National Conference of Catholic Bishops as a national forum from which to issue statements on a vast array of social issues, such as housing, concern for the elderly, welfare reform, food stamps, medical care, and the like. But these statements—all mildly progressive by the standards of American politics—have never received much public attention, and were little noticed even by most Catholics. To the general public and its own membership, the Bishops' social teaching was known mostly for its opposition to birth control and to legalized abortion, and in both cases their teaching cannot be described as greatly altering public opinion and practice.[19]

18. Ibid., pp. 320-21.
19. James R. Kelly, "Catholicism and Modern Memory: Some Sociological Reflections on the Symbolic Foundations of the Rhetorical Force of the Pastoral Letter, 'The Challenge of Peace,'" *Sociological Analysis*, 45(2):137 (Summer 1984).

Nuclear war was strongly condemned by the Second Vatican Council. The American bishops addressed the issue first in November of 1976, stating that it is "wrong to attack civilian populations, but it is also wrong to threaten to attack them as part of a strategy of deterrence."[20] But this declaration was embedded in a letter primarily about issues of sexual morality and did not receive widespread attention.

Not so, however, for the 1983 bishops' letter, "The Challenge of Peace," nor the draft pastoral letter on the American economy released in November of 1984 and scheduled for final redrafting and issuance in the bishops' 1985 fall meeting. How can we account for the widespread publicity given these documents? When the bishops in the 1970s issued policy statements at odds with national policies, no controversy surrounded those documents to match the lively, at times acrid, debates surrounding the two more recent statements. A number of factors deserve specific mention and form a fundamental context for understanding what certainly appears to be the new collective role chosen by the bishops.

1. Both "The Challenge of Peace" and the draft statement on the economy contain specific policy recommendations. They are not confined to enunciations of general moral principles. The former calls into question major planks of U.S. military policy: targeting large population centers, nuclear first strikes,

20. Quoted in Jim Castelli, *The Bishops and the Bomb: Waging Peace in a Nuclear Age* (Garden City, NY: Doubleday, 1983), p. 22.

and the concept of limited nuclear war.[21] This pastoral letter appeared during the height of the nuclear freeze movement and supported the aims of the movement by calling for "bilateral verifiable agreements to halt the testing, production and deployment of new nuclear testing systems."[22] The draft letter on the economy labels "morally unacceptable" the "level of inequality and wealth in our society," calling for an unemployment rate of no more than 3 to 4 percent and job-creation programs, to mention but a few specific policy recommendations.[23] In both letters, then, particular major policies endorsed—but not necessarily initiated—by a current U.S. administration are singled out for moral criticism.

2. This strategy of making specific judgments seems at least partly a response to the antiwar movement's charge in the late 1960s that the American church was too often silent or a johnny-come-lately regarding major moral issues. An even broader context is the criticism surrounding the Vatican's alleged silence during World War II vis-à-vis the rise of the Nazis and the carrying out of the Holocaust. Silence, in this critical vein, is tantamount to a stamp of approval.

3. In writing both letters, the bishops, sensitive to the antiauthoritarian con-

21. The American Catholic Bishops, "The Challenge of Peace: God's Promise and Our Response," in *The Bishops and the Bomb*, Castelli, app., p. 192.

22. Ibid.

23. "Exercepts from Draft of Bishops' Letter on the U.S. Economy," *New York Times*, 12 Nov. 1984.

sciousness of many Catholics, as detailed earlier, openly invited input from a wide variety of sources. The bishops included those they knew would be basically opposed to some of their stances. Moreover, both letters are addressed to the nation as a whole, not only to Catholics. The bishops invited witnesses chosen for their expertise, an invitation that obviously included many who were not Catholic. This overall strategy both widened publicity concerning these documents and left them open to extensive critical commentary from a variety of viewpoints—particularly because the hearings were openly reported in the press.

4. The bishops have explicitly characterized these documents as intended to stir discussion, awaken consciousness, and instruct—but not to obligate Catholics under pain of sin. In fact, they explicitly acknowledge that Catholics may disagree with their conclusions, and they state they are refraining from making moral judgments about how Catholics ought to respond. For example, they judge it inappropriate to suggest that a Catholic employed in a plant manufacturing nuclear weapons leave his or her job. This is a judgment, they affirm, each individual and/or family will have to make.

5. These stances have left the door open for the formation of opposing Catholic organizations. Thus, in reference to the pastoral letter on nuclear warfare, the National Committee on Catholic Laymen, organized by William F. Buckley, Jr., was concerned that "the liberal Catholic bureaucracy in Washington has given our bishops very bad

advice." The Lay Commission on Catholic Social Teaching, headed by William E. Simon, former secretary of the treasury, recruited prominent Catholic business executives and economists to propose to the bishops, as the latter drafted the letter on the economy, a viewpoint more favorable to a capitalism undirected and unconstrained by government. The committee said in a statement issued just before the November 1984 release of the draft pastoral that mechanisms of the marketplace will generate increasing wealth benefiting all sectors of the population; offered as examples were the experiments in free enterprise occurring in mainland China.[24]

The combined effect of these factors and developments is to propel the bishops squarely into the thick of controversy. For in deliberately choosing to avoid the charge of platitudinous utterance and nonrelevance, they have taken stands on issues hotly debated in the everyday secular world of economic and political discussion and policymaking. As of late 1984, it was difficult to forecast how intense the debate surrounding the economic pastoral would become—but probably lively, considering that it addresses clusters of issues affecting the daily lives of American citizens. Throughout 1985, the bishops will continue to receive input from various groups—such as the laypersons' groups referred to previously—some of whom will strongly wish to influence the pastoral's final statement.

No less public and intense will be the forthcoming statement on the role of women in the church. "Unbudging" is probably the best description of the Vatican's stand not only on the ordination of women to the priesthood, but on the sexuality issues cited earlier. Above all, of course, is the underlying assumption in practice of second-class citizenship for women in the official ranks of the Catholic church. It will be interesting to see whether the bishops, even indirectly, challenge Rome's deeply traditional views and the long-standing practices deriving from them or at least attempt to initiate a dialogue with the Vatican concerning women's status in the church. It is impossible to believe that the bishops will not hear some challenging testimony from women consulted in the initial drafting of the pastoral letter.

CONCLUDING REFLECTION

Both the rank-and-file dissent from church authority in personal morality and the bishops' stands on socioeconomic-political questions make manifest the reality of American Catholic pluralism. In the creative analysis of sociologist Joseph Varacalli, the very effort of the American Catholic church "to keep pace with the rationalizing, pluralizing, democratizing, civilizing tendencies of the outer world" means many of these tendencies become mirrored in the church itself.[25] With none of these trends is authoritarian control

24. "Am I My Brother's Keeper?" *Time*, 26 Nov. 1984, pp. 80-82; also, "The Church and Capitalism," *Businessweek*, 12 Nov. 1984, pp. 104-12.

25. Joseph A. Varacalli, *Toward the Establishment of Liberal Catholicism in America* (Washington, DC: University Press of America, 1983), p. 248.

compatible. And while Pope John Paul II may reiterate traditional personal, including sexual, morality, there seem to be few bishops and priests attempting to shape up the laity to the point of realigning their beliefs and practices.

Here, of course, come into play the various interpretive categories cited earlier. Are these trends indicative of a deterioration from the true faith or simply a reordering of priorities in favor of a less authoritarian and more personalized faith? A social scientist cannot legitimately make a choice here, but might simply point out that these newer tendencies are congruent with an acculturation hypothesis. No longer is the American Catholic laity an immigrant population; upward mobility has brought them into parity with other Americans socially, economically, and politically. Catholics are now culturally aligned as well, in terms of a style of belief that is terribly similar to what obtains in the larger culture with its typically American faith in being true to oneself—that is, following one's own inner voice or conscience. There seems little likelihood that these trends will be reversed. Andrew Greeley's recent exhortations to the American hierarchy and to pastors to emphasize strongly the image of God as loving and to emphasize the possibility of a close personal relationship with God—an approach, Greeley believes, based on his research, that will diminish sexual permissiveness—will probably go unheeded.[26]

26. Andrew M. Greeley, "Selective Catholicism: How They Get Away with It," *America,* 30 Apr. 1983, p. 334.

Vitality, nevertheless, characterizes a good deal of contemporary pluralistic Catholicism. Hispanic Catholics are the fastest-growing Catholic minority. The 15 Hispanic bishops were primarily responsible for the 1983 American bishops' letter, "The Hispanic Presence." A plan of pastoral ministry to Hispanics is now in formation, based substantially on input received in a series of grassroots *encuentros pastorales* ("pastoral encounters") to be held in dioceses throughout the country. Vitality also characterizes scores of other Catholic ministries—to the urban poor and homeless, to low-income students in inner-city schools, and to rural migrant workers, to name but a few. Catholic schools are rebounding in enrollments after a drop-off in the late sixties and early seventies. A vigorous Catholic press, from the *Wanderer* and *Catholicism in Crisis* on the right to the *National Catholic Reporter* and *Commonweal* on the left, focuses lively and critical attention on issues of interest to Catholics. No verdict of moribund can be passed on the pluralist American Catholic church of the 1980s.

The strain on the new Catholic pluralism may be greatest, of course, where the bishops seem to be applying pressure. They are, in a way, taking a classic prophetic gamble. For in striving to overcome irrelevance and make an impact on both church and nation, the bishops have placed themselves in an intensely controversial arena. The resistance already generated may well presage a great deal more to come.

A distinct outcome, if there is one, of this contention may depend on whether the American public, including acculturated Catholics, is truly undergoing a massive shift away from support for a New Deal-type social and economic liberalism. Should this be the case, the bishops' gamble at relevance may backfire and diminish further their credibility as moral teachers. They may find themselves relegated again to the sacristy in the consciousness—and consciences—of American Catholics; or, the economic pastoral letter may be widely discussed and, when passed, subsequently ignored; has this fate already befallen "The Challenge of Peace" ? These remarks are not intended to prejudge the outcome, much less to pass judgment on the wisdom or cogency of the bishops' messages. But the basic question of authority, Is anyone out there listening, pondering, and heeding? will not go away quickly. It is certainly among the central questions facing the American Catholic church of the mid-1980s.

ANNALS, *AAPSS,* **480,** July 1985

From Integration to Survival:
American Jewish Anxieties in Transition

By STEVEN M. COHEN and LEONARD J. FEIN

ABSTRACT: Until roughly 1967, the dominant theme of American Jewish history was integration. Could the Jews find here in America the safety that had eluded them everywhere else in their wanderings? And, if so, at what cost to their Jewish beliefs and behaviors? From 1967 onward the theme has shifted. Greater concern is now focused on the maintenance of Jewish identity and commitment. With the shift from the integration of Jews to the survival of Judaism has come a renewal of interest in the meanings and implications of the Jewish experience.

Steven M. Cohen is professor of sociology at Queens College, CUNY. He is the author of several books and articles on American Jewish political values, religious life, communal organizations, and demographic trends, including American Modernity and Jewish Identity *(1983).*

Leonard J. Fein is editor in chief of Moment *magazine. Formerly, he was the Klutznick Professor of Contemporary Jewish Studies at Brandeis University. He is the author of more than 200 articles and three books on diverse aspects of the contemporary Jewish condition.*

DURING the late 1960s and early 1970s, American Jews experienced what developmental psychologists might refer to as a passage or transition. From the time of their arrival in America, integration into the larger society had been the highest priority on the collective agenda of the Jews, as also, commonly, on their personal agendas. As it was generally understood, the task of integration required, in considerable measure, assimilation to American standards and styles. But, since about 1967, a discernible change of priorities has taken place; Jewish survival—that is, the survival of the Jews as a distinct ethnic/religious group—has become a priority of at least equal, and perhaps greater, concern to many individual Jews and, more particularly, to the agencies and institutions that determine the collective agenda of the Jewish community. This shift has had profound consequences for the political, religious, and cultural life of America's Jews, and also for the symbolic expression of Jewish group identity.

As late as 1973, political scientist Charles Liebman could—correctly—observe that

the American Jew is torn between two sets of values—those of integration and acceptance into American society and those of Jewish group survival. . . . the behavior of the American Jew is best understood as his unconscious effort to restructure his environment and reorient his own self-definition and perception of reality so as to reduce the tension between these values.[1]

Liebman was extending the portrait of Western Jewries that had been drawn by many social historians to the particular

conditions of American Jewry. According to this widely accepted view, traditional Jews had emerged out of the confinement of the social—and sometimes physical—ghettos of pre-Enlightenment Europe to be thrust, willingly or not, into a more secular, voluntaristic, and pluralist modern society.[2] The Jews were a special case of the transition from tradition to modernity because it was not at all clear that the modernizing polities in which they lived were, in fact, prepared to extend them the welcome they offered others. At the same time, there could be no adequate test of the modern welcome unless the Jews were first prepared to offer, as it were, unilateral concessions—giving up their religious particularity, their language, their patterns of social interaction. And very many Jews accepted these terms, imagined or real.

But in Russia, where most Jews lived, no such welcome was even extended. And although it was offered in France, the Dreyfus affair suggested it was not seriously intended. In Austria, repeated outbursts of anti-Semitism belied the sincerity of the welcome. And in Germany, finally, the welcome—accepted there with enthusiasm by the Jews— became a curse.

Only in distant America were the Jews offered—incredibly—tolerance, integration, social advancement, and, not least, physical security. Jewish skepticism regarding the American promise

1. Charles S. Liebman, *The Ambivalent American Jew* (Philadelphia: Jewish Publication Society, 1973), p. vii.

2. See, for example, Todd M. Endelman, *The Jews of Georgian England 1714-1830: Tradition and Change in Liberal Society* (Philadelphia: Jewish Publication Society, 1979); and Jacob Katz, *Out of the Ghetto* (New York: Schocken Books, 1978). For a review of the literature and an application to American Jewry, see Steven M. Cohen, *American Modernity and Jewish Identity* (New York: Tavistock, 1983), pp. 6-38.

led many Jews to suppose that the offer was, in fact, contingent; that America was saying, in effect, that it would not treat the Jews as Jews—that is, as Jews had historically been treated in the lands of their dispersion—if the Jews, for their part, would promise not to behave as Jews—that is, in the idiosyncratic, separatist ways in which Jews had historically behaved.

Much of American Jewish history—until the late 1960s—can be read as the story of the Jewish struggle with the terms of the American offer. Many Jews hastened to fulfill their part of the bargain they supposed was intended, and most of these—some of whom actually converted, more of whom sought to pass—discovered, presumably to their delight, that America kept its word. There were, however, some who chose to test the American promise more fundamentally, whether out of faith in that promise or out of tenacity with respect to Judaism and Jewish interests. These keepers of the faith included not only the Orthodox, who sought as best they could to fence out the modern world, but also the Yiddishists and some of the Zionists—the diverse groups devoted less to the safety of individual Jews than to the survival of Judaism itself.

Most Jews preferred to forgo neither the benefits of the group nor participation in modern American society. Instead, they sought a workable balance between Jewish loyalty and modernity, between authenticity and integration. This balance had theological, cultural, economic, associational, and ideological implications. For some, the intention was merely to hedge the Jewish bet on modernity, lest it prove a chimera; for others, it was a more honest effort to insist on genuine pluralism.

INTEGRATION—AND SURVIVAL

Can the Jew expect, in Shylock's words, "to walk, talk, buy and sell with" the Christian without coming to "eat, drink and pray with" him? At the same time, can the Jew refuse to "eat, drink and pray with" the Christian and yet expect the Christian to agree to "walk, talk, buy and sell with" him? A most delicate balance here, and, therefore, a rich diversity of Jewish response, each seeking a way for traditional Judaism—however defined—to adapt to the modern challenge by defining a peripheral, expendable husk that could safely be discarded, and a central, essential kernel to be retained.

Thus—and here we simplify greatly—Reform Jews initially abandoned all that seemed to them excessively separatist, nationalist, legalist, contrary to reason. The abandonment included even the word "Jew," which was, briefly, replaced by the ostensibly more sanitized "Hebrew." In place of these traditional elements, the Reform emphasized the ethical, hence universal, teachings of Judaism, teachings presumably shared with Christians.[3]

In contrast, Zionism elevated and developed that which the Reform discarded or deemphasized: the national character of the Jewish heritage, its connection with the land of Israel, the Jewish need for a national home as a response to persistent anti-Semitism, and the rising nationalist spirit of turn-of-the-century Europe.[4] At the same time, most early Zionists denied the centrality of ancient religious law for Jewish continuity in the modern era. In this, Zionism and Reform Judaism

3. Nathan Glazer, *American Judaism*, 2nd ed. (Chicago: University of Chicago Press, 1972).
4. Arthur Hertzberg, ed., *The Zionist Idea* (New York: Atheneum, 1970).

agreed—and even the modern wing of Orthodoxy was prepared to divide Jewish life into essential and expendable spheres, although, obviously, it drew the line in a very different place from that of both the Zionists and Reform Jews. In the modern Orthodox view, the law was the law as of old, but all the stylistic amendments that had collected over the years could safely be discarded. Dress, language, cultural involvements—these were peripheral.[5] The more traditional Orthodox argued, in effect, that style and substance could not safely be separated, that to discard the one would endanger compliance with the other.

But the prevailing post-Enlightenment view was that all fundamentalist traditions would soon crumble, that they would not be able to withstand either the momentum of modernity or its blessings, much less its evident good sense. If the Reform sought to find Zion in America, and to eviscerate Jewish history by effecting a doctrine called the Mosaic persuasion—a kind of bloodless theology in harmony with America's progressive spirit but not with the sweaty facts of Jewish history and culture—Conservative Judaism, an American invention, sought the best of all worlds. Conservative Judaism modified the liturgy—but did not, as had Reform, whether by praying in the vernacular or shifting the Sabbath to Sunday, make it Protestant. It loosened the bonds of ritual and argued that the law is an evolutionary corpus, requiring periodic amendment. These were, in both style and substance, very American views, and the hope and intention was that they would permit genuine continuity with

Jewish tradition, a continuity the Conservative leaders did not imagine would be possible for the unmodern, even antimodern, Orthodox, or for the un-Jewish Reform.[6]

Even the fabled political liberalism of the Jews can be understood, in part, as an effort to resolve the integration-survival dilemma. For the victory of liberalism would mean a reduction in church influence and also in unbridled nationalism, both sources of anti-Semitism; it would mean tolerance and civil liberties for all; it would, by ameliorating poverty, ensure the domestic tranquility without which anti-Semitism was virtually—so most Jews believed—a forgone conclusion. At the same time, the language of liberalism was the language of the prophetic tradition. Hence the battle for liberalism could serve both to preserve the vocabulary of Judaism and to ensure the safety of the Jews.

The urge to integrate was most powerful among second-generation Jews, who formed the largest segment of adult American Jewry from roughly 1935 to 1975. Their parents, the immigrants, were still—purposefully or not—tied to the tradition. And their children, as we shall see, were sufficiently comfortable in their Americanness to feel free to rediscover the tradition. But for the second generation, it is as if they actually chose to abide Hansen's law. So they sought to forget—quite often, with their parents' enthusiastic approval. And they did not require elaborate ideological systems to frame their forgetting.

In significant respects, it was as if America were, to both the immigrants and their offspring, a faith as much as a

5. Charles S. Liebman, "Orthodoxy in American Jewish Life," *American Jewish Year Book*, 64:21-98 (1965).

6. Marshall Sklare, *Conservative Judaism: An American Religious Movement* (New York: Schocken Books, 1972).

place. Had America not perceived itself as the new Zion? Did American writers and political leaders not imagine that this was God's new promised land, hence Americans God's new chosen people? Jews could not easily shed their sense of chosenness—but how much more enticing, in the end, to be chosen as an American—progress, freedom, expanse, wealth—than to be chosen as a Jew—discrimination, poverty, pogrom! In this regard, it is interesting to note how neatly the American civil religion suited the Jewish purpose, offering a set of rituals and symbols that were familiar in style and, because not Christian, acceptable in substance. Thanksgiving is perhaps the very best example of this—a quasi-religious ritual, Jewish in form and in purpose, and not at all un-Jewish in content. Imagine, for example, what it would have meant had the Pilgrims found wild boar rather than turkey.

The communal agenda of second-generation Jewry reflected its collective insecurity as well as its concern for integration. For decades, central Jewish philanthropic institutions spent large portions of the funds they collected from the Jewish community on social services for non-Jews. The most particularistic endeavors—Zionism, the fight against anti-Semitism—were recast in American terms. There was an enormous pride in those Jews who made it in quintessentially American ways, even when those ways were manifestly un-Jewish. So, for example, most Jews took a very dim view of boxing—but were delighted at the success of Barney Ross. Perhaps the combination of pride and anxiety was best captured in the title of a children's book that was popular in the mid-1940s: a collection of tales of Jewish soldiers and sailors of note, entitled *The Jews Fought, Too.* So, too,

for years one leading Jewish intergroup relations agency issued pamphlets and filmstrips that sought to demonstrate—theoretically to Gentiles, but as surely to Jews—how much Jews were like other Americans, how even their holidays could be understood in general American terms.

This being America, several plausible alternatives were available to the unalloyed integrationists. They could convert, of course, but conversion was an extreme choice, widely seen by other Jews as an act of betrayal, sure to cause pain to one's family. But America permitted a kind of nonsectarian identity, especially in its academic and literary subcultural communities. To become an academic was to join a thoroughly respectable community—indeed, a community that was as committed to redemption as were the Jews: "The truth shall make you free," and so forth. So in the academy, where religion was generally held in disdain, one could do sacred work without having to be Jewish. And one's parents could scarcely complain of their son—rarely, back then, their daughter—the professor, even if the grandchildren were deprived of a Jewish education.

Most Jews who sought integration in modern America were, however, perfectly willing to retain and sustain their Jewish connections, and hence Judaism itself, so long as these did not become impediments to their central objective. And, off to the side but enormously energetic, there was also that minority of Jews for whom Judaic purposes still had a very high—sometimes the highest—priority. Most Jews might well have felt more comfortable if this minority had disappeared, but it would not. It persisted, often as a rebuke, sometimes as a temptation. In the end, it articulated an option that became newly attractive in the late 1960s.

IS THERE SURVIVAL AFTER INTEGRATION?

The renewed interest in and emphasis on Jewish survival may be attributed to a variety of factors. By far the simplest, and surely the most direct, is that by the end of the 1960s, a very large number of Jews had made it in America.[7] In this context, making it means considerably more than economic success alone—although that success, too, fed the growing sense that the problem of integration had been solved.

For decades, Jews have led the American population in educational attainment, professionalization, and income. These trends, in fact, dramatically accelerated among the third generation, which came demographically to dominate adult American Jewry sometime around 1975. One recent analysis of American elites demonstrates that, with just 2 to 3 percent of the population, and 8 percent of the college-educated over-40 male population, Jews constitute about 20 percent of the most elite sectors of American society.[8] In his forthcoming study of American Jewry, Charles Silberman notes that about a quarter of the wealthiest 400 Americans are Jewish, as are roughly two-fifths of the richest self-made millionaires. About 8 percent of each house of Congress is Jewish, and Jews are now entering sectors of corporate power once reserved exclusively for white Gentile Americans.

In addition to the actual fact of Jewish achievement, the conditions that have surrounded and promoted that achievement, its environment, have helped reduce integrationist anxieties among Jews in the last decade or two. America has grown increasingly latitudinarian, increasingly tolerant of diversity in virtually every realm—family, sexual preference, leisure, culture, group identity.[9] In particular, the American ethos has come to accept, if not actually to celebrate, ethnic variety and—of special importance for some Orthodox Jews—fervent religious beliefs as well.

Perhaps even more important to the Jewish perspective, the anger of the 1960s, expressed in burning cities, in the emergence of assassination as a form of political expression, and in student riots—riots in which the children of Jews were active participants and sometimes leaders—led, inevitably, to a disenchantment with America as faith. Having so recently learned that radicalism was a god that had failed, and many having concluded in the wake of the Holocaust that the real God, too, had failed, Jews were now learning that America was no more dependable a god. Quite possibly, the growing literature on America's failure to rescue Jews during the Holocaust, and, more precisely, on Franklin Roosevelt's failure, contributed to this disenchantment.

At the same time that Jews, along with many other Americans, were experiencing massive disorientation, an event took place that reminded Jews of an older, and perhaps more dependable, orientation. Israel's Six Day War—and, more particularly, the weeks of terror that preceded the war, weeks during which visions of a new Auschwitz were

7. "The Jewish Community in Change," *Journal of Jewish Communal Service*, 58: 4-11 (Fall 1981).

8. Richard Alba and G. Moore, "Ethnicity in the American Elite," *American Sociological Review*, 47(3): 373-83 (June 1982).

9. See, for example, *Public Opinion* 6(6) (Nov.-Dec. 1983).

commonplace—provides as precise a point from which to take our analytic bearings as history ever offers.

During those weeks, one could almost sense the old Jewish integrationism battling with the new survivalism. There were Jews who energetically sought to act in the classic manner, delegating certain of their number to intercede quietly at the highest levels of government. And there were others who, perhaps aware of the politeness of American Jews during the Holocaust, favored mass demonstrations.

In the event, the war itself was so like a medieval morality play, with good and evil so precisely identifiable, and the world so enthusiastically pro-Israel, that the old inhibitions crumbled. And the sky did not fall; on the contrary, Israel experienced a spectacular victory. And the noisy Jews of the mass rallies in America—and Europe, for that matter—were not punished; on the contrary, they became, vicariously, heroes. If the weeks before the war had reminded the Jews of Jewish vulnerability, the week of the war provided them, for the first time, the experience of Jewish triumph. Both were profoundly moving experiences; together, they opened the door to a new sense of Jewish pride, to a new awareness of the emotional richness of Jewish identification.

The 1973 Yom Kippur War lacked the exquisite drama and emotional clarity of the 1967 war, but it pointed in quite the same direction. And by now, of course, ethnic identity was not merely an accepted aspect of American life; it was almost a faddish preoccupation.

All these events and developments helped shift the focus of Jewish concern from integration to survival—a shift, as we have said, that has had profound consequences for many aspects of Jew-

ish communal, religious, cultural, and political life.

SIGNS OF
THE NEW SURVIVALISM

The story of American Jewry since 1967 is the story of a growing preoccupation with Jewish survival. The signs of that preoccupation abound. In the religious sphere, for example, we find considerable movement in both Reform and modern Orthodox circles toward the classic religious traditions. Modern Orthodox rabbis, thinkers, and congregants report a sense of having lost out to the more religiously fundamentalist, politically conservative, and socially insular traditionalist Orthodox elements.[10] Reform Judaism has restored much Hebrew liturgy to the worship service, has established parochial schools, and— in a reversal of its antipathy toward Zionism—has formally joined the world Zionist movement.[11] Trends in the Conservative movement are harder to document. Most observers detect a growing polarization, as a more traditionally-oriented minority leans increasingly toward the modern Orthodox to its religious right, while the larger number of rabbis and congregants moves toward liberalization of ritual and liturgy.[12]

The Jewish philanthropic world has undergone a similar revolution. There is no longer talk of using Jewish philanthropic dollars to serve Gentile purposes.[13] In fact, the extent of specifically

10. Charles S. Liebman, "Orthodox Judaism Today," Midstream, 20: 19-26 (Aug.-Sept. 1979).

11. W. Gunther Plaut, "Reform Judaism: Past, Present and Future," Journal of Reform Judaism, 27(2): 1-11 (Summer 1980).

12. Lawrence J. Kaplan, "The Dilemma of Conservative Judaism," Commentary, 62(10):44-47 (Oct. 1976).

13. Charles S. Liebman, "Leadership and Decision-Making in a Jewish Federation: The New

Jewish utilization of centrally supported services has become one important criterion for the award of communal funding. Simultaneously, philanthropists have been providing more funds for Jewish education of all sorts, and especially for that most nonintegrationist institution, the day or parochial school. Indeed, we now find that the philanthropists as individuals have become increasingly involved in personal ritual practice[14]—an unthinkable development just two decades ago—even as the less religiously observant have tended to drop out of the Jewish philanthropic enterprise.[15] Similarly, new professionals in Jewish communal services are not only personally more ritually observant; increasingly, they are graduates of new training programs specifically designed to combine professional training with the study of Judaica.[16]

The shift from integrationism to survivalism is evident also in the symbolic realm. American symbols have largely receded from Jewish public life. In their place, we find considerable investment in Israel and the Holocaust.[17]

Fascination with the Holocaust is one of the most striking developments of the last 15 years. Courses on the

York Federation of Jewish Philanthropies," *American Jewish Year Book*, 79: 149-69 (1982).

14. Jonathan Woocher, "The 'Civil Judaism' of Communal Leaders," *American Jewish Year Book*, 82: 29-51 (1980).

15. Steven M. Cohen, "Trends in Jewish Philanthropy," *American Jewish Year Book*, 80: 29-51 (1980).

16. Bernard Reisman, "Managers, Jews or Social Workers? Conflicting Expectations for Communal Workers," *Response*, 13(3): 41-54 (Aug. 1982).

17. Jacob Neusner, *Stranger at Home: The 'Holocaust,' Zionism, and American Judaism* (Chicago: University of Chicago Press, 1981).

subject are the most popular Judaica offerings on college campuses. By most reckonings, the topic is the most frequent subject of newly published titles in English-language Judaica. Several communities have established Holocaust memorial centers, and there seems to be no end in sight to the movement to erect some sort of memorial in community after community. Direct-mail fund raisers report that one major Holocaust museum and study center regularly achieves one of the highest response rates, if not the highest, in mail solicitations of potential Jewish contributors. United Jewish Appeal missions to Israel now often include a stopover in Poland as Jews increasingly adopt the from-ashes-to-rebirth metaphor as their summary of recent Jewish history.

The Holocaust is, of course, a shattering rebuke to modernity. Whether or not it is consciously perceived as such, it cannot be easy for a people fascinated with the Holocaust to retain their naive faith in the blessings of modernity. The decline of that faith, as also of the passion for America—once the last, best hope of mankind, now a troubled and often clumsy giant—is apparent in Jewish attitudes toward a variety of institutions and symbols. One senses—for we enter here the realm of intuition rather than data—a diminished enthusiasm, or, more accurately, a diminished confidence in the principal social institutions, such as the public school and the polling place, as paths to redemption. This growing skepticism, lapping over into cynicism, is doubtless shared with other Americans of these unsettling times. What, then, of the Jewish faith in liberalism, the underlying ideology of social and communal redemption?

JUST AS LIBERAL,
LESS PASSIONATE

The erstwhile political liberalism of the Jews has been a subject of considerable controversy of late. Both the fact of that liberalism and its value have been debated. In significant respects, the debate—especially at the value level—has been coincident in time with the shift from integrationism to survivalism.

The starting point of the argument that the time has come for Jews to turn from their earlier commitment to liberalism is that Jews are now sufficiently well integrated to be able to turn from making friends to influencing people—from, that is, doing good to defending group interests. Depending on the style of the argument, it may be observed that the effort to do good benefited the Jews very little. The example usually introduced as evidence of that proposition is that for all the help Jews proffered blacks during the prime time of the civil rights movement, they have now not only been abandoned by the blacks, but have learned that anti-Semitism is more common among black Americans—and especially among educated black Americans—than among others.

But even where the ingratitude of others is not cited, the matter of Jewish group interests is. "Is it good for the Jews?" used to be thought an unacceptably parochial question. Perhaps it might be indulged by an as-yet unassimilated immigrant generation that could not view the world from other than a Jewish perspective. But for the children of that generation, "Is it good for the Jews?" became the stuff of Borscht Belt humor, not of sociopolitical understanding.

And now a new generation of Jews comes to announce that "Is it good for the Jews?" is an entirely reasonable, indeed self-respecting, standard according to which the sociopolitical realm may be assessed. Some even insist it is the only appropriate standard.

How, they ask, can a Jew be opposed to a strong America, or support détente, given the Soviet Union's treatment of the Jews and its anti-Israel behavior? Why should a Jew support affirmative action, which is scarcely distinguishable from quotas, a system of selection with such bitter memories for Jews? Given Israel's needs, ought not a Jew support American interventionism abroad, so the precedent is there if Israel, heaven forbid, ever needs to call on it? And in any case, considering that Jews are as affluent as they are, why should they not support the party that favors wealth?[18]

These arguments might be supposed to have particular appeal to a generation turning from integration to survival, from the desire not to be noticed to an insistence on claiming its due.

Yet withal, those who have anticipated and those who have urged a massive rightward shift in the Jewish political understanding have been disappointed. The most that can be said of the political opinions—and behaviors—of American Jews is that they have moved along with the rest of the nation—which means that they remain considerably to the left of the ever-changing national center.[19]

Thus, in the congressional elections of 1982, about three-quarters of all Jews supported Democratic candidates. While 59 percent of the nation was

18. See, most recently, Irving Kristol, "The Political Dilemma of American Jews," *Commentary*, 73(7): 23-29 (July 1984).

19. Steven M. Cohen, *The Political Attitudes of American Jews, 1984* (New York: American Jewish Committee, 1984); Alan Fisher, "The Myth of the Rightward Turn," *Moment*, 8(10): 22-26 (Nov. 1983).

voting for Ronald Reagan, only 30 to 32 percent of the Jews followed suit. In a national survey of Jewish adults conducted just a few months prior to the 1984 elections,[20] we learned that

—self-defined liberals outnumbered conservatives three to two, the reverse of the typical findings in national surveys of all Americans;

—Jewish Democrats outnumbered Jewish Republicans by over four to one, as compared to a three-to-two margin nationally;

—on domestic questions, most Jews favored affirmative action but not quotas; gun control and also the death penalty; equal rights for homosexuals; an end to the building of nuclear power plants; government aid for abortions for poor women; and church-state separation on issues such as public school prayer and tuition tax credits for parents of private and parochial school students; and

—on foreign affairs, a majority of Jews favored dovish policies toward the Soviet Union, including a bilateral nuclear freeze, cutbacks in U.S. military spending—but no reduction in military support for Israel—and staying in the United Nations.

In most instances where comparisons with recent nationwide studies of public opinion have been undertaken, Jews emerge as decidedly more liberal on a variety of issues, including gun control, abortion, school prayer, tuition tax credits, the nuclear freeze, and defense spending.

20. Cohen, *Political Attitudes of American Jews*, 1984.

One of the reasons observers so often mispredict and misinterpret the political leanings of the Jews is that they focus on the attitudes and behaviors of the most Jewish Jews—the more observant, the more ethnically segregated, the more organized. These are, indeed, considerably more conservative than the socially integrated—although still Jewishly identified and active—Jews. It would, however, be a serious error to infer from the views of the more Jewishly active that political conservatism has become, in any sense at all, the normative position of the established Jewish community or of a majority of the Jews. As reflected in the pronouncements of the major Jewish organizations, and in the behavior of Jews in general, that has simply not been the case.

Yet another reason for the assumption that Jews have already moved to the right or soon will is the decline in liberal rhetoric and passion within the Jewish community. One hears less appeal to the traditional slogans, in part because of the shift from integrationism to survivalism that we have been discussing, in part because of trends in secular America. Whether it is inertia or policy that keeps the Jews liberal even as liberal affect wanes, we cannot say—but the liberal inclination of the Jews has plainly survived the decline of liberal rhetoric.

UNITED ON ISRAEL,
DIVIDED ON POLICIES

Israel's continuing peril has been both a stimulus to the release of survivalist energies and a focus for the expression of those energies. Between 1970 and 1984, the proportion of American Jews who had visited Israel grew from 15 percent to nearly 40 percent—and almost one of every six American Jews has visited Israel more than once.[21] The Six Day War and the Yom Kippur War—but not the war in Lebanon—each spurred giving to the United Jewish Appeal to much higher levels. And Israel has also been the focus of dramatically heightened political activity, especially among the affluent. The main pro-Israel lobby, the America-Israel Public Affairs Committee, has increased its membership and its financial resources severalfold and is regularly cited by observers as one of America's most effective lobbies. In addition, there are several dozen political action committees that have been organized to support pro-Israel candidates.

In their commitment to Israel's safety, the Jews have shifted—again, mirroring both shifts in the general society and their own shift from integrationism to survivalism—from the politics of discrete intercession to a more muscular model, in which power and pressure supplement the prayer and pleading of old. The overwhelmingly dominant view among Israel's Jewish supporters in America is that what's good for Israel is good for America, and that is the view they press most insistently on American policymakers. But they are not reluctant, when necessary, to invoke more proximate rewards and punishments in lobbying on Israel's behalf.

The profound commitment to Israel's welfare should not, however, be mistaken—as it often is—for agreement

with all of the policies of the Israeli government. And conversely, expressions of opposition to particular Israeli policies do not necessarily imply a lessened concern for Israel's security. In a 1983 survey, four out of five agreed that "if Israel were destroyed, I would feel as if I had suffered one of the greatest personal tragedies of my life," and a six-to-one majority agreed that "Jews should not vote for candidates who are unfriendly to Israel." But the sample split almost evenly on the questions of whether "Israel should offer the Arabs territorial compromise on the West Bank" or whether Israel should maintain "permanent control over Judea and Samaria." A two-to-one majority favored the suspension of settlements in the West Bank to encourage peace negotiations and a four-to-one majority agreed that "Israel should talk with the PLO if the PLO recognizes Israel and renounces terrorism."[22]

Thus, although Jews feel deeply attached to Israel—or say they do—they are not nearly so attached to Israel's policies. Does this mean that survivalism has its limits? Or does it mean that there is a genuine difference over the policies that will best ensure the survival of the Jews, on the one hand, and of their state, on the other?

We cannot say. But we can note that feelings of threat and vulnerability play a major role in provoking hard-line responses by Jews in the United States—and in Israel, too. In four annual surveys from 1981 to 1984, the most hawkish responses came during the height of hostilities in Lebanon, in August 1982.[23] And no

21. Steven M. Cohen, *Attitudes of American Jews towards Israel and Israelis* (New York: American Jewish Committee, 1983); and Gary Tobin and Julie Lipsman, "A Compendium of Jewish Demographic Studies," in *Perspectives in Jewish Population Research*, ed. Steven M. Cohen, Jonathan Woocher, and Bruce Phillips (Boulder, CO: Westview Press, 1984).

22. Cohen, *Attitudes of American Jews towards Israel.*
23. Steven M. Cohen, *A Survey of American Jewish Public Opinion in the Aftermath of the Israeli/PLO War in Lebanon* (New York: Amer-

matter when, those Jews who see other Americans as more anti-Israel are more likely to oppose compromise with the Arabs. Thus, concern for Israel is wrapped up with and expresses a more widespread concern for Jewish survival, a concern that revolves not only around the Jews of Israel but around the Jews of America as well.

FEARS FOR THE FUTURE OF AMERICAN JEWRY: ILL-FOUNDED ANXIETIES

The concern—"obsession" may be more accurate—with Jewish survival is evident in the repeated references of rabbis, educators, fund raisers, and lay leaders to the demographic, cultural, and spiritual crises that allegedly threaten the Jews. These references are the most pervasive theme of Jewish public discourse.

At their center is concern for the stability and continuity of the Jewish family. It is commonly assumed that Jewish-Gentile intermarriage rates are inexorably climbing, and that the offspring of such marriages—or, at least, their grandchildren—will be lost to the Jewish community. Moreover, this line of thinking goes, fewer Jews are marrying early—if at all—and, of those who are, most will have fewer children than did their parents. They will surely reproduce at a rate far below that required for replacement. Hence there is an immediate threat to the actual physical survival of the Jews.

That demographic threat is seen, at least in part, as a reflection of broader trends affecting the Jewish commitment of the young. Nostalgic recollections of the Jewish life of the European *shtetl* or the immigrant neighborhood suggest an erstwhile richness against which the secularized present appears utterly anemic, hence doomed. The nurturing environment of yesteryear is no more; Jews are now safe, but Judaism is profoundly threatened. Jewish culture cannot be sustained by Judaic illiterates; and as Jewish culture wanes, so, ultimately, must the Jews themselves, who will no longer find a compelling motive to stay Jewish.

In short, the survivalists focus our attention on the threats to Jewish life, both quantitative and qualitative, and on the link between the two. They argue that without drastic intervention, the number of Jews will dwindle, and there will be a more rapid decline still in the numbers of communally and ritually active Jews in particular.

A full examination of this line of thinking and of the evidence on which it rests is beyond our present scope.[24] But as the survivalist temper is so central to an understanding of American Jewry today, it is well to pause for a moment to cite some recent findings that bear rather directly on the matter.

Jewish outmarriage—marriage of a born Jew to a born Gentile—seems to have risen to a rate of one in four nationally, where it has now rested for several years. The estimate obscures dramatic regional variations. Recent studies suggest a rate of 12 to 13 percent in New York City and Miami, 39 percent in Los Angeles, and 57 percent in Denver.[25] The 25 percent overall figure

ican Jewish Committee, 1982); idem, "The 1981-1982 National Survey of American Jews," *American Jewish Year Book*, 83:136-59 (1983); idem, *Political Attitudes of American Jews, 1984*; idem, *Attitudes of American Jews towards Israel.*

24. Steven M. Cohen and Calvin Goldscheider, "Jews, More or Less," *Moment*, 9(8): 41-46 (Sept. 1984).

25. Charles Silberman, untitled study of American Jewish life, forthcoming.

is considerably below the popular estimate among Jews, which is closer to 40 or even 50 percent. Moreover, the assumption that the outmarriage statistic is essentially an estimate of the number of Jews annually lost by Judaism is wildly off the mark. In fact, intermarriage may result in net gains to the Jewish population—albeit typically to the less observant segments—as a result of conversion to Judaism, a rather widespread practice, especially among Gentile women marrying Jewish men, and as a result of the tendency of most Jewish women who marry out to raise their offspring as Jews.[26]

The tendency for highly educated Jewish women to delay childbearing, especially evident in the 1970s, has often been perceived as a portent of lower birthrates, hence ultimately of negative population growth. Recent research, however, finds that Jewish women in their late thirties have an average of more than two children, a level adequate to ensure demographic replacement.[27] Furthermore, fears of a less ritually observant or less communally involved younger generation also seem unfounded. Once young adults marry and have children, their participation levels in these areas match those of their elders.[28]

Those who reject the gloomy prognoses for Jewish life in America can point as well to other signs of health and vitality. These include an upsurge in the publishing of books of Jewish interest; tremendous growth in the number of college students enrolled in Judaica courses; widespread participation by

upper-middle-class young adults in political action on Israel's behalf.

The point here is not whether American Jewry is or is not holding its own in demographic, religious, cultural, and political terms. The point, instead, is that communal leaders typically choose to cite the more pessimistic prognoses and to ignore more promising analyses. In so doing, they link themselves to a distinguished tradition, for the animating rhetoric of Jewish life in the recent past has been the urgent need to save the Jews—to save Israel's Jews from their Arab enemies, to save Soviet Jews from their brutal government, to save Ethiopian Jews from oppression and starvation—and, consistent with all this, to save American Jews from assimilation.

It is easy to trivialize the argument, to accuse the obsessive survivalist of depending on enemies to sustain the Jewish effort. If there be no obvious enemy without, then focus on the enemy within; and, incidentally, in this way, draw the attention of the audience to yesterday's enemies, whose defeat has surely been only temporary. But the point the survivalists make, however much it depends on faulty evidence, is more serious. Jewish life, in the wake of the Enlightenment and of the Holocaust, in the wake of the surprise of safety in America and danger in Israel, suffers these days from an understandable intellectual and ideological confusion. There is massive dissensus regarding its rationale, its commitments, its purpose. Amidst such confusion and dissensus, the enemies of the Jews provide a consensual rallying point. In America, the Jews have finally learned that the enemy is not the pogromist at the gates but the erosion of will within.

But by resting their argument on faulty data, the survivalists risk the

26. Steven M. Cohen and Paul Ritterband, *Identity, Family and Community: The Jews of Greater New York* (tentative title), forthcoming.
27. Ibid.
28. Ibid.

credibility of their case, and risk, as well, missing the evidence of a turn from survivalism toward meaning and purpose.

AFTER SURVIVALISM: A SEARCH FOR MEANING AND BELONGING?

The evidence is admittedly weak and scattered, but the case can be made nonetheless, that significant numbers of American Jews have begun a search for a new central ethos to complement, if not supplant, the survivalism we have been describing.

We have already referred to the recent growth in Jewish studies courses and in other expressions of substantive Jewish purpose. More generally, we now witness a gradual shift in emphasis from the preoccupation with numbers—with Jewish quantity—to a concern with meaning—Jewish quality. The much noted *havura* movement—small groups of Jews, within or outside the synagogue framework, who meet regularly and frequently for purposes of prayer, study, or simply fellowship—is one expression of, and response to, this concern. So, too, is the renewed emphasis on Judaic programming in the Jewish community centers, once powerful exponents of integrationism.

At the deepest level, the concern for integration and for survival now merge. There is a growing belief in elite circles, and a growing sense more popularly, that integration into America permits, and perhaps even requires, a healthy sense of identity—in this case, group identity. The old universalist slogans still have power for some, but they are not nearly as generally potent as they were a few decades back. The disen-

chantment leads some to an insular particularism, but more seem to accept that particularism need not mean withdrawal from the commonwealth. Instead, it implies a reformulation of the terms of the American social contract, a shift from America as a nation of unhyphenated individuals to America as a collection of groups. Social pluralism, once an abstract notion defended by a small minority, now emerges as the popular normative perception.

And, simultaneously, Jews in growing number have come to suppose that the quantitative threats they face are perhaps best addressed by an emphasis on the qualitative possibilities they enjoy, that the best assurance of Jewish survival is the development of a community that offers its members opportunities for personal fulfillment not easily found elsewhere. Once the safety of individual Jews has been assured, the continuing communal emphasis on Jewish survival becomes stale. It gives rise to a redundant ideology, in which the community seeks to survive—in order to survive. The irony of such an agenda is that it may well be self-defeating, because in its preoccupation with survival it is led to deemphasize the ideological, cultural, philosophical, theological, and political debates that may well be the most powerful inducements to Jewish identity, and hence to Jewish survival.

This recognition, in one form or another, is now growing in all branches of American Jewry, and its growth suggests that the coming decades will mark a definitive move beyond the search for integration, beyond the search for survival, into a vigorous search for meaning, for purpose.

ANNALS, *AAPSS*, **480**, July 1985

Jesse Jackson and the Symbolic Politics
of Black Christendom

By JAMES MELVIN WASHINGTON

ABSTRACT: This article examines the significance of the Reverend Jesse Jackson's bid for the Democratic party's presidential nomination. Jackson's candidacy represents a new use of political revivalism, an old evangelical political praxis recast in the modalities of African American Christian culture. This praxis is an aspect of American political culture that has often been overlooked because of past misunderstandings of American folk religion in general, and black Christianity in particular, as captives of an otherworldly and privatized spirituality. This article contends that black Christianity has an identifiable and coherent political style with both passive and active moods. The dominant manifestations of these moods are, respectively, political cynicism and political revivalism, which are the consequence of the correct folk perception that it is impossible to reason with the purveyors of the absurdities of racial injustice. A critical assessment of black Christianity's political symbolic capital seems appropriate.

James Melvin Washington, Ph.D., is associate professor of church history at Union Theological Seminary and adjunct associate professor of religion at Columbia University in New York City. His forthcoming books include Frustrated Fellowship: A Critical History of the Black Baptist Quest for Social Power, 1773-1953 *and two anthologies,* Afro-American Protestant Spirituality *and* Martin Luther King, Jr.: A Prophet for Our Time.

T HE 1984 campaign of the Rever- end Jesse Louis Jackson for the Democratic party's presidential nomi- nation was perhaps the most historic development in an otherwise uneventful public ritual. If politics involves, at its most primal level, the rhetorical manip- ulation of basic public symbols and beliefs to legitimate maintenance or change in the social order, surely, Jackson's extraordinary communica- tion skills proved more than equal to the task. But Jackson lacked a genuine feel for the tribal signals of white America. Furthermore, his own commitment to the folk style of black Christianity ex- acerbated the cultural cleavage between black and white America.

This article seeks to explain why Jackson's rainbow coalition did not win the support of the white majority, and why even some black leaders eschewed Jackson's intriguing attempt to renovate some semblance of a pluralistic vision of American politics. First, I contend that Jesse Jackson is the leader of the black church movement's latest and most ef- fective response to the unjust politics of white supremacists. It is a serious mis- reading to see Jesse Jackson as a lone, charismatic politico. On the contrary, his primary constituency is the black church movement. In order to ascertain why Jesse Jackson's rainbow coalition was unsuccessful, I shall offer a his- torical profile of a religious black po- litical ethos. Second, I disagree with the claim that the black church is apolitical and I describe its political styles. Third, I shall examine the relation between the rise of a culture of consumption in American society and the ineffective- ness of moral suasion in black politics. Then I shall examine the role of political revivalism in what I call the symbolic politics of black Christendom.

WHAT IS BLACK CHRISTENDOM?

I consider all of the predominantly black religious bodies in the United States to be part of the black church movement. I use the word "church" here to mean essentially local groups or con- gregations organized around various Islamic, Protestant, Catholic, and Jew- ish beliefs. Black Protestants are by far the largest of black religious groups in the United States. But if one considers the entire Western Hemisphere, black Catholics certainly are the dominant group.

The focus here, however, is upon black Protestants in the United States. They are so diffuse and varied in their theologies that it would be futile to define them according to doctrine. But there are amazing similarities in their worship styles, which differ more ac- cording to class differentiation than according to denominational affiliation. At any rate, I use Paul Tillich's accent on the prophetic political significance of Protestantism in general as the major distinction of black Protestantism. Ac- cording to Tillich, "the most important contribution of Protestantism to the world in the past, present, and future is the principle of prophetic protest against every power which claims divine charac- ter for itself—whether it be the church or state, party or leader."[1] The powerful presence of this prophetic criticism is the central theme in the formation of prac- tically every black religious movement. Indeed, this political praxis, be it sym- bolic or emphatic, joins forces with different liturgical nuances to form a holistic coterie of beliefs and rituals that constitute the black church movement.[2]

1. Paul Tillich, *The Protestant Era*, trans. James Luther Adams (Chicago: University of Chicago Press, 1948), p. 230.
2. I shall use interchangeably the terms

The ideology and political praxis of this distinctive religious culture championed the progressive liberal tradition in American history as the moral expression most favorable to black aspirations. Identification with this tradition does not, however, exhaust the possibilities available to the black community.

Indeed, there have been three cultural strands and one highly diverse prophetic political response constituting the symbolic capital of the largely unexamined political ethos that is black Christendom. The three cultural strands are folk, bourgeois, and urban. And borrowing Cornel West's designation, I refer to the major counter-hegemonic black political tradition as prophetic African American Christianity.[3] These cultural strata have three historical counterpoints in the form of revivalistic, pastoral, and prophetic political praxes, which function as different strategies for resisting white supremacy. A brief historical review of these political praxes in relation to the three cultural strata will show how they have interacted.

The major historical black denominations include the African Methodist Episcopal church, incorporated in 1816; the African Methodist Episcopal Zion church, in 1821; the National Baptist Convention, U.S.A., Inc., in 1840;[4] and the Christian Methodist Episcopal church, in 1870. Practically all other black religious movements originated in congregations once affiliated with these denominations. In fact the black church movement itself began among black urban dwellers in the late eighteenth century who belonged to congregations within these denominations. Out of what began as ecclesiastical injustice among the Methodists and indifference among the Baptists, the black church movement immediately thrived wherever possible. Moreover, it became the chief engine that pulled and supported many black social reform movements such as the abolitionist movement before the Civil War and the civil rights movement of the 1960s. The black church movement accumulated what Pierre Bourdieu calls "cultural capital" sufficient to nurture its own political ethic and ethos to resist the hegemony of white supremacists.

The ideology of white supremacy is the stepchild of modern Western Christianity. A white tribal aesthetic began to erode the Christian doctrine of the universal Christ in the High Middle Ages by employing what Roger Bastide calls the progressive Aryanization of Christ, which, he believes, "is in strict accordance with the logic of the color symbolism" of the Western world. Indeed, "it did not start, however, until Christianity came into close contact with the other races—with the African race, in

"black church movement," "black Christianity," "black Christendom," and "black Protestantism." These terms all signify this general phenomenon that is simultaneously both religious and political. I believe it indeed constitutes a religious political culture in its own right.

3. Cornel West, *Prophesy Deliverance! An Afro-American Revolutionary Christianity* (Philadelphia: Westminster Press, 1982), esp. chap. 4. The best discussion of the idea and development of political revivalism is John L. Hammond, *The Politics of Benevolence: Revival Religion and American Voting Behavior* (Norwood, NJ: Ablex, 1979), esp. pp. 1-19.

4. The usual date given for the founding of this convention, 1880, is erroneous. The first incorporated black Baptist convention with a national constituency was the American Baptist Missionary Convention, which was incorporated in New York State in 1840. See James Melvin Washington, *The Origins and Emergence of Black Baptist Separatism, 1863-1897* (Ph.D. diss., Yale University, 1979), pp. 35-42.

particular. Christian artists began to avoid the darker tints in depicting Christ in order to remove as much as possible of their evil suggestion."[5] It would be quite easy and woefully redundant to recast the findings of recent genealogists of modern racism such as David Brion Davis, Winthrop Jordan, and Cornel West. In short, the darker the hue, the more akin to evil the thing or person came to be conceived.

Besides resistance to all forms of thingification, the black church movement fought against moral and political cynicism within black America. The movement's attachment to the rather shortsighted moralisms of eighteenth- and nineteenth-century Evangelicalism, its parent religious impulse, often eclipsed the different cultural and psychological application of its innovative form of Christian spirituality. The progressive leaders of black Christianity continuously warned against the boomerang effect of moral laxity, political apathy, and racial divisiveness. They argued that blacks must develop psychic and spiritual callosity against white racism, yet simultaneously seek to influence public opinion. Despite this counsel, however, black political sarcasm continued to grow without much abatement until the huge turnout for Jesse Jackson in the 1984 Democratic primaries. Jackson's use of the techniques of political revivalism proved to be historic.

THE POLITICAL STRATEGIES OF BLACK CHRISTENDOM

Black political revivalism includes the use of sermonic folk discourse and a complex of cultural praxes that are all rooted in the distinctive spirituality of black Christianity. It is comparable to what Anthony F. C. Wallace calls revitalization movements.[6] The ancient processes of spiritual renewal involve the psychic fortification of an entire social grouping. When an essentially religious group consists of persons in an inherently politically oppressive situation—for example, slavery, being colonized, or perverse racist practices such as Jim Crowism, tragic political inequalities, lynchings, burnings, and bombings— it must find ways of maintaining its sense of community.

Revivals function as planned events that intentionally try to reclaim some idyllic moment of group cohesion for communities whose identities are under seige. The black church has been the major practitioner and proponent of revivalism as a means of rejuvenating a community gripped by psychic and economic depression. It uses liturgies forged in the crucible of the slave regime, segregation, depressed urban ghettos, and rural shanties to fight assaults upon the psychic well-being of black people.[7] Despite continuous and powerful white attempts to control the black church movement, much internal struggle, and, most certainly, much struggle with secular black competitors, the black church has maintained political and spiritual brokerage.

From its inception in the late eighteenth century, the black church movement took advantage of the historic

5. Roger Bastide, "Color, Racism, and Christianity" in *Color and Race*, ed. John Hope Franklin (Boston: Beacon Press, 1969), pp. 37-38.

6. Anthony F. C. Wallace, *Religion: An Anthropological View* (New York: Random House, 1966), esp. pp. 30-39.

7. See an extensive discussion of the meaning and goals of black spirituality in James Melvin Washington, *Afro-American Protestant Spirituality* (Ramsey, NJ: Paulist Press, forthcoming).

liberty that the Bill of Rights granted religious bodies. Although white church leaders expressed cultural disdain for black spirituality, they sometimes offered support and protection. Some of them would even express admiration for the spiritual integrity of black people. But they were also protecting their own investments in religious liberty by taking this benevolent approach despite their suspicion that something profoundly revolutionary was occurring among these enslaved Christians. They did not know what to do about this revolutionary activity, however, without running the risk of losing their own religious liberty.

A new prophetic form of Christianity

The slave revolts of Gabriel Prosser, Denmark Vesey, and Nat Turner, all fomented in the clandestine wombs of religious fellowship among the slaves, forced the various states to pass strict laws for the regulation of the religious life of the slaves. This was especially true after Nat Turner's Revolt in 1831.

Meanwhile, between 1829 and 1843, northern blacks and their liberal white compatriots began to raise a mighty prophetic outcry against the American Colonization Society's racist project of returning blacks to Africa. There was certainly a latent bourgeois cultural chauvinism toward Africa in the resistence to the return, but the historical significance of this development was that it became the first united political stance of African Americans. They reached the conclusion that racism was a national, not a southern, problem, and that it would not be eradicated by escaping to the North. Many of them, such as David Walker, Frederick Doug-

lass, Sojourner Truth, and the Reverends Henry Highland Garnet, Samuel H. Davis, Jermain Wesley Loguen, and James William Charles Pennington, helped to form the tradition of prophetic black politics by their fiery denunciations of slavery. Like their white comrades, such as Sarah and Angelina Grimké, Theodore Weld, William Lloyd Garrison, Beriah Green, and Gerrit Smith, they came to the conclusion that slavery was part of a systematic social and economic cancer that left no part of American culture unscathed.

These allies for freedom forged a progressive political alliance, which has had its ups and downs.[8] Although strained, the alliance remains intact today despite the constant defections of some white progressives from the cause of racial and economic justice and despite Jesse Jackson's embarrassing "hymie" *faux pas* and Louis Farrakhan's unfortunate anti-Jewish rhetoric.

Progressive pastoral resistance

Blacks did not form organizations exclusively for protest until the twentieth century, however. The first one was, of course, the National Association for the Advancement of Colored People (NAACP), established in 1909. The other important ones were the National Urban League, founded in 1910; the Congress of Racial Equality, founded in 1942; the Southern Christian Leadership Conference (SCLC), founded in 1957; and People United to Save Humanity (PUSH), founded in 1971. Of these major protest organizations, the

8. The progress of this alliance in the post-Civil War era is shown in James McPherson, *The Abolitionist Legacy: From Reconstruction to the NAACP* (Princeton, NJ: Princeton University Press, 1975).

NAACP, SCLC, and PUSH have always had significant religious bases and often equally powerful religious leadership. Black religious leaders have had far more power in the NAACP than was recognized before the Reverend Benjamin E. Hooks became its executive director. For example, the Reverend Dr. Channing Tobias, the powerful national executive director of the Colored Young Men's Christian Association and a member of Roosevelt's Black Cabinet, served for years as the chairman of the NAACP's board of directors.

Although we cannot review the full history of the leadership struggle here, it must be noted that we are currently in the midst of a major leadership power struggle that began immediately after the deaths of Malcolm X in 1965 and the Reverend Dr. Martin Luther King, Jr., in 1968.

After King's assassination on 4 April 1968, black leaders reverted to the more traditional procedure of dividing leadership responsibilities. The tough persistence of this leadership style had even challenged King's unquestionable reign between 1963 and 1968. The division of labor went along the lines of religious, social, political, and economic leadership. Only the ministers were able to prevail, from time to time, in all of these areas. In fact it might be helpful to see the 1960s as an attempt on the part of lesser-known black leaders such as Whitney Young, Roy Wilkins, James Farmer, and Malcolm X to usurp, if not secularize, the rhetoric of black leaders.

But this disorganized strategy did not work. The ministers simply reverted to their traditional division of labor. Some went into politics. Andrew Young, a minister in the United Church of Christ, became a congressman representing the state of Georgia. Walter Fauntroy, a Baptist pastor and former head of SCLC's office in the District of Columbia, became an at-large U.S. congressional representative for the District. Others, including the Reverend Wyatt Tee Walker, returned to the pastorates of local congregations, where they engaged in major social uplift endeavors such as the reform of public education and the construction of publicly financed housing.

The ministers' social reform projects would have been untenable without Lyndon Baines Johnson's Great Society programs, which Richard Nixon began to eliminate. Nixon urged the creation of programs to stimulate black capitalism. A number of Martin Luther King, Jr.'s disciples denounced Nixon's renunciation of the welfare state. They sensed that a more enduring national move toward conservatism was inevitable.

Nixon's black capitalism became the conservative economic philosophy of quasi-revolutionary black nationalism. Jesse Jackson was the most prominent King disciple to embrace this ironic philosophical partnership between a neoclassical economic philosophy and a liberal social philosophy. The national government failed, however, to stimulate black capitalism, and Jackson therefore returned to the progressive fold and then even moved to the left of it.

By the 1976 presidential campaign Jackson had succeeded in broadening his programmatic base. He embraced the consumers' rights tactics of Ralph Nader, and he aided several black business executives in becoming millionaires. But this tangential support for black capitalism did little to help the deprived.

THE CULTURE OF CONSUMPTION AND POLITICAL CYNICISM

As a result of the depression that stubbornly gripped the black community, Jackson, like other notable leaders of black America, had to ask some fundamental questions. For example, What recourse should the victims of injustice in America take? Better yet, What strategies have they employed to resist systemic unfairness? Since it is obvious from even a superficial knowledge of American history that violent revolution has not been a common strategy, we must look elsewhere. The answer is simple and yet complex: they resorted to individual and group protests against and criticisms of the status quo. But this response proved to be ineffectual in the 1970s and 1980s. America itself had undergone in the 1960s and 1970s what Sydney E. Ahlstrom called a moral and cultural revolution. As we view it now, however, the resistance to an economic restructuring that would be more reflective of a just society proved to be the broken cog in the wheel of this glorious revolution.

Amazing technological advancements certainly pushed America, which still clung stubbornly to its Victorian values, into this tremendous watershed period. Richard Nixon's silent majority was gladly seduced, however, by the simplisms of Jerry Falwell's Moral Majority, and by Falwell's fellow television evangelists, who sent daily pleas across the airwaves for America to turn back the clock. This powerful conservative reaction retreated into the arms of the lapsed moralism of the profit motive. Many— even erstwhile liberals—felt that the American myth of the right to practice what Thorstein Veblen called conspicuous consumption was unfairly under assault.

America had embraced a new order,[9] according to Rifkin and Howard, that was characterized by the demise of liberalism and the rise of a more disciplined entrepreneurial spirit. They believed American religious conservatives would be in the forefront of this new capitalist phalanx. Progressive black Christian leaders have been slow to decipher the meaning and consequences of the rise of this new righteous culture of consumption. But perhaps the presidential campaign experience of Jesse Jackson and the reelection of Ronald Reagan might awaken all progressive religious leaders to the shortcomings of the politics of moral suasion, political revivalism, and prophetic pronouncement without a tough-minded, yet compassionate, political praxis determined to reorient an often unjust American political economy.

Another important issue is at stake here also. That is, blacks who identified with liberalism in both its political and moral expressions overlooked the nihilistic potential of public opinion. The *modus operandi* of classical liberalism's moral adjudications is based on utilitarianism. Alexis de Tocqueville warned about this danger in the 1840s:

Not only is common opinion the only guide which private judgement retains among a democratic people, but among such a people it possesses a power infinitely beyond what it has elsewhere. At periods of equality men have no faith in one another, by reason of their common resemblance; but this very resemblance gives them almost unbounded confidence in the judgement of the public; for it would seem probable that, as they are all endowed with equal means of judging, the

9. See Jeremy Rifkin and Ted Howard, *The Emergence of a New Order: God in the Age of Scarcity* (New York: G. P. Putnam, 1979).

greater truth should go with the greater number.[10]

The founders of the United States believed the Bill of Rights would protect Americans from the nihilistic pragmatism of utilitarianism. They suspected that the success of this form of reaching political compromise depended heavily upon as much social and cultural homogeneity as possible. That is why several of them feared the black presence. And they were correct. James Rawley summarized the challenge presented by the racial factor in American political life and discourse:

Race relations have rarely been treated rationally by Americans. Discussions of them usually turn to inanities, culminating in the question "Do you want your daughter to marry a Negro?" Race is the one thing in our history that has defied the political genius of the American people.[11]

American political ingenuity has also failed to meet the negative challenge that white supremacy poses to its democratic political idealism. Amidst the perennial social amnesia of many white Americans, especially as it regards racial justice, the politics of black Christendom offers a restorationist ideology and political praxis. It levels stinging moral judgments that expose the gilded cage of white suburbia and the fortified townhouses of affluent urban neighborhoods that seemingly remain oblivious to the moral outrage of their impoverished neighbors at home and abroad.

10. Alexis de Tocqueville, *Democracy in America* (New York: Vintage Books, 1945), 2:11.

11. James Rawley, *Race and Politics: "Bleeding Kansas" and the Coming of the Civil War* (Philadelphia: J. B. Lippincott, 1969), p. ix.

THE PASTORAL POWER OF THE JACKSON CAMPAIGN

Although the tradition of black ministers as community activists is an old tradition, it has undergone important changes since the death of Martin Luther King, Jr. *Time* magazine referred to the dispersion of King's phase of the civil rights movement as the creation of leadership in the form of localism.[12] But in truth the strong secondary local leadership had been there all the time. After 1968 it received a new impetus with the return and infusion of talented black clerical leadership.

Clearly, Jesse Jackson rose to the top of this list of leaders. Blessed with photogenic pizzazz, a rich—although often grating—poetic jingoism, adroit political savvy, and the prophetic, pastoral, and priestly responsibility—customary of black ministers, especially after Dr. King's death—to be a community leader, Jackson became one of the prime foci of the hungry cameras of the news media age. But it would be a mistake to conclude that Jesse Jackson is a creation of the news media. His roots are planted deeply within the black church's rich tradition of social, political, and economic activism. He builds upon the tradition of prophetic politics that I outlined previously. Jackson's political ingenuity, however, lies in his ability to reform the techniques of black political revivalism. Jackson, unlike Martin Luther King, Jr., has been able to translate the southern agrarian ethos of the civil rights movements into the language and ethos of urban black America without losing the southern tenor of the movement.

Jackson achieved this transformation by using his gifts as a publicist,

12. *Time*, 6 Apr. 1970.

prophetic politico, and political revivalist. Moreover, the presidential campaign in effect bestowed upon Jackson the presidency of black America, a de facto office held by such notables as Frederick Douglass, Booker T. Washington, Adam Clayton Powell, Jr., and Martin Luther King, Jr. Undoubtedly, Jackson has become a national and international spokesperson for the downtrodden. In fact, Jackson is the most influential black man in America since Booker T. Washington. The key for understanding both how he rose to power and how he continues to acquire it at such an amazing rate lies not with his ability but with his willingness to take advantage of his religious roots.

The PUSH revival

The power of political revivalism rallied black Americans during their three major historic campaigns for civil and human rights in the abolitionist movement, and in the civil rights movements between 1865 and 1914 and those between 1953 and 1965. The use of black religious rituals in social movements came under intense criticism, however, from the black power movement, a secularist impulse, after the rise of this movement in 1965. Actually, those who were embarrassed by the use of black hymns, spirituals, prayers, and preaching in the civil rights movements were oftentimes secular-minded black college students who crassly, often with shadowy verve, appropriated Karl Marx's dictum that "religion is the opium of the people." They were willing to romanticize practically every aspect of black culture except its distinguished great-grandparent, the black church movement.

The abandonment of the black church movement was not universal, however.

In fact, a cadre of bright, courageous black college students and seminarians, such as Robert Moses, James Lawson, C. T. Vivian, Diane Nash, Marion Barry—who is now mayor of Washington, D.C.—John Lewis, Julian Bond, Courtland Cox, and the untempered—although exceptionally bright— Stokeley Carmichael, actually radicalized King's movement. This was especially true of the Student Nonviolent Coordinating Committee (SNCC), which was formed under the leadership of the ubiquitous Ella Baker after the Greensboro, North Carolina, sit-ins started by four local black students from the Agricultural and Technical College of North Carolina. Even though some of the major leaders of SNCC, such as Stokeley Carmichael, later refused to use the exorcisms of black religiosity, many of them were primarily attracted to the movement partly because of its religious fervor for justice. Indeed, as one Protestant minister reported in the *San Francisco Sunday Chronicle* as late as 21 March 1965, the religiosity of the civil rights movement had not waned. It was a sterling, and probably consummate, illustration of black political revivalism: "this movement to procure civil rights is distinctly a religious movement," said the Reverend Andrew Juvinall,

rooted in the conviction that God has "made of one blood all the nations of mankind" and it is His will that all should stand erect in their full manhood. The movement of the Southern Christian Leadership Conference has political and economic aspects but it is most of all a profound spiritual movement.[13]

One of the bright college students who understood this historic alliance

13. Quoted in Daniel Day Williams, *The Spirit and the Forms of Love* (Lanham, MD: University Press of America, 1981), p. 269.

between religion and social change was Jesse Jackson. Jackson was the president of the student body at the Agricultural and Technical College of North Carolina when four of his classmates started the sit-in movement. Jackson graduated from the college in 1963 after successfully assuming leadership of the sit-in demonstrations. In the fall of 1963 he enrolled at Chicago Theological Seminary.

Even as a young seminarian, Jackson was able to organize and mobilize the black community in preparation for Martin Luther King's initial effort to move the civil rights movement to the stubborn Northern urban frontier. Jackson's charisma won the confidence of many of the local black ministers of Chicago. Even then he fervently stressed the need to relate ministry to social and political change.

Of course one could argue that Jackson received his greatest inspiration from Martin Luther King, Jr. That is true. But without his own charismatic gifts, he could have never won the support of stalwart and able colleagues such as the Reverends David Wallace, George Riddick, Willie Barrows, Wilbur Reid, and Calvin Morris. They were all very charismatic figures in their own right. But there was an energy and contagion about Jackson and certainly about the movement itself that elicited their best efforts.

Jesse Jackson's charisma attracted and held the allegiance of several of his early Operation Breadbasket colleagues long enough to make it a forceful movement of national and international stature.[14] But not even his great charismatic powers could retain them past

1971, when Operation Breadbasket became Operation PUSH. PUSH both revived and expanded the Breadbasket program. As such PUSH became a national urban religious movement for social, economic, and political change. It sought to revitalize the moral, psychic, economic, and political health of depressed urban black communities across the United States.

Although Jackson now has formed and heads an openly political alliance called the rainbow coalition, this organization, as well as the earlier ones he has headed, should be seen as part of his deep commitment to an activist understanding of Christian ministry. His primary base, however, is still his Chicago-based Operation PUSH. PUSH gained a major portion of its fervor and its resources as a result of the tough, yet eloquent, prophetic pastoral style of Jackson's leadership of the PUSH congregation, which meets every Saturday for at least two or three hours. This activistic religious assembly numbers well over 5000. With the help of several other ministers, especially the Reverend Mrs. Willie Barrows, Jackson formed a prophetic local bridgehead in black Chicago and was instrumental in the election of Harold Washington as the city's first black mayor. Indeed, between 1968 and 1983, Jackson solidified his contacts with the wider black church movement through his own hectic speaking tours and through close associates in different denominations, such as Bishop H. H. Brookins of the African Methodist Episcopal church. Within the National Baptist Convention, U.S.A., Inc., Jackson drew the major portion of his

---

14. The best account of the history of Operation Breadbasket is the excellent master of divinity thesis by Gary Massoni, "Perspective on Operation Breadbasket" (Thesis, Chicago Theological Seminary, 1971).

national support from the ministerial network. In fact this collegium provided basic psychic and financial support for Jackson's rainbow coalition.

Black Baptist roots

Although Jesse Jackson enjoys friendships that cross denominational lines, his primary religious constituency is the black National Baptist Convention, U.S.A., Inc. But maintaining his relationship with the usually conservative leadership of this denominational movement has not been easy for one so single-mindedly committed to social and political activism.

For 29 years, until 1982, the president of that convention was the conservative Reverend Dr. Joseph Harrison Jackson. He was also pastor of the powerful Olivet Baptist Church of Chicago and one of the late Mayor Richard Daley's faithful cronies. The causes Jesse Jackson favored J. H. Jackson did not: the latter attacked Dr. King's Operation Breadbasket, which the former headed for SCLC; J. H. Jackson opposed the protest strategies of the civil rights movement; and he was part of the Daley machine, which Jesse Jackson courageously opposed.

Despite Jesse's fierce ideological disagreements with Reverend Joseph Harrison Jackson, he never left the National Baptist Convention. One explanation for this is Jackson's basically conservative evangelical theology, which was evident, for example, in his initial opposition to abortion and homosexual rights. The convention's powerful black folk spirituality, its traditional evangelical theology, and, from a historical viewpoint, its atypical political conservatism—thanks to Joseph Jackson—vied successfully for Jesse Jackson's allegiance.

Jesse Jackson was not indifferent to the convention's tentative turn toward political conservatism. He correctly interpreted it more as a by-product of the convention's affection for the spiritual persona of Joseph Jackson than as a result of an inherent conservative bent.

Joseph Jackson is actually a rather consistent anti-communist who earnestly believes that the civil rights movement was a Communist front. With consistent political acumen, he learned how to manage the convention's black populist ethos in order to accommodate his own conservative beliefs. Although he is the pastor of a large urban congregation, he always ran on the platform that he was the defender of the little preachers and the small congregations that constitute the bulk of this denomination.

Jesse Jackson also understood and accepted the convention's powerful populist impulse. Thus his description of himself as a country preacher is both genuine and politically astute.

Because the convention has the capacity to change its political mood, as long as its populist and black cultural nationalist commitments are not violated, its various factions have a history of competing to control the leadership of the convention. The most significant recent melee occurred in 1961. As a consequence of this embarrassingly turbulent meeting, the convention sustained a significant split. The primary issue ostensibly was how long the president should hold office. But the most powerful undercurrent was the issue of whether or not the convention should officially support King's civil disobedience campaign. This issue infused the heated annual campaigns for the convention's presidency. After J. H. Jackson's defeat of Dr. Gardner C. Taylor, pastor of the 14,000 members of the Concord Baptist

Church of Christ in Brooklyn, New York, for the presidency, many of the convention's prominent urban churches banded together to form the more activistic Progressive National Baptist Convention. It seems that Jesse Jackson could also have left for the new convention.

Jesse Jackson remained with the National Baptist Convention, U.S.A., not only because he is theologically conservative, but also because he has strong personal ties to key ministers belonging to that convention. For instance, when Jackson came to Chicago in 1963 as a student at the Chicago Theological Seminary, he was hired almost immediately as the assistant pastor of Fellowship Baptist Church. The Reverend Clay Evans, the pastor of Fellowship, became quite instrumental in establishing Jackson as a powerful presence in Chicago. In fact, Evans's church is one of the largest black churches in Chicago. He has significant local and national friends, such as the late Reverend C. L. Franklin of Detroit, the father of Aretha Franklin, the renowned black recording artist. Jackson's friendship with these powerful stalwarts of the National Baptist Convention is so close that Evans and Franklin both sponsored Jackson's ordination into the Baptist ministry in June 1968, nearly two months after the assassination of Dr. King. Despite a few political disagreements, Clay Evans still serves as the honorary chairman of PUSH's board of directors.

In September 1982, the Reverend Dr. Theodore J. Jemison ran for the presidency of the National Baptist Convention, U.S.A., against J. H. Jackson and defeated him. One consequence of J. H. Jackson's defeat was that Jesse Jackson acquired the influential position of chairman of the convention's Civil Rights Commission. This was not only an important recognition of Jackson's influential assistance in helping Dr. Jemison acquire the presidency; it also gave tacit convention recognition to Jackson's status within the civil rights movement and eventually to his bid for the U.S. presidency.

The influential network of black Baptist ministers that Jackson knows both within the National Baptist Convention and in the other Baptist conventions provides powerful local roots and sustenance to Jackson's role as a minister in the forefront of the civil rights movement. But Jackson could not maintain these links on notoriety alone. He also projects the image of a conscientious pastor of a great movement. He is the confidant of black artists and professionals of national and international repute. This pastoral skill is nurtured by a charisma that is legendary among black Baptist preachers. One could also point to the Reverend Benjamin E. Hooks, executive director of the NAACP, as another example of this special type of black religious and social leader. Hooks also maintains his standing among black preachers because he continues to be the nominal and effective pastor of two independent black Baptist congregations in Detroit and Memphis.

Ministers and leaders such as Hooks and Jackson belong to a strong activist tradition within their own denominations and within the black church movement as a whole. They practice a domineering pastoral style that is in accordance with their religious tradition. Black pastors are independent, set their own agendas, and are deeply admired by their people. The people's admiration, if not love and respect, is based upon reverence for the pastoral office as the most sacrificial and generous vocation a black person can hold. Being on the margin of society, black people have not fully developed a trust and respect for the integrity of other professionals. In fact they have too often been victimized by incompetent professionals and entrepreneurs. It is their pastor who visits the sick, buries the dead, and does innumerable personal favors such as getting them jobs and getting them out of jail. Above all, the pastor defends the poor and attacks injustice. Black people trust their pastor, who is seen as a friend and a prophet.

They admire the Reverend Mr. Jackson because he stands tall in this proud tradition. But he is fast earning himself a distinctiveness comparable only to that of Booker T. Washington. He is amassing a huge black patronage system. Similar to King, but only from the materialistic vantage point, he is more like a cardinal who is a prime candidate for a new kind of black American papacy in which the world itself can become his parish.

Fusion politics

Despite his strong religious base, in order to expand his influence Jackson must continue to use fusion politics to survive politically. Besides divisiveness within the black community, Jackson must lead black America in a movement against a new form of racism. As John Hope Franklin notes, "The chief barriers to racial justice today are subtle and much less conducive to media coverage."[15]

The general mode of domination in American society is, as it always has been, more a matter of cultural than of social relations. There has been a change in American cultural relations, however, that increases the subtlety of obstacles to racial justice. After a long, arduous struggle, America no longer needs to mimic European society. For better or worse, America is now the major standard-bearer of Western culture. However, the reality of an expanding black and Hispanic underclass accents the depth of the racist classism that beguiles a republic that has lost sight of its original moral social vision.

Jesse Jackson was the only candidate in the 1984 presidential campaign who pinpointed this critical relation between the breakdown of democratic values and the demise of a just political vision. He said repeatedly that "the rainbow coalition is, first, a moral cause, not just a political campaign" and that the nation's "genius must not be in how much we consume, but in how much we share." But in the minds of white America, he is a black man trying to demonstrate his worth. As they used to say on the streets of the black ghetto, "The Negro is an insanity which overtakes the white man." Martin Luther King, Jr., said the same thing in far more eloquent terms:

Ever since the founding fathers of our nation dreamed this noble dream, America has been something of a schizophrenic personality, tragically divided against herself. On the one hand we have proudly professed the principles of democracy, and on the other hand we have sadly practiced the very antithesis of those principles. Indeed slavery and segregation have been strange paradoxes in a nation founded on the principle that all men are created equal.[16]

15. Quoted in Susan Bloch, "A Continuing Climate of Racism," *Duke*, 71(2):14 (Nov.-Dec. 1984).

16. Martin Luther King, Jr., "The American Dream," a speech given at Lincoln University, 6 June 1961, in Philip S. Foner, ed., *The Voice of*

Jesse Jackson's very presence in the presidential campaign represented a new threat to white supremacy. He had the audacity to act as if his race did not disqualify him from becoming the president of the United States. Black Americans generally viewed Jackson's self-confident presence as a refreshing assertion of group pride. White Americans, on the other hand, read Jackson's political style as a brazenly cocky demeanor that threatened the political and psychic space that white male hegemony has traditionally claimed in American society. America's majority people viewed his participation as a symbolic attack against the racist cultural grid that constitutes the psychic infrastructure of the central public ritual of the United States.

Although he did not win the Democratic primary, the Jackson campaign demonstrated that the right black candidate can indeed muster significant support. Jackson won over 3.5 million popular votes; he won over 60 congressional districts, with half of them in the South. Jackson was victorious in most of the largest urban centers in the North as well as in the South. In fact, he captured the popular vote in Louisiana, South Carolina, Mississippi, Virginia, and the District of Columbia. But as Jackson says himself, "Most of all, we have gained a new confidence relative to our politics."[17]

Jackson's woefully misunderstood and maligned alliance with Louis Farrakhan was one large part of that new corporate political self-esteem. Lu Pal-mer, the leader of the important political action group called Chicago Black United Communities, has observed that "the joining of Jesse Jackson and Louis Farrakhan represents a new dimension of unity in the Black community. Those two symbolize the coming together of different thoughts, ideology and religions around one common cause: Black empowerment."[18] We forget how deep the public division was between Martin Luther King, Jr.'s southern crusade and Malcolm X's northern urban militancy. Jackson and Farrakhan were trying to heal this wound.

Maulana Karenga correctly pinpoints the nature and depth of the opposition to Jackson's campaign from the American Jewish community, Israel, the news media, the black political establishment, even from most of the white Left, and of course the old-line Democratic party stalwarts. Jackson's urban victories probably could not have been achieved without Farrakhan. While Farrakhan's untempered anti-Jewish rhetoric embarrassed Jackson and his black and white progressive cohorts, the alliance between the two men was more political than religious or philosophical. Jackson's enemies, with the assistance of the black *Washington Post* reporter Milton Coleman, unjustifiably maligned either Jackson's character or his political savvy. Jackson finally had to sever his ties with Farrakhan. He learned the hard way, as did Martin Luther King, Jr., that the news media, the eyes and ears of the great white American middle class, expect and demand moral perfection.

With the pressures inside and outside the black community, black leaders had

Black America: Major Speeches by Negroes in the United States, 1797-1971 (New York: Simon & Schuster, 1972), p. 934.

17. Jesse Jackson, "The Rainbow Coalition Is Here to Stay," *Black Scholar*, 15(5):72 (Sept.-Oct. 1984).

18. Maulana Karenga, "Jesse Jackson and the Presidential Campaign: The Invitation and the Oppositions of History," *Black Scholar*, 15(5):62 (Sept.-Oct. 1984).

to understand that great psychic and spiritual fortitude is part of their unwritten job description. Thus strong black religious leaders have usually been at the forefront of black protest because only the strong ones could deal with the pressure.

Nevertheless, Jackson, like most astute leaders of the black religious community, understood that successful politicians are priests who know how to manage the core narratives, symbols, and beliefs of a people. The more social trust exists, the more likely it is that these rituals can solidify public opinion. Yet every social network has a gnosis. Access to the collective memory, interaction rituals, and private interests of different social configurations, especially if they have political power, is difficult. In fact the ability to manipulate the collective gnosis of the powerful depends greatly upon how well those who seek it understand the nature of what Michel Foucault calls pastoral power: "This form of power cannot be exercised without knowing the inside of the people's minds, without exploring their souls, without making them reveal their innermost secrets. It implies a knowledge of the conscience and an ability to direct it."[19]

If this description is true, then Ronald Reagan is undoubtedly the most effective manager of pastoral power in America. He has demonstrated his ability both to acquire and to manage the symbols and the dynamics of power. But he also has that rare priestly gift of knowing the gnosis of his flock, available only from the oracle at Delphi.

Merely acquiring pastoral power is not enough. The major leaders of the black church movement have always understood how to acquire and administer pastoral power. But when they tried to translate that into a larger following beyond their own racial boundaries, they usually did not succeed. This is not their failure, however. It illustrates the sad failure of American pluralism.

THE POLITICAL FUTURE OF BLACK CHRISTENDOM

Progressive African American Christians, such as Jesse Jackson, have drawn on the spiritual and practical wisdom of the conventicles of a political culture that is older than the United States. In the crucible of slavery and free black denizenship, blacks sought to devise various means of resisting oppression.[20] Some of these forms of resistance have been far more subtle and effective than many observers and scholars realize.

20. Northern and southern antebellum free blacks often had an unclear legal status because jurists could not agree on whether or not they had the rights of natural or naturalized citizens. According to James H. Kettner, "free Negroes appeared to occupy a middle ground in terms of the rights they were allowed to claim in practice, a status that could not be described in the traditional language of slave, alien, or citizen." James H. Kettner, *The Development of American Citizenship, 1608-1870* (Chapel Hill: University of North Carolina Press, 1970), p. 319. The word "denizenship" was often used to describe this status. And although there was much disagreement about the appropriateness of using this designation, it is a useful word for capturing the complexity of the free blacks' legal status. See ibid., pp. 287-333, for an excellent summary of the juridical discussion. See also Leon F. Litwack, *North of Slavery: The Negro in the Free States, 1790-1860* (Chicago: University of Chicago Press, 1961); and Ira Berlin, *Slaves without Masters: The Free Negro in the Antebellum South* (New York: Pantheon Books, 1974).

19. Hubert L. Dreyfus and Paul Rabinow, *Michel Foucault: Beyond Structuralism and Hermeneutics,* 2nd ed. (Chicago: University of Chicago Press, 1983), p. 214.

The task before progressive black religious scholars now is to describe and analyze this phenomenon so that we can learn from its successes and failures. We need to determine when each form coalesced to respond to major threats to the black body politic and what the representative views and advocates of each phase were. With this information in hand, we can be better prepared to address the pressing issues not just of the 1980s, but, more important, those of the twenty-first century.

A large part of this reorientation of the scholarly world and the black church itself has already been advocated by the leaders of the black theology movement that began in 1969 upon the publication of James Hal Cone's *Black Theology and Black Power*. Unlike an earlier generation of black religious scholars and church leaders, Cone argues for the cultural distinctiveness and political necessity of black Christianity. He disagrees with earlier black religious leaders who argued that black Christianity is a Jim Crow arrangement. Cone also believes that black Christianity has now, as in the past, a revolutionary as well as therapeutic role to play in the advancement of black America and oppressed peoples throughout the world. In other words, despite black Christianity's seemingly "ambiguous politics"[21] and apparently "deficient political wisdom,"[22] it moves with integrity toward where Paul Lehmann argues "the empirical church points." According to Lehmann, the church points, "despite its ambi-

guity, to the fact that there is in the world a *laboratory of the living word*, or, to change the metaphor, a *bridgehead of maturity*, namely, the Christian *koinonia*."[23]

It is true that Jesse Jackson's aspirations for political office were frustrated. But beyond simply indicating the blatant role of white tribalism, other factors need to be considered, such as the following: (1) distrust of Jackson's identification with the persona of a black Southern country preacher; (2) the demise of what John Diggins calls the lost soul of American politics and the concommitant, unquestionable dominance of a culture of consumption; and (3) bourgeois cultural disdain for the moralistic and agrarian political revivalism of black Southern culture, the primary *modus operandi* of the symbolic political aspirations of black Christendom.

Despite the unrelenting criticisms, whether constructive or destructive, of the symbolic struggle waged by the black church movement, Jesse has steered progressive black Christians into new, uncharted waters. He helped us to see that the politics of black Christendom are the ethical exorcisms that oppressed African American Christians can use to defend their collective egos against the callousness of white supremacy. The project of black Christendom is the maximum realization of human freedom. The pedagogy of black Christendom seeks to train black people to acquire symbolic capital in order to continue "the acquisition of a reputation for competence and an image of respectability and honourability that are easily converted into political positions as a local or national *notable*."[24]

21. Manning Marable, *How Capitalism Underdeveloped Black America: Problems in Race, Political Economy and Society* (Boston: South End Press, 1983), pp. 195-214.

22. Peter J. Paris, *The Social Teaching of the Black Churches* (Philadelphia: Fortress Press, 1985), pp. 83-105.

23. Paul L. Lehmann, *Ethics in a Christian Context* (New York: Harper & Row, 1963), p. 131.

24. Pierre Bourdieu, *Distinction: A Social*

Black Christians have always found it difficult to justify the direct accumulation of economic capital because of a prior commitment to a biblical eschatology that looks with suspicion upon all attempts to idolize material things. But perhaps the recent attempt of the historic black denominations to form a Congress on Black Churches augurs well for building solidarity across congregational, denominational, class, and even economic lines, a necessary development if these churches intend to have an impact on a highly organized society with a new, highly refined form of racism.

The most subtle and effective aspect of the politics of black Christendom, however, is the spiritual praxis that nurtures and supports the psychic infrastructure of black America. The positivistic obsession of the social sciences, however, has often ignored both the reality and the importance of what William Stringfellow rightly calls the politics of spirituality.[25] Indeed, I agree with Ida Rousseau Mukenge's salient assessment of the indispensability of this central praxis to the future direction of the black church movement:

As we move through the last decades of the twentieth century, the special role of the church in maintaining mental health and psychological stability is pre-eminent. In fact, the present interpretation of the historical and contemporary church suggests that this is the role the black urban church *must* perform.[26]

While we need not embrace intellectual suicide, it is imperative that prophetic self-criticisms of the black church be heard.[27] The politics of black spirituality, which are inherently symbolic and psychological, must be embodied in church programs that recognize and resist the systemic nature of injustice lest they fall prey to the pitfalls of undisciplined subjectivism.

Certainly the symbolic politics of black Christendom are not vacuous. This set of political praxes consists of ideologies and strategies embraced by the oppressed to defend themselves against the crushing sincerity[28] of the powerful whose benevolence is a false love that represents the postponement of justice and that is an arduous attempt to soothe the conscience without making the sacrifices genuine penance demands. But as Jackson has shown, the black church movement itself can and must refine its politics to meet the new challenge. Indeed, it seems that a cadre of anointed martyrs will be needed before this powerful, yet infantile, culture of consumption sees the wisdom of the ancient need for reciprocity and responds institutionally to the religious call for justice, love, and mercy.

Critique of the Judgement of Taste, trans. Richard Nice (Cambridge, MA: Harvard University Press, 1984), p. 231.

25. William Stringfellow, *The Politics of Spirituality* (Philadelphia: Westminster Press, 1984).

26. Ida Rousseau Mukenge, *The Black Church in Urban America: A Case Study in Political Economy* (Lanham, MD: University Press of America, 1983), p. 204; see also Cheryl Townsend Gilkes's excellent article, "The Black Church as a Therapeutic Community: Suggested Areas for Research into the Black Religious Experience," *Journal of the Interdenominational Theological Center* 8: 29-43 (Fall 1980).

27. An example of such criticism is James H. Cone, "Black Theology and the Black Church," in his *My Soul Looks Back* (Nashville, TN: Abingdon, 1982), pp. 64-92; and West, *Prophesy Deliverance!*

28. Lionel Trilling, *Sincerity and Authenticity* (Cambridge, MA: Harvard University Press, 1972), pp. 1-25.

ANNALS, *AAPSS*, **480**, July 1985

The Growth of Religious
Reform Movements

By ROBERT WUTHNOW

ABSTRACT: Moral Majority, pro-life groups, charismatic renewal, antinuclear coalitions, religious feminist groups—all typify American religion in the 1980s. Neglected in most studies of denominationalism and church-sect dynamics, these reform movements provide the sinews that crosscut denominational boundaries and shape the course of religious organizations. Such movements have deep roots in American history, but evidence indicates that their numbers have grown dramatically during the past quarter century and that millions of Americans are currently involved in them. Reform movements play an important role in revitalizing commitments to the churches, but they also raise the specter of a stultifying bureaucratization of American faith.

Robert Wuthnow received his Ph.D. in sociology at the University of California, Berkeley. He taught for two years at the University of Arizona and since 1976 has taught at Princeton University, where he is professor of sociology. His books include The Consciousness Reformation, Experimentation in American Religion, The Religious Dimension, The New Christian Right, *and* Cultural Analysis.

EARLY in 1984, a few weeks after the Reverend Sun Myung Moon went to jail for alleged tax fraud, a social movement came into being under the sponsorship of an unlikely partnership of religious activists. Calling themselves the Coalition for Religious Freedom, the movement's leaders seemed persuaded that Orwell's vision of totalitarianism was coming painfully near to fulfillment in the very year for which it had been predicted. In Moon's arrest they saw the ugly specter of a police state in which government bureaucrats brazenly wiped out all traces of America's heritage of religious freedom. These were not Moonies themselves, fired by a desire to free their leader; far from it, they were generally staunch doctrinal enemies of the Unification Church, including Protestant fundamentalist leaders such as Tim LaHaye of the Moral Majority's board of directors and Robert Grant of Christian Voice. Yet Moon's cause was theirs, too, for at stake was the right to advance minority religious programs without fear of state regulations.

What makes the Coalition for Religious Freedom interesting is neither the specific issue to which it responded nor the spectacle of Moonies and fundamentalists joining forces at protest demonstrations—although both made headlines—but the fact that literally scores of such movements have emerged in recent years. The most publicized have generally been associated with the so-called New Christian Right: movements such as the Moral Majority, Christian Voice, Religious Roundtable, National Federation for Decency, and National Christian Action Coalition, to name a few. But these have been visible only because of national politics and religious television. Other such movements, with vastly different political

views, goals, and organizational styles, have been at least as numerous, if not more so. Their causes range from nuclear arms control to liturgical renewal, from gender equality to cult surveillance, from healing ministries to evangelism. They address issues both specific to the churches and of general concern to the broader society. Yet they are clearly rooted in the religious realm, taking their legitimating slogans from religious creeds and drawing their organizational resources, leadership, and personnel largely from churches and ecclesiastical agencies.

Some of these movements command enough resources and have sufficient potential for influencing American values to have recently attracted the attention of journalists, social scientists, and religious leaders. Yet the importance of religious reform movements for an understanding of the character and quality of American religion itself has been for the most part overlooked. There have been, to be sure, countless discussions of so-called new religious movements and their impact on American religion since the 1970s, and over a longer period the role of historic movements—such as Methodism, Mormonism, and Pentecostalism—in shaping American religion has been virtually synonymous with the study of American religious history itself. But these examples fit well within the two prevailing sociological models of American religion—church-sect theory and denominationalism—while the kind of reform movements under consideration here generally do not.

Church-sect theory has tended to highlight two important processes in the history of American religion—or for that matter, in the history of Protestantism. One is the tendency for splinter groups to break away from established churches, forming sects that are usually smaller in size, devoted more enthusiastically to distinctive theological and moral positions, more demanding of their adherents' loyalties, and thus in greater tension with the secular world than their churchly progenitors. Related to this process, as evidenced by countless schisms, mergers, and successive schisms, has been the tendency for sects to mature into established churches themselves, thus ceasing to be quite so small, quite as theologically or morally orthodox, as demanding of their members, or as uneasy with the secular world. The great break of Wesley's followers from the Anglican establishment, the subsequent growth and accommodation of Methodism with modern culture, the rise of Methodist sects along the fringes of this broader religious movement, and their subsequent maturation into established churches has been taken as archetypical of these processes.

The fact that some established churches—such as Mormons or Christian Scientists—or relatively well-established churches—such as the Unification Church—did not begin as splinter groups but as independent movements has necessitated adding a third category—cults—to the church-sect duo. But the idea of a gradual evolution from embattled minority to established institution has not been fundamentally challenged, since most cults seem to have gone the route of sects.

Denominationalism has simply been the more aggregate perspective from which to view the mosaic of American churches, sects, and cults. If "church" continues to carry connotations of a local congregation, then "denomination" points to the fact that most churches are identified with some larger federation or ecclesiastical organization at the national level, and "denominationalism" refers to the several hundred such denominations that coexist in American society and give American religion its distinctively pluralistic character. Denominations—and thus denominationalism—have a relatively enduring quality that makes questions about such matters as membership, size, doctrine, and organizational style of primary interest.

The difficulty with both of these conceptual devices is that they ignore religious movements—reform movements—that do not result in separate sects, that do not grow into established churches, and that do not produce new or distinct denominations. As yet, for example, the Coalition for Religious Freedom shows no signs of drawing people away from other churches, of constituting itself as a separate religious sect, or of creating a new denomination. Its very survival, depending as it does on resources from churches with radically different doctrines, requires that it avoid any such tendencies. Much the same can be said for the Moral Majority, the National Christian Action Coalition, and any number of similar groups. Their orientation is toward a specific objective and their tactics involve mobilizing resources toward the attainment of this objective, but they are not for the most part concerned with becoming membership organizations that take the place of existing churches or sects.

AN AMERICAN TRADITION

Religious reform movements are not a recent invention, nor are they unique to the United States. Despite the advent of denominationalism, which grew with the fracturing of Christendom by the

Reformation in the sixteenth century, the religious settlements that were constructed in the wake of the Reformation imposed state churches or territorial churches in most of the Protestant areas of Europe, including England, Scandinavia, and major German principalities such as Saxony, Hesse, and Brandenburg. By the middle of the eighteenth century a number of so-called free, dissenting, and nonconformist sects had managed to become established alongside the official churches—a fact that received considerable emphasis in subsequent treatises contributing to the development of church-sect theory. Nevertheless, the predominance of state churches meant that many of the influential developments shaping European Protestantism came about through the workings of internal reform movements, not from splinter groups or separatist sects.

Two of the most important examples of such reform movements were the Oxford movement in England and the Pietist movement in Germany. Known also as Tractarianism, the Oxford movement was contained wholly within the Church of England. Originating at Oxford in 1833, it led to a revival of interest in liturgy and worship, a renewal of emphasis on conservative doctrine, and greater cooperation between Anglicans and Roman Catholics. Not unlike some of the movements that have developed in recent years, the Oxford movement also championed greater separation of church and state. Indeed, one interpretation suggests that its founding owed much to a wave of ill feeling toward Parliament for interfering in the church's affairs.

German Pietism developed much earlier than the Oxford movement, dating from the preaching of Jacob Spener in the 1660s, but it too grew largely within the established church and continued to influence Lutheranism well into the nineteenth century. The thrust of Pietism was what many contemporary evangelicals would now recognize as an emphasis on personal conversion or rebirth, small group fellowship, and disciplined attention to such moral virtues as abstinence from card playing, dancing, and the theater. In some areas the movement came under such violent attacks from ecclesiastical and civil authorities that some groups that became known as radical Pietists did break away from the church. One of these groups was the Moravian sect that eventually emigrated to eastern Pennsylvania. The main following of the Pietist movement, however, received encouragement from the authorities in Brandenburg-Prussia, including several prominent positions at the University of Halle, which thus permitted the movement to flourish and even play an important role in shaping the Prussian Enlightenment.

In the United States, separation of church and state, combined with the ethnic and religious pluralism that was fed by European immigration, reinforced the spread of multiple denominations, including splinter groups and sects. The dynamincs of sectarianism, sect-to-church transformations, and pluralism among competing denominations thus came to play a much more prominent role than it had anywhere in Europe. Nevertheless, the history of American religion has also been typified at least since the beginning of the nineteenth century by a rich tradition of religious reform movements both within denominations and across denominational lines.

Some of the first religious reform movements in the United States were organized within the mainline denominations to mobilize resources for the evangelization of native Americans, immigrants, and peoples in other lands, including Europe. One of the first of these was the American Board of Commissioners for Foreign Missions. Founded in 1810, this movement quickly became bureaucratized, but it began as a grassroots development, the leadership of which gained supporters through local prayer meetings. Four years later another missionary society was founded by the American Baptists, and by 1860 three more were in operation, a number that eventually grew to 94 by the end of the century.

Distinctive of the pluralistic religious context in America, many reform movements were founded that spanned denominational boundaries. The early decades of the nineteenth century, usually characterized as a time of rising denominational strife between Congregationalists and Unitarians, New and Old School Presbyterians, Baptists and Methodists, was also a period during which reformers created movements that conscientiously avoided denominational labels in order to carry ministries into new areas. The American Bible Society, founded in 1816, provided a model that many other movements would emulate. Although it became an increasingly bureaucratized organization, its origins in fact lay in more than 30 local Bible societies that had sprung up in at least 24 different states during the preceding 12 years. The establishment of a centralized agency merely facilitated the publishing and distribution of Bibles on a national scale. Other movements that resulted in nationally coordinated cooperation across denominational lines included the American Tract, established in 1823; the American Sunday School Union, in 1824; the American Education Society,

in 1826; and the American Society for the Promotion of Temperance, in 1826.

While these movements quickly became institutionalized, others had a significant impact on the formation of American religion without ever becoming formal organizations. Fed largely by popular zeal, they contributed in important ways to the vitality of local churches. One example was the prayer meeting movement that developed in New York City in 1857 and 1858. Starting in a single church, the movement spread throughout the city, drawing an estimated 10,000 participants by the end of the first six months. Remaining genuinely interdenominational rather than forming new sects or churches, it was estimated to have added some 500,000 new members in all to the city's churches.

As the nineteenth century drew to a close, religious reform movements began to appear in response to the rising problems associated with industrialization and urbanization. Among these movements were numerous temperance societies, such as the Anti-Saloon League (1895), which came into being to battle the liquor industry that was felt by many to be the source of the ills visible in the cities. These movements, at first limited mainly to local communities, grew to the point of playing an important role in bringing about the adoption of the Eighteenth Amendment in 1919.

More typical as a consequence of industrialization and urbanization than the temperance movement, however, was the emergence of a whole variety of reform movements aimed at creating more effective organizational structures for carrying out the churches' tasks in the new urban environment. Movements such as the Salvation Army and the Young Men's Christian Association (YMCA) developed outside of established denominational structures and functioned similarly enough to the churches in some respects to earn them labels as sects or denominations. But in neither case were these labels entirely accurate. Growing from fewer than 9000 members in 1890 to more than 35,000 members in 1915, the Salvation Army relied on unpaid and uneducated volunteers rather than trained clergy, organized brass bands and youth groups rather than worship services, and devoted its resources to the construction of orphanages and lodgings for immigrants rather than churches.

The strategy of the YMCA was not altogether different. Beginning during the Civil War with fewer than 10,000 volunteers, it grew to 263,000 by 1895 and then mushroomed to 720,000 by the start of World War I. It too focused on recruiting lay volunteers rather than members, started special-interest groups such as reading clubs and student organizations rather than competing head-on with the churches, and, in the early years at least, emphasized evangelism and relief for the poor.

Other movements worked largely with the cooperation of local churches or through denominational hierarchies to extend the reaches of American religion into segments of industrial society. For example, the Gideons International, founded in 1899, used local churches to recruit business and professional men who were interested in distributing Bibles and drew on the contributions of church members to fund their operations. Movements aimed at broadening the churches' appeal in other ways included the Catholic Church Extension Society, established in 1905; the Pocket Testament League, in 1908; the Knights of the Immaculata Movement, in 1917; and the Association of Baptists for World Evangelism, in 1927. Utilizing current publishing and managerial technologies, most of these movements worked mainly to coordinate efforts that had previously proven successful in scattered localities and to amass the enlarged funds and personnel necessary in order to put out publications, hold conferences, and pay professional staffs.

The reform movements, then, that have emerged in American religion during the past several decades—clergy-led civil rights protests, antinuclear peace coalitions, feminist movements, pro-life organizations, charismatic and evangelical renewals—are part of a venerable tradition in American history. Most result neither in new religions nor in distinct denominations, but such movements have repeatedly shaped the direction in which religious efforts are focused.

NUMBERING RELIGIOUS REFORM MOVEMENTS

Estimating the exact number of religious reform movements presents nearly insurmountable problems because of the wide variety of membership sizes, causes, and organizational styles encompassed by these movements. They range from purely local movements, sometimes concentrated within a single church, to highly bureaucratized organizations on a national or international scale. Some are special-interest groups designed only to give formal identity to an otherwise inward-looking association of persons with similar concerns, while others are oriented toward effecting change within their denomination, in government, or in values and life-styles. They range from spontaneous, grass-roots membership movements to paper organizations, which serve solely to satisfy tax laws or give official recognition to an issue of bureaucratic concern. Nevertheless, some progress can be made toward estimating the number of such movements by restricting the definition of religious reform movements to nationally incorporated nonprofit voluntary associations that meet the Internal Revenue Service's qualifications as religious organizations, other than churches or denominations. This is the definition utilized by the *Encyclopedia of Associations,* an annually updated, multivolume series that provides data on associations of all kinds, including the category of "religious organizations."

As of the 1984 edition, the *Encyclopedia of Associations* reported that there were 818 religious organizations in the United States. Associations of all kinds totaled approximately 16,000; thus, religious organizations made up about 5 percent of the total. This figure, it should be cautioned, included many well-established, highly bureaucratized organizations—for example, the National Council of Churches and the American Bible Society—that seem only remotely involved in reform as such and that carry few of the popular connotations of the term "movement." Still, these are organizations that seek to mobilize resources for the attainment of a specific goal, generally through means other than the sale of products, investment of capital, application of law, or simple wielding of bureaucratic power—means that usually involve the mobilization of voluntary commitment and the translation of that commitment into organizational, economic, or symbolic resources aimed at realizing a specified ideal, belief, or program. This is particularly evident in the case of newer, spontaneous, special-interest groups devoted to broader social reform, such as the Methodist Federation for Social Action or the United Church Coalition for Lesbian/Gay Concerns. But it applies equally to many of the better-established organizations as well.

Additional perspective on the importance of these movements can be gained by examining trends in their formation. As the *Encyclopedia of Associations* lists the founding date of each organization, and as information on defunct organizations—relatively few—is retained, it is possible to calculate how many such organizations were in existence at different points over the past century. Even a few figures point to the tremendous growth that has taken place in these movements during the past few decades: prior to the Civil War only 20 such organizations were formed; during the remainder of the nineteenth century only 61 more came into existence; then between 1900 and the close of World War II, 257 new organizations were founded; and since World War II a staggering 460 have come into being. In other words, almost twice as many religious organizations have emerged in the past 40 years than in the 40 years before that, and more than five times as many have been formed in this recent period than during the whole of the nineteenth century. Perhaps even more significant is the fact that in the past 25 years alone 293 organizations—36 percent of the total—have been founded.

THE SCOPE OF INVOLVEMENT

Estimating involvement in religious reform movements is as difficult as the problem of calculating the number of such movements. The *Encyclopedia of Associations* cites membership figures for some of the movements it lists, but these are available for a relatively small proportion of the total; and even the figures reported are woefully inadequate, either because of inflated self-reports or because only full-time paid staff are listed. Thus, as in other studies of religious movements, it is virtually impossible to make an accurate estimate of involvement in these movements without engaging in direct data-collection efforts.

The task of collecting such data is made simpler by virtue of the fact that many specific movements, including those operating less formally at the local level, can be grouped into broader classes according to their major objectives. This was the tactic employed in a nationally representative survey of the adult U.S. population in June 1984 by the Princeton Religion Research Center and the Gallup Organization. A total of 10 general kinds of movements—6 of which were specifically identified as religious ministries and 4 of which were included for comparison purposes because they often appear linked to religious movements in popular accounts—were listed, and respondents were asked to indicate which ones they had "heard anything about," which ones they had "had any contact with," and which ones they were personally "involved in."

In terms of familiarity, "ministries dealing with world hunger" were the most visible; nearly two-thirds—63 percent—of the persons interviewed had heard of them. Other movements that at least half the respondents had heard of included "healing ministries"—58 percent; "home Bible study or fellowship groups"—58 percent; "religious coalitions against nuclear warfare"—51 percent; and "prison ministries"—50 percent. Of the remaining movements, "group therapy sessions" had been heard of by 39 percent, "social protest or activism" by 35 percent, "the charismatic movement" by 35 percent, "positive thinking seminars" by 35 percent, and "holistic health activities" by 26 percent.

As might be expected, actual contact with movements was considerably more limited than was having merely heard about them; and the two did not necessarily correspond to one another. The largest proportion of respondents had been in contact with home fellowship groups—28 percent; ministries dealing with world hunger—15 percent; and healing ministries—11 percent. The smallest proportions were those in contact with protest groups—5 percent; holistic health groups—6 percent; and religious coalitions against nuclear warfare—6 percent. In between were the charismatic movement—10 percent; positive thinking—10 percent; group therapies—8 percent; and prison ministries—8 percent.

Actual involvement was lower than being in contact, never representing more than a small fraction of the public except in the case of home fellowship groups, in which nearly one person in six—18 percent—claimed involvement. World hunger ministries came in next—7 percent; then positive thinking—5 percent; group therapy—4 percent; and healing ministries—4 percent. These were followed by prison ministries and the charismatic movement—each 3 percent; and by social protest, holistic health, and coalitions against nuclear war—each 2 percent.

These figures appear relatively modest as percentages of the entire adult population. Yet in assessing their significance it must be remembered that many well-established denominations make up no larger percentages of the population than this. The 7 percent claiming involvement in world hunger ministries is comparable, for example, to the 7 percent listing membership in the Southern Baptist Convention—the largest of all Protestant denominations in the United States—and the 5 percent involved in positive thinking seminars is comparable to the 5 percent claiming membership in the United Methodist Church. Even the 2 or 3 percent involved in antinuclear coalitions, holistic health, or the charismatic movement is larger in absolute size than most American denominations. Indeed, of the 108 Protestant denominations included in the 1980 edition of *Churches and Church Membership in the United States,* the membership of each of 106 churches comprised 1.3 percent or less of the total population. Membership and involvement vary in intensity, of course. No one would argue that sending a check periodically to a world hunger ministry is quite the same as being a Southern Baptist. Yet, when less than a third of the population attends church weekly and well over half the population changes denominations at least once during adulthood, the degree of involvement in religious reform movements compared to that in denominations must not be underestimated.

In all, taking into account the fact that involvement in some of the movements asked about sometimes overlapped, 29 percent of the public was involved in at least 1 of the 10 movements. Given that many other kinds of movements could have also been included, this is a relatively substantial proportion. It in no way rivals the 65 to 70 percent that typically claims membership in a church or synagogue, nor does it equal the 40 percent that attends religious services in a typical week. But it makes up a figure that in absolute terms is larger than the number of all the Roman Catholics in the United States and is, by comparison,

almost half again larger than the combined memberships of the 10 largest Protestant denominations.

REFORM MOVEMENTS
AND RELIGION
IN THE EIGHTIES

The number and extent of reform movements in American religion at the present requires a great deal more investigation than they have yet received in order to assess the potential importance of these movements. Much of the current debate has focused, of course, on movements associated with the New Christian Right as these appear to have both the greatest current appeal and the greatest potential for effecting change in American institutions. Because of the relative neglect that has surrounded religious reform movements as a general class, however, it seems most valuable to direct attention to some of the broader implications of these movements in general, quite apart from particular cases. Two implications seem especially worthy of consideration: the relevance of reform movements for religious revitalization, and their role in the growing bureaucratization of American religion.

The role of reform movements in religious revitalization is perhaps the most straightforward: many such movements have as their explicit aim some form of religious renewal. The charismatic movement that has grown both in nondenominational organizations such as the Christian Renewal Ministry, established in 1968, and within denominational frameworks such as the Presbyterian Charismatic Communion, established in 1966, is a clear example. Oriented toward a more intimate sense of the Holy Spirit, these and numerous movements with similar aims have worked to bring about spiritual renewal by sponsoring conferences, holding retreats and workshops, and providing information to local churches.

Other movements have focused on different aspects of renewal in areas such as evangelism, scripture, doctrine, and liturgy. Many of these movements have emerged in mainline denominations and have in some instances had a notable impact on the practices of these denominations. For example, movements such as the Forum for Scriptural Christianity among Methodists and the Evangelical and Catholic Mission in the Episcopal church—established in 1966 and 1977, respectively—have arisen among laity and clergy who wished to see a return to more traditional beliefs and practices but who chose not to join other denominations or to originate new denominations.

More generally, reform movements appear to be one of the major mechanisms by which denominations redirect their policies and evoke renewed commitment from their members. The availability of different movements within a denomination provides a variety of hooks capable of catching the interests of different members. For one member it may be working to create more intimate fellowship through Bible study groups; for another, the appeal of channeling one's energies toward combating the nuclear arms race. Denominational pluralism merely heightens the importance of these movements, as members can easily switch religious preferences if their own denomination does not offer a sufficient menu of digestible entrées. Thus, the religious marketplace generates not only a single charismatic, feminist, or peace movement, but proliferates distinct denominational brands of each.

The negative role of religious reform movements, however, is that in addition to effecting revitalization they also seem inherently prone to adding layers of bureaucracy to the already highly bureaucratized structure of American religion. Robert Michels, in his book *Political Parties*, first stressed the general importance of this tendency—an "iron law," as he termed it—almost 70 years ago. Michels's conclusions were drawn mainly from observing the socialist movement in Germany as it evolved from an informal but highly enthusiastic reform movement in the 1870s to a highly regimented and less-than-revolutionary political party in the years prior to World War I. He could have drawn the same conclusion had he been able to observe many of the religious reform movements that have arisen over the past 50 years.

The extent to which American religion has become bureaucratized is immediately evident from the lists of religious reform movements that have become institutionalized in recent decades. Many of the current religious organizations that operate in addition to already complex denominational agencies probably developed at one time because of a grass-roots movement that was concerned with expanding the churches' ministry into new areas. But now these organizations function mainly as formal bureaucracies of professional staff to ensure that people continue to be recruited into these movements.

Ministries have thus become more highly specialized, resulting in a proliferation of organizations devoted to the coordination and supervision of these ministries. Most large denominations, for example, have specialized organizations concerned chiefly with ministries by and for women. The Christian Women's Fellowship, founded in 1949, with a current membership of 161,000 women from the Disciples of Christ denomination, and Lutheran Church Women, founded in 1962, with a current membership of 223,000, are but two examples. Children's ministries have also evolved from relatively small, informal movements into vastly complex structures dealing with thousands of members. For example, the Christian Service Brigade, founded in 1937, and Pioneer Ministries, founded in 1939, now minister to 48,000 and 100,000 children, respectively, by providing materials, training, and supervision to thousands of lay volunteers.

Other movements, while also contributing new layers of bureaucracy, have emerged less from the demands of large-scale ministries than from the increasingly differentiated hierarchy of religious professionals that has emerged in American religion. The religious establishment now consists not only of local clergy—general practitioners of the soul—but also of professional counselors, educators, educational consultants, newswriters, researchers, church architects, campus clergy, church-growth specialists, missions planners, and staff development specialists, to name a few. As in other professional areas, the growth of these specialties has resulted in a desire for greater communication, sharing of common interests, and coordination. Thus a host of new movements has arisen over the past few decades that has resulted in numerous professional associations for highly specialized groups. Even a brief list of these associations gives an idea of the kinds of interests represented: the Association of Christian Church Educators, founded in 1947; the Religious Newswriters Association, in 1949; the American Association of Pastoral Counselors, in 1963; the Church Music Association, in 1964; the Committee of Southern Churchmen, in 1964; and Campus Ministry Women, in 1970.

On a broader scale, the cost of a growing bureaucracy is that an increasing share of the spontaneity, energy, and enthusiasm initially generated by reform movements becomes channeled into professional staff positions whose responsibilities gradually shift from attaining the desired reform to maintaining the offices, career lines, and salaries of the professionals themselves. Max Weber recognized this cost more than a half century ago when he wrote of the "iron cage" that was gradually imposing itself on Western culture.

As church leaders and parishioners face the remainder of the 1980s and look to the remaining decade of this century, then, one of the dilemmas that will surely need to be confronted repeatedly is the problem of balancing religious revitalization against bureaucratic effectiveness. The denominational structure of American religion is not simply a static entity maintained by individuals who each choose within his or her secret heart of hearts a religious preference. It is rather a dynamic organism enlivened by the rich flows of energy and resources that are mobilized by religious reform movements. Opponents of particular manifestations of these movements will inevitably decry their prominence in American life, and church bureaucrats will invariably find their jobs made more difficult by the proliferation of these movements. But the very vitality of American religion will depend—as it has in the past—on the freedom of such movements to voice their demands.

Religion and the Changing Role
of Women

By BARBARA HARGROVE, JEAN MILLER SCHMIDT,
and SHEILA GREEVE DAVANEY

ABSTRACT: As the role of women in the society at large has changed, religion in America has responded to the changes in a number of ways. New professional roles in church and synagogue have been opened to women, including, in most mainline denominations, that of ordained clergy. Lay leadership positions as well are increasingly being filled by women. Along with these structural changes, a number of theological issues have been engendered, including the recovery of women's share of religious history, changing images of God and the church, and issues relating to sexual equality and justice. On the other hand, some religious groups have taken the lead in opposing women's assumption of more public roles and also movements to free women from the domestic role through, among other things, abortion, birth control, and divorce. These issues have been joined to larger movements over which religious groups and denominations have become polarized. They have also affected the churches' expectations of a large pool of female volunteer workers. Thus the general pattern of changing roles for women has changed the structure, both social and ideological, of American religion.

The authors are colleagues at the Iliff School of Theology in Denver. Barbara Hargrove, professor of the sociology of religion, is currently vice-president of the Association for the Sociology of Religion. Her most recent books include Women of the Cloth, *with Jackson Carroll and Adair Lummis. Jean Miller Schmidt, associate professor of modern church history, serves on the American Academy of Religion's Board of Directors and has published articles on women and religion, United Methodist history, and American religion. Sheila Greeve Davaney is associate professor of theology. Her publications concern process theism and feminist theology. Her current research is on the relationship between social theories of knowledge and liberation theologies.*

WRITING about women in American religion, while an exhilarating challenge, is often an exercise in frustration as well. Traditionally in this society, as in others, the experience of women has not been examined in the histories of religious institutions nor has it found full expression in the theological frameworks of these structures. The current women's movement has led to attempts to rectify this exclusion, but so far the recovery of the history of women and the articulation of women's experience within theological perspectives have been partial at best. They have been partial not only because women in general have been ignored, but because in a predominantly white society, greatly influenced by the politics of race, the experience of women of color has been almost completely erased by those, including white women, who have had access to the academic and professional institutions that carry out historical inquiry and theological reflection.

Thus there is the double frustration of knowing that we are only beginning to recover the content and meaning of women's lives at all, and in particular that the task of retrieving and appreciating the experience of women of color is still fundamentally in front of us. As it has been white women who have been first to make their way into the professional structures where such issues arise, it has been their history that has been recovered first and their understandings of their faiths that have been most prominent in theology. The frustration, then, is to know that the experience and thought of many women of color and of working-class background is not available for us to discuss. So, with the painful knowledge of the partial nature of our information, we will begin with a discussion of women in the dominant religious traditions, then turn to women from groups and religious heritages that have been marginalized.

WOMEN'S SEPARATE SPHERE

By the mid-nineteenth century in America, two major developments of particular significance for religion and the role of women had occurred. One was the forging of the mainstream of American evangelical Protestantism largely as a product of the Second Great Awakening, with its egalitarian revivalistic spirit, new measures encouraging women to speak in mixed prayer meetings and congregations, and voluntary associations in which women became active participants.[1] The other was the widespread agreement in American culture on a new standard of womanhood, the segregated woman's sphere prescribed by the cult of domesticity. According to this view of gender complementarity, men were to be active in the public sphere of work and politics, while women's peculiarly religious and moral nature suited them to reign in the private sphere of the home. From this base it was assumed that women would influence the character not only of their husbands, sons, fathers, and brothers, but of society itself. The notion of woman's sphere "not only assigned distinctive roles, characteristics, and spaces to the

---

1. Much has been written on the relationship between evangelical Protestantism in America and an expanded role for women. See, for example, Donald Mathews, *Religion in the Old South* (Chicago: University of Chicago Press, 1977); and Nancy Hardesty, Lucille Sider Dayton, and Donald Dayton, "Women in the Holiness Movement: Feminism in the Evangelical Movement," in *Women of Spirit: Female Leadership in the Jewish and Christian Traditions,* ed. Rosemary Ruether and Eleanor McLaughlin (New York: Simon & Schuster, 1979).

female sex, but also construed this sexual division as a principal safeguard of social order."[2]

As of 1860, only about 15 percent of the adult women listed in the U.S. census were gainfully employed outside the home, a fact that gave widespread credence to the doctrine of the spheres. In actuality, there was considerably more elasticity to the boundaries of woman's sphere than this ideology would suggest. Many women worked outside the home before marriage, large numbers of women found a place for themselves on the boundaries of woman's sphere in women's organizations devoted to religious or reform activities, and the first women's rights movement arose to protest the doctrines of true womanhood almost as soon as they had been formulated.[3] In addition, the role of women in nursing and relief work during the Civil War had a permanent effect on the expansion of woman's sphere.

The entrance of women into lay leadership in Protestant churches during the nineteenth century came through the creation of organizations for women only. From the 1860s to the 1890s, women's foreign missionary societies were founded in 33 denominations and home missionary societies in 17.[4] Begun in order to support female missionaries and to do women's work for women and children, these women's missionary societies were especially successful at fund raising and the dissemination of missionary information at the local level. They thus provided an effective outlet for the considerable energies and leadership abilities of volunteer laywomen, to whom other avenues in the church were closed.

The desire to train women for lives of usefulness led to the development of the missionary training school. By 1916, there were some 60 religious training schools in America, the majority of which were primarily for women and staffed by women.[5] The curriculum generally required one or two years and was both comprehensive and highly practical. It included studies in religious pedagogy, hygiene, citizenship, social and family relationships, and fieldwork experience in the city, as well as classes in Bible, church history, and the history of missions. A whole range of church workers were trained in these schools, including Sunday school teachers and deaconesses. Although never involving large numbers of women, the deaconess movement afforded women in the Luth-

2. Mary P. Ryan, *Womanhood in America: From Colonial Times to the Present,* 3rd ed. (New York: Franklin Watts, 1983), p. 116. Ryan suggests three distinct patterns of gender system in America: (1) the integral position of women in the patriarchal household economy of the seventeenth century; (2) the segregated woman's sphere of industrial capitalism in the nineteenth century; and (3) the more symmetrical but still unequal relationship of the sexes in the 1960s and 1970s. Barbara Welter described this cult of true womanhood in her *Dimity Convictions: The American Woman in the Nineteenth Century* (Athens: Ohio University Press, 1976).

3. Ryan, *Womanhood in America,* p. 119. This woman's rights movement began at Seneca Falls, New York, in 1848 and lasted until the granting of woman suffrage in 1920.

4. Rosemary Skinner Keller, "Lay Women in the Protestant Tradition," in *Women and Religion in America: The Nineteenth Century,* ed. Rosemary Radford Ruether and Rosemary Skinner Keller (New York: Harper & Row, 1981), pp. 242-93. The entire volume is a useful resource.

5. See Virginia Lieson Brereton and Christa Ressmeyer Klein, "American Women in Ministry: A History of Protestant Beginning Points," in *Women of Spirit,* ed. Ruether and McLaughlin, and in *Women in American Religion,* ed. Janet Wilson James (Philadelphia: University of Pennsylvania Press, 1980); the statistic about the women's training schools is on p. 178 in James.

eran, Methodist, and a few other denominations the opportunity for full-time service as professional lay workers in world mission stations and as social workers and nurses in deaconess hospitals or immigrant communities in American cities.

Outside the church, movements such as the Women's Christian Temperance Union, led by Methodist laywoman Frances E. Willard, were the means by which countless Victorian ladies left the sanctuary of their homes to support the causes of temperance and woman suffrage—and eventually a wide range of social reforms—for the sake of home protection. Because these independent women's organizations served as a training ground for lay leadership, they were bound to affect the status of women in the churches.

THE STRUGGLE FOR STATUS WITHIN THE CHURCHES

A combination of factors led to greater awareness of this issue by the 1920s. One was the consolidation of women's missionary societies with general missionary boards, which usually was accomplished without consulting the women. Although a few women were given positions of leadership on the new combined missionary boards, the general result was a loss of power for women within these denominations. A parallel development was the closing of the women's training schools or their absorption into denominational theological schools in the years after World War I. The passage of the Nineteenth Amendment granting woman suffrage and the impact of higher criticism on biblical interpretation in many denominations also contributed to the reevaluation of women's status in the churches. A direct

consequence was the struggle for full laity rights for women in Protestant churches. Increasing professionalization of roles in society as a whole in the first few decades of the twentieth century also led to the creation of new positions for women as professional lay workers within the churches.[6]

Throughout the nineteenth century, women were licensed as evangelists in churches—including holiness and black churches—which recognized the authority conferred by charismatic gifts of the Spirit. Here women's successful soul-winning was regarded as validation of their call to preach. In 1853, Wesleyan Methodist pastor Luther Lee preached the ordination sermon for Congregationalist Antoinette Brown, probably the first woman to be fully ordained to the Christian ministry in an American denomination. In identifying prophetic charisms with historic ministry, Lee went beyond earlier defenses of women's right to preach and claimed a biblical basis for their right to be ordained as well.[7]

From the 1880s on, women began to press for ordination in mainline Protestant denominations. While some few were ordained early in the more independently organized or charismatic de-

6. These developments are discussed in Brereton and Klein, "American Women in Ministry," pp. 178-86.

7. The holiness evangelist Phoebe Palmer defended women's right to preach on the basis of the gift of the Spirit to the Church at Pentecost, with its promise that "your sons and your daughters shall prophesy." She did not press for ordination for women, viewing the whole system of ordination as unscriptural. The term "prophetic charisms" is Rosemary Ruether's in her *Sexism and God-Talk: Toward a Feminist Theology* (Boston: Beacon Press, 1983), p. 199. It should be noted that in some of the utopian and sectarian movements in the nineteenth century, women played major roles as founders, leaders, and theologians.

nominations, and more were after the 1920s, significant numbers of women were granted ordination only from the 1950s.[8] In general, the more priestly the conception of ministry, the slower that church would be to admit women to the ranks of ordained clergy. Only in the 1970s would Lutheran and Episcopalian churches vote to ordain women, and then with considerable dissent from both members and clergy.[9]

WOMEN IN IMMIGRANT CHURCHES

The pattern of developments just outlined is descriptive primarily of native-born, white, middle-class Protestant women. In turning to women of other religious traditions, races, and classes, it is important to keep in mind the extent to which immigration shaped the priorities of both women and the churches and synagogues that ministered to immigrant peoples. In the century after 1830, the influx of immigrants to America changed the nature of our society and its religious institutions. Nearly 40 million people came: Irish in the first wave; Germans and Scandinavians dominating the next phase; and after 1890, a vast exodus of Eastern European Jews, southern Italians, and Balkan peoples.[10]

As a result of this immigration, Roman Catholics, once a tiny and ignored minority, became the largest church in the country. Faced with the challenges of preserving and fostering the Catholic faith among millions of immigrant members, and of establishing credibility in an alien society, the Catholic church relied heavily on the efforts of Catholic nuns or sisters—that is, women religious. Their numbers grew from under 40 to more than 40,000 during the nineteenth century, and by the close of that century there were almost four time as many nuns as priests in America.[11] During the Civil War some 640 sister-nurses in military hospitals not only performed a significant ministry but also brought about a dramatic change in public attitudes toward Catholicism. The major preoccupation of Catholic sisters, however, was with teaching, particularly in the parochial schools developed in every diocese after 1884.

In these schools and in girls' academies in which nuns taught, Roman Catholic young women were given a sense of responsibility for nurturing the Catholic faith in the homes they would someday run and for the religious education of their children. Together, Catholic teaching and the American cult of domesticity reinforced woman's traditional role as wife and mother. Like their Protestant counterparts, married

8. Anna Howard Shaw was ordained in the Methodist Protestant church in 1880, and women were ordained in the United Brethren church in 1889 and 1984. Some Congregationalist, Unitarian, Baptist, and Disciples women were ordained early in the twentieth century. The Methodist church and the Presbyterian Church in the United States gave full clergy rights to women in the 1950s. Due to the domestic interlude of the 1950s, in which the housewife reigned over the suburbs, the 1950s was also a time when becoming a minister's wife was an accepted avenue to ministry for women.

9. Jackson Carroll, Barbara Hargrove, and Adair Lummis, *Women of the Cloth* (New York: Harper & Row, 1983), p. 102.

10. The impact of immigration is given ample attention in Sydney Ahlstrom, *A Religious History of the American People* (New Haven, CT: Yale University Press, 1972).

11. See Mary Ewens, "The Leadership of Nuns in Immigrant Catholicism," in *Women and Religion in America,* vol. 1, *The Nineteenth Century,* ed. Rosemary Radford Ruether and Rosemary Skinner Keller (New York: Harper & Row, 1981), pp. 101-49.

Catholic women also served the church through volunteer work in altar and rosary societies.

Since Vatican II, communities of Roman Catholic women religious have become modernized, discarding the distinctive nun's habit and encouraging a much more public role for their members. Especially since the 1970s, women religious and laywomen have combined their efforts to urge the ordination of women to the priesthood and access for women to positions of real power in the American Catholic church.[12]

Transitions in the role of women in Judaism likewise are related to patterns of immigration to America. German Jews settling in eastern and midwestern cities between 1840 and 1880 brought with them Reform Judaism, the most radical departure from traditional Judaism in terms of the position of women. Unlike Orthodox Judaism with its different spheres of religious behavior, the man's revolving around the synagogue and the study of the Torah and the woman's centering on the home, Reform Jewish women participated fully in the life of Reform temples. They could sit in family pews rather than being segregated in a curtained-off area in the synagogue, and they counted as part of the *minyan,* or quorum of 10 necessary for public prayer. Through temple sisterhoods and the National Council of Jewish Women—established in 1893—Reform Jewish women engaged in a wide variety

of volunteer religious, educational, and philanthropic activities.[13]

Orthodox Judaism in America was largely constituted by the migration of over 2.5 million Eastern European Jews between 1880 and 1920. Orthodox Jewish women maintained their traditional responsibilities for husband, family, and the moral purity of the home through strict observance of dietary laws and ritual purifications. Jews who were no longer Orthodox but could not accept Reform Judaism were attracted to Conservative Judaism, established in America after World War I. Conservatives adjusted the status of women somewhat, and Conservative and Reform Jewish women often worked together in organizations such as Hadassah, the women's division of the Zionist Organization of America, founded in 1912.

Jewish women lived within a pattern of "seeming acceptance combined with implicit exclusion"[14] until very recently. In 1972, Sally Preisand became the first woman to be ordained a rabbi. In Reform, Reconstructionist, and Conservative Judaism women began to study to become rabbis and cantors. Jewish feminism, a self-conscious movement since the 1970s, has sought full participation for women and girls in Jewish life, including public ceremonies, and has struggled to reconcile the integrity and full personhood of Jewish women with talmudic tradition.

RELIGIOUS INVOLVEMENT OF WOMEN OF COLOR

A major factor in determining women's religious roles in America has

12. For example, Helen Sanders, *More Than a Renewal: Loretto before and after Vatican II: 1952-1977* (Nerinx, KY: Sisters of Loretto, 1982). Women of the Eastern Orthodox branch of Christianity share the desire to enter more fully into the decision-making structure of the churches, as illustrated in *Survey of Greek Orthodox Women in Respect to Philoptochos Society* (New York: National Office of the Greek Orthodox Ladies Philoptochos Society, 1981).

13. See Charlotte Baum, Paula Hyman, and Sonya Michel, *The Jewish Woman in America* (New York: Dial Press, 1976).

14. Norma Fain Pratt, "Transitions in Judaism: The Jewish American Woman through the 1930s," in *Women in American Religion,* ed. James, p. 226.

source of religious education, with women religious finding a more focused educative career but forming a decreasing proportion of the faculty of parochial schools. As in the past, women's voluntary associations in local congregations and at district, national, and international levels remain for many of their members the primary channel into public influence and responsibility.

However, major changes in the economic structure of society have made inroads into patterns of activity by women of all backgrounds. Traditional women's roles have been reduced in proportion to the increased reliance on specialization and technology. Modern conveniences have reduced the time spent in household maintenance, but they have also increased the cost of housing to a point where for a high proportion of families an outside income beyond that of the typical husband and father is needed. Nonspecialized work like that of the homemaker is not highly valued in modern American society, being ranked often in the general category of unskilled labor. For all these reasons, the women who once were able to spend their spare time serving religious organizations as volunteers are now joining their less affluent sisters in working outside the home.

As women have been able to open more and more doors to public involvement in the society at large, many who were trained in church societies have moved into more general denominational and ecumenical organizations previously considered the preserve of men. They have served as presidents and moderators or in similar leadership roles in a number of denominations that allow lay leadership, and as heads of ecumenical organizations at all levels.

WOMEN AND THE CLERICAL ROLE

The primary professional role in the church for women, as for men, is that of the clergy. It was not until the 1970s that Protestant women began filling the seminaries and pushing for ordination in significant numbers, as part of the larger pattern of women's movement into professional roles in the society as a whole. Jewish women rabbis and cantors now serve some congregations, and their number is growing. Orthodox and Roman Catholic churches still deny ordination to women; but as laywomen begin to push for more leadership roles in those churches, they demonstrate their hope to follow their sisters into full professional status in their traditions.

Many of the women who have been ordained have taken their place as professional leaders of local congregations. A considerable number of ordained women, however, have been placed in various staff positions of the denominational hierarchies. Their influence is in some ways more widely felt as it comes from those points in the structure, but it may be less powerful at the grass-roots level. As the number of women clergy increases, their presence will inevitably become more evident to the rank and file. Currently many mainline Protestant seminaries have nearly as many women as men enrolled in degree programs leading to ordination, and in 1980 nearly a third of the students at the Reform Jewish seminary were women.[17]

17. See Carroll, Hargrove, and Lummis, eds., *Women of the Cloth,* chap. 4, for details about this process in American Protestantism. The figure on Jewish women comes from June Sochen, *Consecrate Every Day: The Public Lives of Jewish American Women 1880-1980* (New York: State University of New York Press, 1983), p. 1.

been that of social class. Obviously the volunteerism of middle-class women was not an option for working-class women, white or nonwhite. In addition, any consideration of the religious involvement of women of color must take into account both internal developments within their own traditions and patterns of interaction with the dominant white culture.

Under slavery, black women struggled in various ways to hold families together, to give religious nurture to children, and to work for the improvement of their people. Free black women in the North went as missionaries to Africa, were prominent in the abolitionist movement, taught black children, and were widely recognized by whites and blacks alike as successful evangelists. After the end of the Civil War, black women took an increasingly active role in the independent black denominations, fighting some of the same battles as their white sisters for access to leadership positions, as well as serving in women's roles such as stewardess and deaconess.[15] With the growth of a sizable middle class among American black people, women have assumed volunteer work within both black and integrated churches.

The economic status of the majority of blacks in American society, however, has led black churches to devote themselves to service to their communities in far more holistic ways than is true for the majority of white churches, and these services often are carried on by the

whole church rather than being vince of women, as in so ma churches.

Much of the movement of outside the home has been s resisted by Hispanic culture, and Hispanic Catholic women tend to their religion through personal pi home and family settings. In ger where ethnicity is a primary part o religion, women are likely to be stro reinforced in the kind of personal family piety that can be utilized to ma tain a group's ethnic identity.

In the Hispanic Protestant church growing out of missions in the Soutl west, women have played a major role a converts, teachers, lay workers, and clergy wives. As the Hispanic tradition of *machismo* delegates the observance of religion to women, a major concern has been to involve Spanish-speaking men in the life of these congregations and to recruit them for ministry.[16]

White home-missions women and deaconesses serving Native American, Asian American, Hispanic, and black communities through schools, settlement houses, clinics, and homes for women and children have come to respect and have been changed by the experience and heritage of these peoples.

WOMEN VOLUNTEERS IN THE CONTEMPORARY CHURCH

Whereas the typically American patterns of involvement in religious structures that were established in the nineteenth century still hold for many church and synagogue women, a number of strains are increasingly felt. Women volunteers continue to be a primary

---

15. For the story of that struggle in one independent black denomination, see Jualynne Dodson, "Nineteenth-Century A.M.E. Preaching Woman: Cutting Edge of Women's Inclusion in Church Polity," in *Women in New Worlds,* ed. Hilah F. Thomas and Rosemary Skinner Keller (Nashville, TN: Abingdon Press, 1981), pp. 276-89.

16. Clotilde Falcón Náñez, "Hispanic Clergy Wives," in *Women in New Worlds,* ed. Thomas and Keller, pp. 161-77.

One of the issues currently being debated in the churches is the possible influence on the clerical role of a significant number of women serving as clergy. Generally speaking, much of a pastor's time is spent in nurturing and supportive activities resembling those traditionally expected of women. Yet the evidence is growing that women in the clerical role often bring with them a different style, more likely to be open and democratic, more willing to involve the laity at significant levels of church life.[18] It is hard to evaluate such trends as yet, as a large number of women have only recently gone into the ministry, and many of them attended seminary and sought ordination after many years as active laywomen in local congregations. Later cohorts of women whose career paths have been more similar to that traditionally expected of men may or may not alter this pattern.

It is also difficult to evaluate the future possibilities for women of color in the ministry. In many of the more sectarian churches they still can serve as preachers and evangelists, but in the more middle-class churches there is often a strong conservative element, perhaps to compensate for the low status often given people of color in this society. This conservative tendency is compounded by concerns about the status of men in these communities and by a desire on the part of women to help to elevate their brothers in the opinion of the society as a whole. Many women who are particularly capable of leadership are therefore somewhat reluctant to compete with men for positions in the clergy.[19] However, a growing number of black women are attending seminary and graduating with the hope of being ordained in their churches. A significant number of black women have served high posts in major denominations that are predominantly white, and a much smaller number of Hispanic women are also making their presence felt in denominational structures.

THE CONSERVATIVE REACTION

The women's movement in the society at large has not only facilitated the rise of women into leadership in the churches, but also has called into question many of the assumptions of the cult of domesticity that has played a vital role in some religious understandings of the Christian life. Women, less reliant on men economically and more able to adjust or limit family size, have moved out of familiar family patterns into new modes of living.

For some groups this is a direct violation of accepted religious norms. They consider the earlier form of the dominant wage-earning husband and the full-time homemaking—and church-volunteering—wife and mother to be instituted by God. Patterns that would grant full equality to women in home and church are attacked as irreligious. Thus many of the religiopolitical battles of the 1980s over abortion, the Equal Rights Amendment, and the like are rooted in the religious definitions of women's role that are being challenged by modern economic and social structures.

Professional leadership by women clergy may be a particular problem for some women in this tradition as the pro-

---

18. See Carroll, Hargrove, and Lummis, eds., *Women of the Cloth,* chap. 7.

19. See, for example, Katie Cannon, "Black Women and the Church," in *Face to Face: An Interreligious Bulletin,* Special Issue on Women and the Religious Communities, 5: 30-32 (Spring 1978).

fessional woman may be seen as taking the place of the righteous volunteer. On the other hand, it was out of associations of women volunteers that much of the pressure arose to push the churches into ordaining women and taking their religious work seriously. In general, women in the so-called mainline churches, where their social background may be more professional, tend to be most supportive of professional women in religious institutions, and indeed the same may be said of men in those organizations.[20] The principles of economic justice are applied to these roles as to other segments of the society, and refusal to grant women positions for which they are qualified is seen as scandalous.

Generally speaking, then, there is considerable ferment in American religious institutions at present concerning the role of women. They have in the past tended to legitimate certain patterns of participation in the society that no longer fit well for a high proportion of the country's women, including the ways in which they participate in religious organizations themselves. New patterns of legitimation are emerging, often through leadership in the religious organizations by women; but religious traditions do not change easily, and there is likely to be considerably more unrest before any religious consensus emerges, if one ever does.

WOMEN AND THE THEOLOGICAL ENTERPRISE

While the presence of women has exerted a certain amount of influence within the life and structures of religious institutions throughout America's his-

tory, it has only been in recent decades that women have begun to have crucial and far-reaching effect within the field of theology.[21] Until the current wave of feminism, women neither were significant participants in the theological discipline nor were considered by male theologians to have lives and experiences worthy of theological reflection. This once all-male province has, however, undergone radical change as women have begun to enter theological studies in ever greater numbers and to challenge the prevailing male understanding of theology and its subject matter. The result of this challenge is that during the last decade and a half there has emerged a theological perspective known as feminist theology that has defined as its task both the critical analysis of traditional —that is, male—theologies and the construction of new theological visions more adequate to the emerging experience of contemporary women.

Feminist theology, growing out of the women's movement, has reflected to a significant extent the racial, economic, and religious makeup of that movement. That is, most theology has been done by white, middle-class, and usually Christian or post-Christian women.[22]

21. Theology is not the only arena of theological studies to feel the impact of feminist analysis. Parallel developments have occurred in biblical studies, the historical fields of inquiry, history of religion, and ethics as women bring to bear their feminist perspective on these academic areas.

22. While Jewish women have participated in large numbers in the women's movement, their presence in the theological discipline has not been as visible as that of their Christian counterparts. There are a variety of reasons for this, including the fact that Judaism has not had the same history of theology as a discipline as has Christianity. Increasingly, however, Jewish women are formulating a specific theological response to their experience as feminists whose religious and cultural heritage is Judaism.

20. Some of these patterns of support are documented in Carroll, Hargrove, and Lummis, eds., *Women of the Cloth,* chap. 6 and p. 102.

While women representing other experiences and different traditions have participated in feminist theologizing, only now are these voices challenging in full force the prevalent white and Christian character of this theological development. Because of this, we will turn first to the predominant strand in feminist theology, and then look explicitly at the unique contributions and critical challenges emerging from the perspectives of Jewish women and women of color.

Sensitized by the civil rights movement and reflecting the rising tide of feminist consciousness developing with the present-day women's movement, feminist theology emerged as a distinctive theological approach during the 1970s. Many voices have been heard, speaking from a variety of perspectives and offering quite diverse proposals for this new understanding of theology and its task. Precisely because of their diversity it is impossible to identify one position as the only true feminist position; variety, creativity, and experimentation have been the watchwords of feminist theologians as they have sought to create new visions of reality. However, although there is no monolithic feminist theological stance, feminist theology has been characterized by common critical perceptions and shared constructive concerns. Resonating with the insights of precursors of feminist theologians such as Elizabeth Cady Stanton[23] and Valerie

Saiving,[24] feminist theologians have called for a mode of theologizing that is self-consciously provisional, that is not afraid to acknowledge its interest-laden character, and that openly declares the commitments out of which it is emerging.

Many women theologians have declared clearly that the context out of which they work has as a primary, although not exclusive, concern the experience of women and the possibility of the transformation of that experience into a fuller and more humane existence. Thus, for many women theologians there exists a self-conscious prior commitment to women, and it is out of and in relation to this perspective that religious symbol systems and their attendant understandings of reality are analyzed and judged.

Critical aspects
of feminist theology

This conceptual starting point and existential locus of commitment has led

---

23. Suffragette Elizabeth Cady Stanton compiled, in the closing years of the nineteenth century, a controversial work entitled *The Woman's Bible,* originally published in two volumes in 1895 and 1896. In it she set forth all of the biblical verses pertaining to women and developed a series of feminist-inspired commentaries on these passages. Her convictions that religion played a profound role in the oppression of women and that women

would not be free until the religious elements of subjugation had been recognized and transformed have reemerged more than 70 years later as central concerns of feminist theology.

24. In 1960 theologian Valerie Saiving published an article entitled "The Human Situation: A Feminine View" in *Journal of Religion,* 40:11-112 (Apr. 1960). In this article Saiving suggested that central Christian understandings of sin and salvation emerged from and reflected male, not female, experience. She posited that sin interpreted as pride, and fulfilled human life understood in terms of self-sacrifice and self-giving, may adequately reflect the experience of men but do not describe accurately nor respond salvifically to the experience of women, who have been socialized to have little sense of self and who lack pride even in minimal terms. Saiving's insights that many theological positions flow from and reflect the theologian's own experience and that therefore theology carried out by males is not responsive to the condition of women have been developed as central themes of feminist theology.

feminists to call for the reassessment of Western theological visions in light of the age-old oppression of women. Convinced that theological assertions and religious visions, no less than political, economic, and social structures, must be scrutinized in relation to the realities of oppression, women have undertaken the critical evaluation of their inherited religious traditions.

Much of the first stage of feminist theology was characterized by this critical agenda. Led by Mary Daly[25] and Rosemary Ruether[26]—women engaged in what might be termed theology of opposition—the ideas of God, of Jesus, of human nature, and of the purpose of reality were all examined to determine to what extent they contributed to the subjugation of women; the patriarchal character of Western religious traditions was unmasked and the powerful alliance between religion and oppressive social structures was clearly and critically brought to light. In all this a new theological norm emerged; theological visions were, for the first time in history, being scrutinized in terms of what they meant for women. Women, historically denied participation in the theological enterprise and ignored as subject matter for theological reflection, were now arguing that women's experience was to be the critical principle according to which religious symbols and theological systems were to be evaluated.

25. See Mary Daly, *Beyond God the Father: Toward a Philosophy of Women's Liberation* (Boston: Beacon Press, !973); see also idem, *Gyn/Ecology: The Metaethics of Radical Feminism* (Boston: Beacon Press, 1983).

26. Rosemary Radford Ruether, *Liberation Theology: Human Hope Confronts Christian History and American Power* (New York: Paulist Press, 1972); see also Ruether, *Sexism and God-Talk*.

Constructive aspects of feminist theology

As feminist theology has refined its methods and broadened its areas of inquiry, it has retained this critical tenor as it has sought to uncover the male character of its inherited traditions. Such theology of opposition, however, has not been the only concern for women theologians. Increasingly, women have turned their creative energies to the constructive task of transforming their understandings of reality and of deity into more liberating and humanizing visions. And it is in relation to these constructive efforts that the great diversity and indeed conflict among feminist theologians emerges with clarity.

There are a number of women theologians who are attempting not only to uncover male biases in their received traditions, but, more important, to recover resources within these heritages that are more supportive of women's efforts toward liberation. Thus there are those feminists who seek alternative ways of conceiving God that are not tied to male imagery.

These women also have as a primary concern the unearthing of the contribution of women, which had been buried and hidden until recently, and the reconstruction of female experience and history. In the words of one such theologian, Letty Russell, they search for "a usable past."[27] There is much debate within this perspective over method, over what constitute adequate criteria, and over what is usable. Nonetheless, thinkers such as Rosemary Ruether, Elisabeth Schüssler Fiorenza, and Letty

27. Letty M. Russell, *Human Liberation in a Feminist Perspective* (Philadelphia: Westminster Press, 1974), pp. 72 ff.

Russell, concurring with other feminist colleagues in the biblical and historical fields, agree that there are liberating dimensions of their religious traditions that might be appropriated by contemporary women, and that it is the task of feminists both to reconstruct the lost history of women and to determine those historical elements that are worthy of commitment today. A somewhat analagous movement has begun as well within conservative Christian circles as evangelical women, such as Virginia Ramey Mollenkott,[28] Nancy Hardesty, and Letha Scanzoni,[29] are attempting to delineate a theology that is both biblically grounded and supportive of women.

Other feminists have opted to remain within their traditions, although they are less concerned with the biblical heritage of either Christianity or Judaism. Some, such as Sheila Collins, are less sanguine about the search for a usable past and instead call for the radical renaming of reality—not in loyalty to the past, but in light of the possibilities that have emerged in the modern world.[30] Another approach feminists are taking is to seek out not biblical visions, but later alternative theological and philosophical positions that resonate with the commitments of women. While much of Western philosophy and theology have been powerful contributors to the oppression of women, there have always been thinkers who raised dissenting voices. Feminists are now exploring and weighing the possibilities of these alternative visions. One such option that feminist theologians are considering is that development termed process thought. Increasingly women are seeing liberating possibilities in this perspective, which posits a deity who shares power, who is reciprocally related to the world, and whose very life depends upon the fulfillment and liberation of all people for its own richness.[31]

And finally, there are growing numbers of women who seek what might be termed spiritual visions but whose symbols are self-consciously female in nature. That is to say, there is a growing interest in a Goddess-centered vision of reality. Thinkers such as Carol Christ, Merlin Stone, Starhawk, and Mary Daly have increasingly articulated their positions utilizing Goddess imagery and symbols. In Christ's words, "As women struggle to create a new culture in which women's power, bodies, will, and bonds are celebrated, it seems natural that the Goddess would re-emerge as a symbol of the newfound beauty, strength, and power of women.[32] Thus these women turn not to the authorities of scripture, tradition, or male-created philosophy but to the resources of female history, literature, experience, and imagination. Their conviction is that female hope of true liberation does not lie in the rehabilitation of male models of reality embodied in patriarchal religion or philosophy, but in the new vision that is

28. Virginia Ramey Mallenkott, *The Divine Feminine* (New York: Crossroads, 1984).

29. Letha Scanzoni and Nancy Hardesty, *All We're Meant to Be* (Waco, TX: Word Books, 1974).

30. Sheila Collins, *A Different Heaven and Earth* (Valley Forge, PA: Judson Press, 1974).

31. For a variety of articles, see Sheila Greeve Davaney, ed., *Feminism and Process Thought* (New York: Edwin Mellen Press, 1980); and also Marjorie Suchocki, *God Christ Church: A Practical Guide to Process Theology* (New York: Crossroad, 1982).

32. Carol P. Christ, "Why Women Need the Goddess: Phenomenological, Psychological, and Political Reflections," in *Womanspirit Rising,* ed. Judith Plaskow and Carol P. Christ (New York: Harper & Row, 1979), p. 286.

emerging as women bond together and seek a new form of non-oppressive existence that the world has not yet known.

While these developments have held prominent positions within feminist theology, there have been other voices that have offered profound challenges to these trends and have suggested that feminists engaged in theologizing must incorporate within their process ongoing and far more rigorous self-criticism. Leaders in this area have included black and Jewish feminists who, while participating in the previously explored developments, have also raised serious questions about the character and direction of feminist theological reflection.

Acknowledging that the majority of feminist theology has been carried out by Christian or post-Christian women, Jewish feminists have pointed to the disturbingly anti-Jewish tone of much of this work and have urged their non-Jewish counterparts to be alert to the dangers of such a facile and unrecognized anti-Jewish bias. Whether this anti-Jewish orientation finds expression in the misunderstanding of Judaism as a rejection of Christianity or in a view of Jesus as the one who offers an alternative to a negatively and naively interpreted Jewish understanding of power and judgment, Jewish feminists such as Judith Plaskow have argued that failure to root out this anti-Semitism will damage the prospects of an inclusive and progressive feminist theology. Furthermore, Jewish women led by thinkers such as Plaskow, Rita Gross, and Susannah Heschel are currently seeking to construct a new theological perspective appropriate to women whose religious roots lie in Judaism.[33]

Women of color, led by black women, have raised a parallel criticism of theology, pointing out the pervasive white character of this perspective. Black women have argued that the almost exclusive emphasis upon sexual oppression without attention to the dynamics of racism and classism results in an incomplete and superficial analysis of oppression that does not address the condition of women of color. Speaking of the white bias of much feminist theology, Jacquelyn Grant asserts that it is not only inadequate but oppressive insofar as it universalizes the experience of white women.[34] Thus women of color are arguing strongly that only when the experience of all women finds serious expression in feminist theology will this development lay claim to the loyalties of black, Hispanic, and other nonwhite women.

Moreover, women of color such as Grant, Delores Williams, and Ada Maria Isasi-Diaz are further arguing not only that their particular experiences in a white-dominated culture must be seen as oppressive, but also that their lives must be recognized as offering original and creative resources for the development of a truly non-oppressive vision for the future. The values of their com-

33. See Judith Plaskow, "Anti-Semitism: The Unacknowledged Racism," in *Women's Spirit Bonding*, ed. Janet Kalvin and Mary I. Buckley (New York: Pilgrim Press, 1984), pp. 89-96; see also Susannah Heschel, ed., *On Being a Jewish Feminist* (New York: Schocken Books, 1983).

34. See Jacqueline Grant, "A Black Response to Feminist Theology," in *Women's Spirit Bonding,* ed. Kalvin and Buckley, p. 122; see Gloria T. Hull, Patricia Bell Scott, and Barbara Smith, eds., *All the Women Are White, All the Blacks Are Men, but Some of Us Are Brave: Black Women's Studies* (Old Westbury, NY: Feminist Press, 1982); Pauli Murray, "Black Theology and Feminist Theology: A Comparative View," *Anglican Theological Review*, 60: 3-24 (Jan. 1978).

munal experience require criticism, as do those of white women, but they also require close scrutiny for the visions of hope, courage, and determination that they offer all women.

CONCLUSION

This brief survey can only serve as an introduction to the movement of feminist theology. From its beginnings in protest to its stage of creative construction, from its origination in the experience of white Christian women to its search for a global vision in which all women can speak from and to their own experience, feminist theology has sought to delineate new forms of thought and life that are more conducive to humane and liberating existence. The diversity of opinion is immense; and as feminist theology has developed, it has become clear that while shared female oppression binds women together, race, class, and religious heritage can divide them. It is the hope of all feminist theologians that these differences can and will become new resources for a deeper vision rather than continued sources of di-

vision. However, it is also clear that unless feminist theology becomes truly inclusive it will fail to live up to its promise of new possibilities for a transformed future.

How much those visions of transformation have penetrated American society at this time is difficult to say. No matter what else it may indicate, however, such a restructuring of personal and social identity, when provided through institutions that are understood to be purveyors of sacred values, must almost inevitably move the society further in the direction of social change. Even resistance to feminist theology is likely to change the structure of religion, and of male-female relationships as well. Modern society has tended to relegate both religion and women to an isolated sphere, out of touch with the broader forces of economic and political life. As women are emerging from that enforced isolation, a significant number of them may bring religion into the public sphere with them, and in ways not previously envisioned. Some kind of transforming power seems present; only the future will tell what becomes of it.

ANNALS, *AAPSS*, **480**, July 1985

Religion and Region in America

By SAMUEL S. HILL

ABSTRACT: A decline in the differences between regions has been occurring in a number of demographic and socioeconomic aspects. Religion is one of several areas in which regional differences persist. Zelinsky's classification of seven religious regions remains standard. Americans migrating from one part of America to another are aware of this, and recent research supports popular perceptions. Migrants have been shown to be more likely to adapt to the level of religious commitment of the new region than to be dislocated by the move. As long as this remains true, migration should not be accompanied by a decline in the distinctiveness of religious regions. The continuing strength of the historically prominent denominations in the several regions is impressive.

Samuel S. Hill holds an M.A. in English from Vanderbilt and a Ph.D. in religion from Duke. He has been professor of religion at the University of Florida since 1972. He has also taught at the University of North Carolina at Chapel Hill from 1960 to 1972. Among his publications are Southern Churches in Crisis *(1966),* The South and the North in American Religion *(1980), and the* Encyclopedia of Religion in the South *(1984).*

CONVENTIONAL wisdom has it that American society is becoming more and more homogeneous. Under the impact of television, the syndication of newspaper articles and even companies, and widespread travel, Americans are becoming more alike, so we are told. Regional differences, thus, should be decreasing in favor of a greater national—American culture-wide—consensus.

The religious life of the American people should reflect any such decline in regional peculiarity. To this supposition a second would be added by a number of observers—namely, the growth of secularism in its scope and in the power of its hold on our society under conditions of modernization. In other words, a growing proportion of American citizens is "practicing the absence of God"—a vest-pocket definition of secularism. They are taking religious faith less seriously, although without actually repudiating it and thereby becoming either atheists or agnostics. If these popular perceptions are in fact true, the strength of religion should be decreasing. It would follow that religion would be a less significant factor in any attempt to assess regional differences or similarities.

On both points, the evidence disputes conventional wisdom. Religion is proving to be a more tenacious element in our national life than many have supposed. That condition extends even to the formidability of the religious factor in particular places. Religion is not proving to be an undifferentiated sentiment or merely a tradition to which we cling; instead, it is something of an aggressive, attracting force. In a nutshell—with elaboration to come—"religious commitment rises among migrants to regions of higher native commitment, such as the South, and falls among migrants to regions of lower commitment, such as the West."[1] That tells us something about the strength of religion in America and about the importance of region.

MIGRANTS NOTICE DIFFERENCES

Americans actually moving from one region to another know quite a bit firsthand about regionalism and religion. They are apt to note very early in a new place which religious groups are in the area and to discern which ones are prominent. Moving to Utah from virtually anywhere impresses a family with the Mormon church's remarkable dominance, not only in the number of churches and adherents but also in its influence over public laws, customs, and attitudes. To transfer into the Southeast opens one's eyes to the strength of a particular cluster of Protestant churches, the Evangelical ones that stand largely in the revivalist tradition. There often seem to be "more Baptists than people," as the joke has it, or at least the number of Baptist churches is overwhelming. The public influence of the southern-style Evangelical denominations is nearly as great in the South as Mormon influence is in its stronghold areas. This shows up to many moving in from "the North"—the blanket reference to all non-southerners—and in many ways, most notably in policies about the sale and use of alcoholic beverages.

These examples are among the most striking, but it takes a long list to show fully the impact that a shift in religious patterns through migration can make on a person's or family's life: black

1. Roger Stump, "Regional Migration and Religious Commitment in the United States," *Journal for the Scientific Study of Religion*, 23:292 (Sept. 1984).

Americans moving from almost any-where to anywhere; Jews moving from centers of Jewish cultural—and demo-graphic—strength to places where there are few Jews and Jewish amenities; Protestants moving to a heavily Roman Catholic area such as an industrial city in the Northeast or to a Hispanic center in the Southwest; people transferring from many places to a normless area such as southern California or penin-sular Florida; and, more specifically, a Kentucky Disciple of Christ moving to New England, a Pennsylvania Quaker to Minnesota, or a Southern Baptist to Montana.

THE FACTOR OF ETHNICITY

Any treatment of religion and region must be alert to factors that we typically associate with religious patterns in spe-cific locations. In particular, ethnicity contributes in a variety of ways to the religious affiliation of individuals and families. The great majority of Amer-icans of Czech or Irish descent—also of Italian, Hispanic, or Polish—are Ro-man Catholics. Americans whose cul-tural tradition is German are likely to be Catholic or Lutheran. Black citizens tend to hold on to the forms of Chris-tianity that achieved success in the Christianization of slaves; hence they tend to belong to Baptist or Methodist churches. White southerners overwhelm-ingly reflect an Anglo-Saxon heritage, as modified by regional history, which makes the Baptist and Methodist—and Presbyterian and Episcopal—commu-nions their natural religious homes.

Some regions are more accustomed to outsiders, to diversity, and to alter-native religious forms than are others. The Mormon region is remarkably sol-id; the South somewhat less so. Al-though some parts of the South have long been home to coexistence—not always peaceful—between Roman Cath-olics and Evangelical Protestants and to the greater diversity that is now char-acteristic of southern cities and towns, the normative role played by left-wing Protestantism there has determined popular perceptions of the basic nature of the Christian religion.

Parts of the Midwest are dominated by Lutherans—often ethnic Lutherans—and parts of the Southwest by Amer-icans of Mexican or other types of Latin descent. Thus, in some large territories and numerous local areas, the spirit of pluralism is absent because diversity is a stranger. Manifest ill will rarely bares its ugly face, but persistent provincialism and ethnocentrism make it difficult for long-time residents to do much more than tolerate strange religious forms. True affirmation of others' right to differ comes slowly; efforts toward un-derstanding and cooperation are nearly as foreign as the alien religious bodies themselves.

By contrast, Americans living in lo-cales that have been heterogeneous for a long time are apt to take it for granted that organized religion comes in multi-ple forms. Cooperative ventures are more common under such conditions. To the degree that the religious people are more secular or liberal, they may simply not concern themselves with the religious posture of others. Also, in some cases they may be committed Christians who hold to a theology that distinguishes positions but does not eval-uate interpretations as more and less valid. Typically in large cities, hetero-geneous cultures, and areas where re-ligious commitment is moderate to low, then, diversity is the expected social condition and toleration is apt to be a cultural value.

We should note that places and areas to which this description applies have a kind of regional status themselves. They may be true regions, a sizable expanse of territory such as the Pacific Northwest, the least churched area in the United States. More often they are metropolitan areas where religious toleration results from some blending of personal indifference with modernity—that is, with diversity and the spirit of pluralism.

SEVEN RELIGIOUS REGIONS

The standard classification of the United States into religious regions was developed by Wilbur Zelinsky in 1961 on the basis of relatively complete data compiled in 1952.[2] Seven religious regions are delineated.

New England. Roman Catholicism pervades and is widely dominant, but old Protestant traditions—namely Congregational, Baptist, and Episcopal—are strong. The region is also the homeland and heartland of Unitarianism.

The midland region. The midland region stretches from the Middle Atlantic states to the Rockies. Methodism is found throughout and Catholicism dominates many places. The Jewish population is notable in the larger cities. Most mainline Protestant bodies appear in considerable strength.

The upper middle-western region. Two religious bodies stand out for size and permeation, Lutheranism and Catholicism. But this region continues to

2. Wilbur Zelinsky, "An Approach to the Religious Geography of the United States: Patterns of Church Membership in 1952," *Annals of the Association of American Geographers*, 51: 139-93 (June 1961).

show the influence of the westward movement from New England in the number of Congregationalists. Most other mainline groups have a significant presence.

The southern region. From Virginia to Texas, Baptists or Methodists rank consistently either first or second; usually the Baptists are most numerous. While the size of these two bodies is massive, other British or indigenous Protestant bodies are well represented, including the Presbyterian, Episcopal, Campbellite, and sectarian groups such as the various Church of God bodies and the Assemblies of God.

The Mormon region. Only negligible numbers of Protestants, Catholics, and Jews appear in Utah, southern Idaho, eastern Nevada, and northern Arizona. Nothing elsewhere in the nation compares with the dominance of the Latter-Day Saints in the intermountain area.

The Spanish Catholic region. The Spanish Catholic region covers the sections of Texas, Arizona, and California reasonably near Mexico and most of New Mexico.

The western region. From Washington down to Oregon and northern and interior California, we find a religious region that is the least recognizable of the seven. Many groups are present, but none is especially large, no one dominates any large zone, and many people are unchurched.

Two notations are needed to clarify Zelinsky's mapping of the American religious regions. The first is that several sizable groups, not being reported in the 1950s data, are not figured into his construction: black Protestant bodies, the Churches of Christ, and most Eastern Orthodox memberships. The second is his modification of the seven regions to include one subarea—Pennsylvania Germans—within the midland region; and to include four subareas—the Carolina piedmont, peninsular Florida, French Catholics, and Texas Germans—within the southern region. While unexceptionability and precision do not characterize this—or any such—mapping of American regions, Zelinsky's effort to describe religious patterns continues to be useful. This construction remains the standard for religious demography in the country.

FIVE RELIGIOUS TYPES

More recently, James R. Shortridge has attempted a new approach in the regionalization of American religion.[3] He concludes that there are five regions, and his are not coordinated with points of the compass or Census Bureau areas. Instead they are clusters or concentrations scattered rather widely around the United States. A less tidy formulation of region than Zelinsky's and than popular perceptions, it does have merit, reflecting levels of subtlety not present in most depictions.

Shortridge's five religious types are (1) intense, conservative Protestant; (2) diverse, liberal Protestant; (3) Catholic; (4) super Catholic; and (5) transition, by which he means a religious type made up of a variety of styles and not identical with any of the other four. The transition type is the closest of the five to the national norm. The term "transition" itself refers to a type in between any and all the others.

3. James R. Shortridge, " A New Regionalization of American Religion," *Journal for the Scientific Study of Religion*, 16:143-54 (June 1977).

The intense, conservative Protestant type is found in much of the South, in Utah and adjacent areas, and parts of the northern plains. "Diverse, liberal Protestant" describes the Middle West and the West Coast. The Catholic type is concentrated in parts of the Northeast and the upper Middle West. Super Catholic areas are French Louisiana and parts of the Spanish Southwest. The transition type is found here and there, but especially in the upper South and Southwest, and in various places in the West. In addition, Shortridge notes the presence of religious islands across the nation, for example, Catholic cities in various seas of Protestantism and diverse, liberal Protestant cities set within intense, conservative Protestant areas.

One suspects that Americans migrating from one section to another would recognize Shortridge's religious types as well as Zelinsky's cultural regions. At any rate, professional geographers reach quite similar conclusions as to major religious regions, even when taking different approaches, as in the cases of Zelinsky and Shortridge. Moreover they generally agree that regionalism is persisting in American society. In fact, writes Shortridge, "a 'self-sorting' process seems to be occurring with people of like minds clustering together to form new culture areas and reinforce old ones." [4] This judgment is corroborated by John Shelton Reed, who has recently observed, "The kinds of people going to California already look like Californians. Conservatives tend to go to the South."[5]

A somewhat surprising element in recent American religious patterns is the dearth of new denominations. The

4. Ibid., p. 152.
5. Interview of John Shelton Reed, *Charlotte Observer*, 25 Nov. 1984.

vigor of religion in American society these days is not often expressed by the formation of new bodies. In fact, the years around 1900 were the last period in which a plethora of new bodies appeared. At that time, nationwide, new conservative Protestant groups were coming into being, many of them known as holiness—emphasizing the life of perfection—or Pentecostal—practicing speaking in tongues. In the meantime, the 1920s witnessed some rupturing owing to the Fundamentalist-Modernist controversy. And in the wake of liberalizing trends characteristic of the 1960s, new Presbyterian and Episcopal bodies were created. A number of denominations live with considerable internal stress in the 1980s, reflecting the determination of conservative segments to mobilize until they have their way. Thus all is not serene in the contemporary picture. But the form this unrest typically takes is not the formation of new denominations.

TRADITIONAL GROUPS REMAIN PROMINENT

As Americans migrate they are apt to find that the denominations traditionally strong in the new region are remaining prominent there. A recent study has disclosed that throughout the twentieth century regional differences in religion have grown stronger. Rather than convergence across regional lines to create a more homogeneous society, the trend has been toward stronger regional differences—in religion, that is, and not with reference to every demographic and socioeconomic variable. Going further, the prominence of a religious body in a given region has contributed to the region's growth and thus to the region's persistent divergence from other regions. In geographer Roger Stump's

words, "The development of divergence through the reinforcement of established patterns suggests . . . that . . . groups [have] a distinct advantage in regions where they [are] already prominent."[6]

The historically strong religious bodies in given regions are difficult to dislodge from prominence. Their continued strong presence is predictable because the flow has been in that direction throughout this century. The persistence of Mormons in Utah, Baptists in the South, Lutherans in the Dakotas, and Catholics in New Mexico, for example, results in the ongoing divergence of those places from other areas or regions of the country.

Regionalism is not dying out in the United States, and the religious factor is one major reason.[7] The denomination that has been dominant, or at least very prominent, for a long time has several advantages working for its continuing position: its extensive infrastructure within the region; its visibility; its reputation for stability; its very size, which serves as a critical mass for promoting enlarged membership; and the mere fact of its being the ranking denomination.[8] For these and other reasons, nothing succeeds like success in the persistence of the prominent denominations and in the continued divergence between religious regions in the United States.

Earlier we noted that the formation of new denominations is not common in recent America. What is new, at least in its intensity and general distribution, is

6. Roger Stump, "Regional Divergence in Religious Affiliation in the United States," *Sociological Analysis*, 45(4) (Winter 1984).

7. See esp. Raymond D. Gastil, *Cultural Regions of the United States* (Seattle: University of Washington Press, 1975).

8. Stump, "Regional Divergence in Religious Affiliation."

the decreasing importance of denominationalism. Historically one tended to
belong to the denomination of one's
family or, in some cases, one chose to
affiliate with a particular denomination
because of its reputation or the social
status it conferred. There is now a
tendency to belong to a congregation
rather than a denomination. This is
particularly true among conservative
Protestants, those standing in mainstream American Evangelicalism.

Especially when Christians of this
orientation move from one place to
another, they search for congregations
of like mind. A family may have belonged to a Methodist, Presbyterian, or
Baptist church but seek out a more
intense, intimate, and biblically conservative congregation in the new place of
residence. Several communities of faith
are growing in numbers and strength as
a result of this shift, among them the
Evangelical Free church, various independent fellowships, and an assortment
of Bible churches. For people interested
in such communities, status is not important but a sense of belonging is.
Open positions on doctrinal issues are
set aside in favor of sharper definitions
and firm standards in both belief and
moral practice.

Thus, family or style of expression
has become the principal consideration
for a sizable company of Americans. A
couple of generations back, people moving about—or casting about for something better in their home community—
would have inclined toward finding a
church of their traditional denomination to affiliate with. Conservatives, or
former moderates moving in a newly
conservative direction, are apt to dis-
regard that factor in preference for the
right sort of congregation, no matter
how it is affiliated.

Implied in that discussion is the decrease in the significance of social class
as a factor in church preference in recent
years. Some continue to choose—perhaps change—denominations because
of the class status one or another is
reputed to enjoy. But the extent of that
pattern of behavior is diminishing. This
seems to be due to the sharper differentiation among choices these days.
Conservatives manifest a new boldness,
both as congregations and as individuals. They are very clear on what they
stand for, to themselves and to outsiders, and people disposed differently
should probably locate themselves elsewhere. Moreover, it is no longer a
liability to belong to such churches. The
public has become more accepting of
eccentric—that is, off-center—practices.
Also, conservatives are little concerned
with what others think about them.

SACRAMENT WORDS

Mention of conservative Protestants
invites attention to formulations by
which we can distinguish conservatives
from liberals, mainline bodies from eccentric ones, and so on. One useful
schema is sacrament words, those central terms used by various bodies to
indicate what is absolutely central to
their belief and their animation. Six
such terms are very common in American Christianity: (1) "Word of God,"
meaning Bible and the principle of authority; (2) "Body and Blood of Christ"—
that is, Communion in the setting of
worship; (3) "born again," the personal
experience of the divine spirit, which
divides life into a before and an after; (4)
"Body of Christ," the church as authority and repository of grace; (5) "New
Testament Christianity," the restoration
to today's church of the exact beliefs and

practices of the earliest church; and (6) "love your neighbor," or understanding faith mainly in ethical terms.

In one sense most Christian denominations honor all six sacrament words. At least each of the six terms points to an aspect of the Christian religion that is ingredient in the whole. In priority, however, they differ markedly. For Catholicism, "Body and Blood of Christ" and "body of Christ" head the list. For Lutherans and Presbyterians, "Word of God" is the foundation for everything. For many Methodists and Congregationalists—now United Church of Christ—"love your neighbor" is the heart of the matter. For revivalistic bodies, "born again" looms largest. In the Campbellite tradition—Disciples of Christ and Churches of Christ—"New Testament Christianity" is the historic watchword. And so on.

Regional religious differences are illuminated by seeing how prominent one or more of the sacrament words is in a regional culture. Catholics moving from the Northeast or Middle West to the South, for example, bring the two body metaphors into a culture dominated by "born again." Lutherans of "Word of God" persuasion find alien the "body of Christ" emphasis when it, rather than "Word of God," stands as the authority. Church people oriented toward "love your neighbor" are perplexed by others' fastidious concern with "New Testament Christianity."

Most Christians agree on most basic Christian teachings. But the particular configuration that characterizes a denomination or a regional culture-religion, built upon the foundation of one or two sacrament words, differentiates one type from another. Often a quasi-doctrinal factor such as sacrament words is salient for distinguishing one

denomination from another and, more important here, for distinguishing one region's religious assumptions or religious imagination from another's.

In view of the modifications we have referred to in the reasons for which people belong to the denominations they do, region would appear to be more prominent than socioeconomic factors. Instead of affiliating with a denomination reputed nationwide to be of the desired social status—upper class, working class, or something else—Americans are now more likely to note what options are available in the local community and choose according to style or orientation. Thus, those migrating are less likely than earlier to decide in advance what their choice will be. Instead they look around and, in many cases, choose specifically on the basis of suitability to their tastes and convictions. There is also a growing, if still small, tendency to import churches similar to ones left behind in the old location in hopes of mission to the new community as well as providing a spiritual home in the new place of residence.

MIGRATION'S IMPACT

Any treatment of region and religion in the United States must take note of the impact of migration that is such a familiar feature in a mobile society. Recently, Roger Stump especially has attended to this issue through statistically based research. He has reached some fascinating conclusions.

In seeking to discover what regional migration does to religious commitment, scholars have applied two conceptual schemes. One is the dislocation model; the other, the adaptation model. According to dislocation theory, when people move from one region to another they experience what is popularly called culture shock, with the result that they realize integration into the structures and life of the new home community slowly and awkwardly, if much at all. In fact, in the case of religion, their level of interest and commitment is likely to decline. In other words, the dislocation they undergo tests severely the genuineness of their religious commitment and suggests that their commitment was not to belief and affiliation in the abstract but to belief and affiliation in a particular—familiar—setting.

Adaptation theory holds that migrants fit into their new environment rather readily, adopting the values accorded high standing there and easing into affiliation with the organizations popular there. Briefly stated, they "adopt patterns of behavior compatible with the norms of their cultural milieu."[9]

Stump's research bears out the validity of the adaptation model. When Americans migrate from one region to another, the level of their commitment befits the level of religious commitment in the new region. Their new level can be higher or lower, depending on the region of new residence, and it can differ from their personal quality of commitment in the region moved away from. People moving into the South, a region where higher levels of native commitment exist, are likely to adopt a higher level of commitment themselves. Conversely, migrants to the West, "where the dominant cultural patterns deemphasize religion," are more likely to experience a decline.[10]

It may be surprising to many that so apparently private—and perhaps culture-transcendent—an aspect of life is heavily influenced by where one lives, indeed the place to which one migrates. We are apt to regard as predictable migrants' adaptation to a number of other local cultural norms. This research indicates that religiosity too bears some correlation with the prevailing culture, even though it is different from what migrants have been accustomed to. Also, we should notice that what is adapted to is not denominational affiliation as such but rather level of commitment.

What Stump's research reveals goes well beyond what happens to people in the process of moving from one region to another. Just as significant are its implications for regionalism—specifically, for the persistence of regional cultures. His findings contest the popular opinion that migration will lead toward the breakdown of particular regional cultures and the homogenization of American life. Instead, he writes,

The results given here indicate that migration need not lead to the decay of regional differences; indeed, if migrants readily conform to regional norms, migration should reinforce those differences. Regional variations in religious attitudes and behavior should thus persist in the United States at least as long as migrants continue to adapt to their new surroundings.[11]

RELIGIOUS REGIONALISM PERSISTS

Many indicators thus point to the persistence of both religion and regionalism in the United States.[12] The vitality

9. Stump, "Regional Migration and Religious Commitment," p. 292.

10. Ibid., p. 302.

11. Ibid., pp. 302-3.

12. A basic work in the history of American religion with reference to geography is Edwin Scott Gaustad, *Historical Atlas of Religion in America* (New York: Harper & Row, 1976); for the recent scene, see Jackson W. Carroll, Douglas W. Johnson, and Martin E. Marty, *Religion in America: 1950 to the Present* (New York: Harper & Row, 1979).

of religion is being maintained in the face of strong pressures toward secularization, itself a powerful force. But the Evangelical resurgence taking place throughout America is also a significant feature of the contemporary scene. In addition, the traditional and mainline churches seem to have regained a sense of direction after a couple of decades of decline in membership and standing. For millions of mainline people, anyway, there never has been any doubt that they would keep on being faithful Christians through their Catholic, Lutheran, Presbyterian, and Episcopal churches. Much the same can be said for a great many Jews. Most mainline religious people have not gotten the word that their kind is said to be abandoning personal and family faith.

As for regionalism, many recent studies disclose its persistence. It is true that we have focused here on one aspect of regionalism—religion—but the evidence extends beyond any small number of factors. We have observed that with regard to some socioeconomic and demographic variables, a national homogenization is occurring—perhaps in clothing styles, foods, accents, and some educational and political values. But real differentiation continues to mark the American people as "*pluribus*" as well as "*unum*." Ethnic pride and local tradition join with historic patterns to assure a richly diverse culture for the foreseeable future.

I would like to offer a concluding unscientific postscript. Students of the role of religion in American culture would profit greatly if, somehow, a question on religious preference could be restored to the decennial census list. Items in this area of the life of Americans appeared on the long list down to 1950. Respect for the concerns that prompted its removal is not difficult to come by: it could be said that now more than ever we need to be vigilant about violation of the sacred boundary between church and state in a democratic society. Nevertheless, one wonders if little is gained and much is lost by the exclusion of religion-related questions from census interviews. Alternatively, it is desirable—if also unlikely—for the Census of Religious Bodies produced decennially from 1906 through 1936 to be reinstituted.

At all events, religion remains a vital and pervasive force in the United States. Consideration of the phenomenon of regionalism only serves to reinforce awareness of that fact. And when the two are treated in coordination, we learn how conservative American society is proving to be in this era.

ANNALS, *AAPSS,* **480,** July 1985

Religion's Very Public Presence

By PEGGY L. SHRIVER

ABSTRACT: The 1984 election emphasized the public role of religion in both parties; much uneasiness about the proper place of religion in politics was revealed. The United States was originally envisioned by some religious groups as a voluntary Christian commonwealth. Although that dream is less persuasive today, religion supplies a continuing definition and critique of the public good. Growing religious diversity produces conflicting views, necessitating rethinking by mainline Protestants. A major difference is between those who nourish nationalism and an individualistic religion and those with a world-encompassing vision and a communal faith. Religion provides sustaining hope and a commitment to wholeness, and it contributes politically, often through coalitions. The role of the religious convictions of politicians was heatedly debated with modest resolution in the 1984 campaign. American democratic ideals are being tested, and religion, in dialogue with science, is challenged to help shape the nation's future.

Peggy L. Shriver has a doctor of humanities degree from Central College in Iowa. She was active as a civic volunteer while raising three children, then became staff executive with the Presbyterian Church, U.S., in Atlanta, Georgia. Currently assistant general secretary with the National Council of the Churches of Christ in the U.S.A., she lives in New York City at Union Theological Seminary, where her husband is president. She is author of The Bible Vote: Religion and the New Right *and numerous articles.*

A N ecumenical prayer breakfast, drawing an estimated ten thousand to the Dallas Reunion Arena, was a major feature of the 1984 Republican National Convention. It was the same site as the 1980 Dallas National Affairs Briefing sponsored by the fundamentalist New Right's Religious Roundtable, at which Southern Baptist Bailey Smith offended many in the public with his comments about God not hearing the prayer of a Jew. Ronald Reagan spoke to both gatherings, and in 1984 Jerry Falwell spoke, too, in benediction over the Republican party. In San Francisco the Democrats listened to the spellbinding rhetoric of a black preacher, Jesse Jackson; considered seminary-trained Gary Hart; and chose as their candidate the son of a Methodist pastor, Walter Mondale. Religion's public presence is very public indeed!

Some Americans are choking on what they feel is too much religion in politics. They include not only those accused by President Reagan of being intolerant of religion but many deeply committed religious citizens who respect both their church and their state. They may sense that religion has important contributions to make to the body politic, but they are troubled by the uses made of religion by politicians and by the clashes of divine right that may stifle rather than illumine political debate. Religion in America has always played a complex public role, and its complexity has grown with the diversity of the nation. It is both too easy and quite impossible to dismiss religion from politics. We need patience to discern the importance of past and present contributions of religion to society, the different religious traditions engaged in public life, and the limits imposed by a pluralistic democracy.

A VISION OF THE PUBLIC GOOD

Vision is one of the major contributions to public life that religion offers. If politics is the organization of the public good, religion helps define both who constitutes "the public" and what is meant by "good."

Enforcement of Sabbath observance and temperance were two specific issues that mustered large religious troops in predominantly Protestant early America, but they were part of a larger vision of a Christian civilization that called forth the energies and hopes of religious citizens in shaping a new nation. Joined to the refreshingly new concept of religious liberty, this vision was perceived as a voluntary Christian commonwealth, to which citizens would flock through the efforts of good people working together with enlightened goals. As William Lee Miller pungently notes, "By enacting the First Amendment and ending established churches in the states, the early American leaders deregulated the religion market."[1]

That dream of a Christian America, not only noncoercive and winsome to its own citizens but persuasive globally, has faded in the twentieth century, argues Robert T. Handy in his recently revised and enlarged classic, *A Christian America: Protestant Hopes and Historical Realities*. He observes that the Protestant era, in which this dream had been sustained, ended by around 1930, although the upsurge of religious vitality after World War II tended to delay awareness of the dream's passing. The Protestant era was eroded by large waves of immigrants from predominantly Roman Catholic cultures; by the

1. William Lee Miller, "The Seminarian Strain," *New Republic*, 9 July 1984, p. 191.

cynicism and secularism bred through World War I, rapid urbanization, and economic depression; and by its own new self-criticism in theology, biblical studies, and ethics.

To those who felt neglected, oppressed, ignored, or blocked out of the Protestant dream, this loss has not been serious. Furthermore, a chastened church is likely to become a more genuinely Christian church. But the evaporation of a dream takes away a significant guiding and driving force for any group of people. Protestant Christians are engaged in finding and constructing a new guiding vision, and now, in the 1980s, this is taking Protestants in various directions. Protestant fundamentalists, such as the Moral Majoritarians, are in fact dusting off the old images of a Christian America and outfitting it as a moral America, in deference to today's religious pluralism, although some fundamentalists do not bother to make that adjustment. The role of America as the city on a hill, a beacon to the rest of the world, given by God a special position of leadership—and the right to be number one in military strength—so long as it cleanses itself of certain moral degradations is compatible with the early Puritan vision. Mainline churches, those that once composed the leadership of the Protestant era and are now central to the National Council of the Churches of Christ in the U.S.A., are struggling to redefine their role in the nation as well as rethinking the nation's place in the world and its peculiar mission.

If there ever was a consensus on the public good in the United States, the abolition of slavery drove a wedge into that comfortable view, challenging both what is good for society and who rightfully belonged in it. Religious people argued on both sides, some taking a courageous stand against slavery. But Protestantism was painfully slow to address the problems of racism and segregation both in society and in its own structures. Similarly, although the rights of women were encouraged in some evangelical circles, the women's suffrage movement was not a key element of the Protestant vision for our democracy. Indeed, battles for women's rights within both Protestant and Roman Catholic churches and in Judaism are far from over. Protestant fundamentalists are attempting to reverse the trends. The poor, disenfranchised by their own despair, have intermittently been championed by the churches, particularly in ecumenical bodies such as the National Council of Churches, and by Roman Catholics, whose immigrant poor have slowly become solid members of the middle class. Unfortunately, Protestantism in some periods of American history resisted the full participation of Catholics in society and political life, as Al Smith was to discover and John F. Kennedy was to overcome. To be sure, however, many church people have led social reform movements that brought about healthy changes in the nation.

The mainline churches and their National Council of Churches, which also includes several Orthodox and small evangelical peace churches, have tried during recent years of national turmoil to expand the concept of the public to include the poor, minorities, women, and even the people of other countries who are adversely affected by U.S. policies. These are strong stands, taken by churches weakened in their own self-esteem with respect to the body politic as they begin to perceive themselves as a minority in the pluralism of modern America. Such stands are difficult enough to take when denominations are feeling secure and confident, but they are especially difficult when both Protestantism—ecumenical-style—and Americanism are under seige. By attempting to listen to anxieties of Christians the world over regarding problems posed by the nuclear age and multinational economic expansion, the National Council of Churches has set itself an agenda of peace with justice, which is quite out of harmony with prevailing political views.

Taking independent stands on public issues has always been a Protestant prerogative. Under the administration of President Jimmy Carter, the National Council of Churches gradually explained itself to this nonecumenically educated Southern Baptist, and the doors of the White House creaked open to the council's leaders as a common position regarding various public policies became evident. The doors have slammed shut again as a new president, schooled by fundamentalist conservatives to see evil in the ways of the National Council of Churches, has resisted contact with these formerly establishment leaders. Statements firmly critical of directions taken by the Reagan administration—such as the National Council of Churches' Governing Board document "The Remaking of America?"—have done little to unlock that door. Politicians are quick to note that ecumenical leadership has not convinced its own denominational ranks to follow in full force.

Definitions of the public and public good by conservative fundamentalists differ considerably from the definitions of mainline Protestants, especially those involved ecumenically. Fundamentalists lift into public view a group of people neglected by politicians because they have been previously aloof to politics,

and left alone by mainline churches because their bristly religiosity is not easy to embrace. Like the thistle, they tend to stand rigidly alone and to permit little ground to others. Much of the public is perceived by them as alien, hostile to the goals of a moral and religiously awakened America that is fulfilling its destiny to spread Christianity to all the world. For the fundamentalists, America's good is to be militarily superior so that it can freely carry out its destiny, and to be morally upright so that God will continue to bless it. Other religious people would not argue with the desire to make the nation morally upright, but they would question the narrowness of the issues of morality and would oppose some of the solutions of the religious Right for rectifying the nation's ills.

Aware of themselves as a vulnerable minority, Jews have been sensitive to including minorities in the public that other groups have only fitfully or recently noticed. Their vision of America has emphasized this country's precious and distinctive tradition of religious liberty rather than its destiny as a citadel of Christendom. They, and many other religious people, are not comfortable with the assurances of Jerry Falwell or of Pat Robertson of the 700 Club and the Christian Broadcasting Network that Armaggedon is near at hand, possibly as a Middle East nuclear conflict, in which converted Jews will join right-thinking Christians in a painless rapture out of the fray and into Christ's millennium.

Much is being written about the new political maturity of Roman Catholics, as they confidently claim their substantial place in the public arena. Roman Catholics now constitute the largest single organized religious bloc in the nation—they number over 50 million. Although there are at least half again as many Protestants, they are fractured into several hundred groups. Both the maturity of the Roman Catholics' arrival in politics and their skill in moral suasion regarding the welfare of the nation are evident in two bishops' pastoral letters, "The Challenge of Peace" and "Catholic Social Teaching and the U.S. Economy." The Pentagon and the State Department paid lavish attention to the peace pastoral's several drafts, and the bishops' thoughtful, searching exploration of one of the primary issues of our time was front-page news throughout the nation.

Why did the nation attend to the bishops' voice when similar positions had been uttered with much lesser effect by several Protestant groups? It was spoken at a timely moment, as the nation was being aroused from a nuclear numbness by talk of limited nuclear war. Furthermore, it was a new initiative at the highest levels in the American Roman Catholic hierarchy. It was a thorough, rigorous, competent piece of work, respected by Protestants as well as Catholics. Not only were the authors fresh actors on the political stage, but they openly invited participation in the process of their thinking—and they got it! It is clear also that the bishops do not deliver a 50-million-strong Catholic vote, as the voices of protest and dissent made evident. A similar attentive furor accompanied the drafting of the letter on the economy. A countergroup was already in place, calling itself the American Catholic Committee, to defend the American economic system. It includes former AT&T president William Ellinghaus, Alexander M. Haig, Jr., William E. Simon, J. Peter Grace, Clare Booth Luce, and American Enterprise Institute scholar Michael Novak.

TRANSCENDENCE AND PERSONAL/COMMUNAL TENSION

Religious traditions infuse the values and loyalties of individual citizens. Some of them baptize an already healthy nationalism. Others nurture a citizenry that subjects the nation to critical judgment higher than the state, that recognizes the legitimacy of other nations and cultures as among God's beloved, and that therefore suspects actions defined by national self-interest and national security alone. Having a transcendent context of global good, this kind of citizenry is sensitive to such attitudes as an imperialistic view of Central America as simply the backyard of the United States. A religiously educated citizenry is wary of reducing any other group of people on earth, including the Soviets, simply to the status of the enemy, because they acknowledge them as part of divine creation, and because in the Christian faith they are enjoined to love their enemies. In that spirit, various religious bodies and ecumenical groups have provided tours to other nations to break down the dividing wall of hostility. There have been people-to-people and church-to-church tours to Central America, the Soviet Union, China, and other places where a more profound understanding is imperative for peaceful and just relations.

Those religious groups that choose to nourish nationalism fare better these days than those with a transcendent, world-encompassing vision. In a time when our nation's ego is bruised, when even its terrifying nuclear power is limited by the very terror evoked by that power, and when its economy is buffeted by forces it cannot control, the global vision is suspect, almost in disrepute, but all the more necessary. To stand as mediator between narrow national self-interest and the interests of global health is a religious role that invites harsh criticism and misunderstanding. Sometimes the mediation is clumsily exercised and risks manipulation or the charge of naiveté in the world of power politics. But a world only of power politics poses an even greater risk in the view of many religious citizens.

The tensions between religious views that encourage nationalism or personal individualism and those that strive to encompass the whole human community are tugging not only the voting public but at the politicians, too. Religion influences political leaders, as William Lee Miller assumes in tracing the backgrounds of recent Democratic nominees for president:

A curious feature of the campaign for the Democratic Presidential nomination seems to have gone unremarked. The candidates for the nomination had been reduced at the end to one Baptist preacher, one son of a Methodist minister, and one graduate of the Yale Divinity School. The immediate predecessor of this year's Democratic nominee was a born-again Baptist deacon who taught an adult Bible class and quoted Reinhold Niebuhr. His predecessor was the son of a Methodist minister who himself went to Garrett Seminary, in Evanston, Illinois, and while a student served as pastor in Methodist churches in the area. And *his* predecessor was Pinky Humphrey, who in his boyhood would sit in the back pews of the Methodist church in Doland, South Dakota, with the son of the minister of that church, and make paper airplanes out of the church bulletins. This last mentioned minister's son, Julian Hartt, became a theologian of distinction at Yale while his boyhood friend was becoming mayor of Minneapolis and Senator from

Minnesota. In the fall of 1958 he was the academic adviser for a new student at the Divinity School, a Nazarene from Kansas and Bethany Nazarene College in Oklahoma, named Gary Hartpence.[2]

A serious curiosity about the role of religion in the lives of U.S. congressional leaders led Peter L. Benson and Dorothy L. Williams to do an unusual piece of research described in *Religion on Capitol Hill: Myths and Realities*.[3] Having discerned that 86 percent definitely believe in God, with only 5 percent leaning toward not believing, and that 75 percent had a moderate to total commitment to religion, they also ascertained a connection between religious beliefs and values and the way congressional people voted.

In their attempt to make sense out of the diversity of religious perspectives of their random sample of 80 responses, Benson and Williams developed a typology, with responses falling into each group as follows: legalistic religionists accounting for 15 percent; self-concerned religionists, 29 percent; integrated religionists, 14 percent; people-concerned religionists, 10 percent; non-traditional religionists, 9 percent; and nominal religionists, 22 percent. They found that the essential filter for discerning a relationship between religion and voting was whether one had an "I" or a "we" approach to life, as shaped by one's religious heritage. For some religious groups, such as those in all traditions that might be called fundamentalist, personal accountability to God, obedience to moral law, and individual encounter with the Divine are the primary focus of religion. For other groups,

2. Ibid.
3. Peter L. Benson and Dorothy L. Williams, *Religion on Capitol Hill: Myths and Realities* (New York: Harper & Row, 1982).

especially those with an ecumenical view, the communal dimension of faith, the accountability before God to one's neighbor, and the releasing power of forgiveness are primary. The emphasis of the fundamentalist groups tends to translate into an individualism that says that good individuals, not government, make a good society. The emphasis of the ecumenical groups is disclosed as a collective moral view that says that in a systemic world a good society helps make good people, thus government is important. Although common sense and good theology would insist that both views have some hold on the truth, but not an exclusive hold, the tendency for the extremes of these positions to do battle persists.

When the communal vision is joined with the personal encounter with God, the strength of both religious emphases is enhanced. A contribution of religion to public life is also hope, which provides motivation and staying power for the long haul of a just, peaceful, morally sound political vision. A recent study sponsored by Connecticut Mutual Life— *The Impact of Belief*—and another coordinated by the National Council of Churches—the *Annenberg/Gallup Religion and Television Study*—both document the political participation of religiously committed people, which is greater than that of the average citizen. Among heavy viewers of religious television, 75 percent had voted in the 1980 election. Citizens to whom religion is very important are more involved in their communities, attend more meetings, vote more, and belong to more civic groups than those who are not very committed religiously. They tend also to be an active part of a church community, which sustains them with friendship and encouragement.

This is further elaborated in the Urban Policy Study, conducted in the early 1970s in the Chapel Hill area of North Carolina by Donald W. Shriver and Karl A. Ostrom. The study found that

the core ethical dispositions of the Judeo-Christian tradition are best nourished when (1) political activity in public life, (2) worship in a religious community, and (3) interpersonal dialogue on the meaning of faith for all of life *are found together in the lives of people.* Without exception we found that merely talking about public issues in the context of congregational life without active involvement leads to a *lower* level of ethical maturity than is found in the public at large!

But one of the most surprising of all our findings was that people's general spirits, and their freedom from such psychosomatic complaints as insomnia and stomach trouble, are more clearly associated with a sense of political well-being than they are even with happiness at home or satisfaction with one's friends.[4]

COALITIONS, COMMITMENTS, AND HUMAN COMMUNITY

Religion at its best assists a democracy to blend its many self-interested voices into a chorus rather than a cacophony, because it encourages the numerous publics to care about the total public. C. S. Lewis's *Tales of Narnia* depicts the sinful state of Narnia's populace in the person of dwarfs among the creatures of the land. The dwarfs' motto is "The dwarfs are for the dwarfs." A religious conversion of the dwarfs would change their motto to "The dwarfs are for Narnia, and the dwarfs are part of Narnia." Unfortunately, religious groups sometimes degenerate into their own self-interested faction in the body pol-

4. Donald W. Shriver, Jr., and Karl A. Ostrom, *Is There Hope for the City?* (Philadelphia: Westminster Press, 1977), pp. 109, 155.

itic, seeking in the halls of justice only justice—or even privilege—for themselves.

The coalitional style has been an effective method for religious groups and similarly concerned secular groups to band together on particular issues without requiring creedal unanimity. The Anti-Saloon League, formed in 1895, with its loose national federation of state and local leagues, is a coalitional forerunner of the Moral Majority, with even a similar sense of American civilization battling for its life. The civil rights and anti-Vietnam war coalitions of the sixties have since dissolved; but a new coalition is forming around the nuclear threat, and this coalition involves some of the same groups and individuals as did those of the sixties, as well as many newcomers concerned with peace. Religious and secular groups intermingle in these coalitions, in which the force of numbers, combined with a common goal, is the overriding strategy.

Conservative religious groups, historically extremely independent and disparaging of ecumenism as least-common-denominator watered-down religion, have banded together in coalitions over the past five years that are themselves a practical ecumenism, if not an intentional witness to Christian unity. The Moral Majority, a political coalition that includes mainly fundamentalist Protestants, contains a smattering of Jews, Roman Catholics, Mormons, and morally indignant persons of no particular religious background. Christian Voice, another coalition, appeals openly only to Christian fundamentalists. A variety of such groups and television personalities with a religious following sit around the Roundtable, join Library Court, or participate in coalitions of coalitions such as Coalitions for Amer-

ica and the Council for National Policy. Familiar religious rightists like Ed McAteer, of the Roundtable; Tim LaHaye, of the Moral Majority; Robert Billings, also of the Moral Majority; and James Robison, a television evangelist, join politicians like Paul Weyrich, Howard Phillips, Philip Crane, and direct-mail entrepreneur Richard Viguerie to map strategy on issues of mutual concern.[5]

In 1980 *Newsweek* summarized the issues of the religious Right cogently, and the list has not changed significantly since then:

The concerns of born-again politics are defined by Falwell's agenda for the '80s—a pro-family, pro-life, pro-morality platform that, in a triumph of political packaging, turns out to be considerably more "anti" than "pro." Among other things, Moral Majority—and its evangelical allies—are against abortion, ERA, gay rights, sex education, drugs, pornography, SALT II, the Department of Education and defense cuts. They are for free enterprise, a balanced budget, voluntary prayer in the public schools and a secure Israel.[6]

Despite the defeat of the Equal Rights Amendment; support for equal access by religious groups to public school space during off-hours, which the National Council of Churches also supported; Nancy Reagan's adoption of the drug issue as her particular concern; the push for voluntary prayer in public schools; anti-abortion efforts of the current administration; and the largest military budget in history, there is still muttering in the extreme Right that a new political party may be the only way

5. For a more elaborate listing of groups, leaders, coalitions, and issue agendas, see Peggy L. Shriver, *The Bible Vote: Religion and the New Right* (New York: Pilgrim Press, 1981).

6. Helen J. Mayer et al., "A Tide of Born-Again Politics," *Newsweek*, 15 Sept. 1980, p. 32.

to effectuate all their goals. Having married into a Jesse Helms-like anti-communism, these political perfectionists find soft spots in the Reagan administration. Uncompromising zeal, fueled by righteous indignation, passionate certainty, and a sense of divine authority, is both the penetrating power of the religious Right and its Achilles' heel in a democracy, in which graceful compromise is essential to the maintenence of unity and order. There is some evidence that a defection from the Reagan administration would not gain unanimous approval within the leadership ranks of the religious Right.

The Jewish community has its own diverse factions that identify with various other religious segments of the society. The issue of Israel has caused some strained relations with mainline Protestants, who try to adjudicate the interests of all parties in the Middle East, but some Jewish leaders find them insufficiently attentive to their interests. Tension over Israel has made alliance with Moral Majoritarians more attractive to some; it has also encouraged the exploration of that and other delicate issues with more moderate evangelicals. Rifts between Jews and blacks, magnified by incidents in the Jesse Jackson campaign, complicate the historic alliance around civil rights and economic-justice issues.

Roman Catholics at times join hands with the National Council of Churches, especially on issues of peace and justice. On subjects such as abortion or tuition tax credits for private schools, they reach out to conservative religious groups that share their views. It is clear, however, that although the Catholic church hierarchy may have a firm and consistent stance on issues such as abor-

tion, their congregational constituency is of a much-divided mind.

From the Dallas speech of President Reagan at the prayer breakfast to the silencing of the campaign on 7 November, the role of religion in politics has been headline news. Much silliness as well as thoughtful exchange entered the public debate. Just possibly the general public became a little more aware of the issues at stake. President Reagan sensibly saw an inseparable relation between politics and morality, and he declared religion to be the fountain of morality, which is at least a partial truth. But he branded as intolerant of religion anyone who opposed voluntary school prayer. The general secretary of the National Council of Churches, in a less noticed retort, branded intolerant those who see as intolerant people who disagree about sincerely held, theologically based religious positions on school prayer! Both Walter Mondale and Geraldine Ferraro immediately realized that the issue of religion in politics was a genuine campaign issue, and clouds of rhetorical clarification billowed from all sides.

Whether one's religious convictions should influence one's views as a politician became the nub of the debate, with bishops, archbishops, governors, presidential and vice-presidential hopefuls, assorted clerics, and innumerable journalists all providing definitive views. Mondale and Ferraro stepped off on the wrong foot by seeming to imply that religion is simply a private matter, not influential in one's public decision making. Archbishop O'Connor implied at least as awkwardly that no sincere Catholic could vote for a politician who did not oppose abortion, thereby apparently endorsing Reagan. Jesse Jackson, freed from the encumbrance of being a nominee, said,

You know real religious fervor by the fruit it bears. You certainly do not say let's pray in school and then cut breakfast and lunch for poor children. For a man who does not go to church regularly, who is not an officer in the church, to try to somehow become a national theologian and to exploit genuine religious fervor is not a healthy atmosphere.[7]

My own candidate for "national theologian" would be Governor Mario Cuomo, whose speech at Notre Dame was the clearest effort to acknowledge the role of church teachings and the obligations of a politician to a diverse electorate. Statements by the Roman Catholic bishop James W. Malone to the National Conference of Catholic Bishops and the prior public statement of the United States Catholic Conference were helpful concerning church teaching, but they did not wrestle with the dilemma of the politician who is also religious.

Although there is no elbow room in this overview of religion's public presence to sort out the subtleties and counterpoints of this debate, there is still an overriding temptation to add another clarifying word. Every citizen, church, secular group, and politician has the right in a democracy to attempt to sway the electorate toward a particular ethical or religiously derived view. Where there is no public consensus, all citizens as well as politicians ought to seek remedies in the law that allow some latitude for other views. Sometimes the best legislation in circumstances of greatly divided opinion is none at all.

Before being elected, the politician has an obligation to the voter to express

religiously held moral convictions, but also to promise to abide by the law and to respect the views of others to whom one is accountable. Once elected, a politician should seek a legal compromise that accommodates as many different publicly held moral views as possible, while advocating his or her own position as part of the debate. After a law is passed, however, the political leader must either oversee the law of the land or resign out of conscience, as should have been clear in the election campaign. Citizens, likewise, may choose civil disobedience to a law found abhorrent to conscience and take the consequences of breaking the law. Through democratic process, citizens and politicians disturbed by bad law may continue to pressure for change. Churches may exhort citizens to do any of these things appropriate to religiously tutored conscience. This, of course, sounds much neater in the abstract than when applied to emotion-laden issues such as abortion.

CHALLENGES FOR THE FUTURE

A group of Christian visitors touring the United States before attending the Vancouver Assembly of the World Council of Churches commented soberly to some American church leaders, "You are engaged in a battle for the soul of America." Not sure of all that was implied in their observation, I have tried to construct a collage from the concerns of many visitors from afar and what they have been challenging American Christians to consider. Admittedly risky and impressionistic, this is what comes to mind:

Every nation has to do battle to reaffirm its ideals in every generation. The United States is no exception, and in times of rapid change and global upheavals the transmission of past ideals is particularly difficult. Having attained a high standard of living far above most of the rest of the world, and now having that standard challenged by oil cartels, world inflation, and global shifts in industry, how far are you prepared to go simply to protect your economic interests? Has a materialistic culture won out over your democratic ideals? Many of you no longer bother to vote or to exercise your precious civic liberties. Your nation, in its past generosity, has welcomed to its shores people from all over the world, but today it is feeling inundated by refugees and displaced persons from Southeast Asia, Central America, and other areas of political and economic strife. How will you handle this situation today? Will these newcomers, fleeing one oppression, merely enter another? Your problems of race and poverty are exacerbated by these new populations, by economic instability, by high unemployment, and by a rampant individualism that seeks to protect its own welfare alone. Do you still try to believe in the worth and dignity of each individual so that collectively you care for all citizens?

You are in all probability the most powerful nation on earth, and you are a major arms merchant to the world, but you act as if you are insecure and continue to bleed your economy for more weapons. The other countries fear both your power and your insecurity. You have far better things to export! Your experiment in democracy, your freedom of speech and religious liberty, your concern for the poor and for human rights, your energy and imagination, your frank and boistrous popular culture, your economic ingenuity, your sense of potential, your willingness to roll up your sleeves, your problem-solving attitude, your openness. Please, don't blow it!

If such observations have even some validity, they are both a judgment and a challenge. Religion's public presence will help to shape the choices made by our nation, as well as our awareness and definition of the issues to be addressed. It is impossible to think of the future, however, without introducing the most obvious influence upon and discerner of it—modern science and technology. The relationship of science and theology, of technology and religious ethics, is characterized at best as peaceful coexistence and more often as two mutually exclusive ways of perceiving the world, deprecatory of one another. Issues in the public sphere are often profoundly grounded in technology and the new thrusts of modern science. Genetic engineering, nuclear power, environmental degradation, euthanasia and prolonged deferment of death, abortion, computer communication and privacy, energy choices and trade-offs, automation and the work ethic, technology transfer to other countries, and star wars military space technology, for example, stir deep anxieties of a religious and ethical nature even among secularists. Scientists are increasingly uncomfortable with the world they are helping to create and with the decisions made with an expertise that defines itself as value free.

Christianity has its uncomfortable memories of an embarrassing battle with Galileo, who was recently reinstated by the Roman Catholic church. The search for truth imperils authority and becomes itself imperiled. As Leon Kass says insightfully, "If philosophy *was*, and modern science *is*, the attempt to replace opinion by knowledge, and if every society is rooted in certain dominant opinions—whether about the gods or justice or the equal rights of man— science essentially endangers society by endangering the supremacy of its ruling beliefs." And he notes, "The sciences not only fail to provide their own standards for human conduct; their findings cause us to doubt the truth and the ground of those standards we have held and, more or less, still tacitly hold."[8]

As keeper of those standards that are rooted in religion, including the most basic questions of the value and nature of humanity and the nature of nature itself, religious leaders must attempt a new engagement with scientific thinkers about truth and values. Both have been chastened to induce a new humility, which is itself hopeful for more productive dialogue.

8. Leon Kass, "Modern Science and Ethics," *University of Chicago Magazine*, p. 27 (Summer 1984).

In sum, religion brings to public life a sense of the context in which our collective life is lived. It struggles to enlarge the community's and its own understanding of who should be respected and included in the public. Religious citizens and leaders subject their own understanding and that of their nation to the scrutiny and critique of a higher law and wisdom, even though that law and wisdom may be imperfectly perceived. Conscious that they are not alone in their efforts, nor unmercifully judged in their shortcomings, they press on in hope and, when they are truly faithful, in humility.

ANNALS, *AAPSS,* **480,** July 1985

Civil Religion in
an Uncivil Society

By N. J. DEMERATH III and RHYS H. WILLIAMS

ABSTRACT: Civil religion denotes a religion of the nation, a nonsectarian faith that has as its sacred symbols those of the polity and national history. Recent scholars have portrayed it as a cohesive force, a common canopy of values that helps foster social and cultural integration, but this perspective may now be at odds with a complex reality. Ours is an increasingly differentiated society with the rise of group politics and subcultures. The forms of civil religion remain, but the cultural cohesion it purportedly reflects is dissolving. Civil-religious discourse has become a tool for legitimating social movements and interest-group politics. A critical examination of the current uses of civil religion must lead to a critical reanalysis of the society at large as well as the concept itself.

N. J. Demerath III is currently professor and chair of the Department of Sociology at the University of Massachusetts, Amherst. Previously, he taught at the University of Wisconsin, Madison. He is author or coauthor of several books and articles concerning the sociology of culture, religion, and political movements.

Rhys H. Williams is a graduate student in sociology at the University of Massachusetts, Amherst. His interests include politics, religion, and culture.

F EW concepts have made a quicker transition from the nation's scholarly journals to its op-ed pages than civil religion. Although the phrase has a long European pedigree, "civil religion" was given special American meaning toward the end of the 1960s, a decade that reaffirmed our political ideals even as it witnessed a deepening sense of political conflict. Civil religion seemed an idea whose time had come, a source of unifying hope in the midst of fragmentation and despair. Since then, the concept has become almost self-illustrating as its very use tends to create the reality it describes. It has become a kind of intellectual incantation on behalf of our cultural virtues, whatever our structural liabilities.

Rather than another celebration of the concept and the collectivity for which it stands, this article offers a more critical perspective. Indeed, in offering a critique of the literature concerning American civil religion, it cannot avoid a critique of contemporary America itself. The article begins by tracing the roots of civil religion as a concept, noting two quite different traditions. It then considers the evidence on behalf of a civil-religious syndrome in this country, noting its limitations. An examination of recent political developments suggests that civil religion may no longer be functioning as its more idealistic proponents have portrayed it. This leads in turn to the relationship between the civil religion and an increasingly fractured culture. It is here that the tension between what the nation ought to be and what it has become emerges with special poignance.

BACKGROUND AND CURRENT CONCEPTIONS

Like one of its principle icons, the Statue of Liberty, the American concept of civil religion comes from France. The term itself was coined by the eighteenth-century French Enlightenment philosopher Jean-Jacques Rousseau. He intended it to denote a constructed religion, a form of deism that would instill in citizens a love of country and a motivation to civic duty. It was to be a religion both of and for the state. Most Enlightenment thinkers predicted and applauded the demise of traditional Christian orthodoxy that was to accompany surging education, democratization, and industrialization. They considered reason the only necessary and emancipating replacement. In fact, France's First Republic even attempted to institutionalize worship of the goddess of reason. But Rousseau had realized that reason alone was insufficient to bind the masses to the state. There was still a need for religion, albeit of a new type. He described its purposes and forms in this way:

But there is a purely civil profession of faith, the articles of which it behoves the Sovereign to fix, not with the precision of religious dogmas, but treating them as a body of social *sentiments* without which no man can be either a good citizen or a faithful subject.

The dogmas of this civil religion should be few, clear and enunciated precisely, without either explanation or comment. The positive clauses are:—the existence of a powerful, intelligent, beneficient and bountiful God: the reality of the life to come: the reward of the just, and the punishment of evil-doers: the sanctity of the Social Contract and of the Laws. The negative element I would confine to one single article:—intolerance, for that belongs to the creeds which I have excluded.[1]

More than a century later, in the early 1900s, another French thinker gave the

1. Jean-Jacques Rousseau, "Of Civil Religion," in *Social Contract,* ed. Ernest Barker (London: Oxford University Press, 1960), pp. 305-6.

concept a somewhat different bent. The sociologist Emile Durkheim agreed with Rousseau that society could not be held together by reason and practical political motives alone. Yet Durkheim went further in arguing that it was absolutely essential to any social order that it have at its core the cohesion and shared values fostered by religion. After studying accounts of a traditional Australian tribe without marked differentiation between its religion and its politics, Durkheim concluded with his classic circularity: "If religion has given birth to all that is essential in society, it is because the idea of society is the soul of religion."[2]

Of course, Durkheim was not naive enough to believe that a large and complex nation-state could have the same type of religious system as an aboriginal tribe. His point was more subtle. A healthy society depends upon the affection and respect toward the collectivity fostered by religious sentiments and rituals. At the deepest level, religion is a basic component of any society's deep culture, its irreducibly preconscious core. But this must be continually reenacted and reinforced:

There can be no society which does not feel the need of upholding and reaffirming at regular intervals the collective sentiments and collective ideas which make its unity and personality. Now this moral remaking cannot be achieved except by the means of reunions, assemblies, and meetings where the individuals, being closely united to one another, reaffirm in common their common sentiments; hence come ceremonies which do not differ from regular religious ceremonies, either in their object, the results which

they produce, or the processes employed to attain these results.[3]

Thus Rousseau and Durkheim produced the two classic accounts of civil religion, although their differences are critical. For Rousseau civil religion was to be constructed and imposed from the top down as an artificial source of civic virtue. For Durkheim civil religion welled up naturally from the bottom, from the very depths of the social experience itself. From this perspective, religious society and civil society were coterminous; the polity was but another extension and representation of a collectivity that was nothing if not religious at its base. Rousseau and Durkheim represented two quite different intellectual traditions in Enlightenment political philosophy and functionalist sociology. Not surprisingly, the result is a conceptual legacy in logical tension as civil religion becomes a canopy of common cultural values extended over a structurally differentiated and secularizing society. We shall return to this tension later.

Meanwhile, accounts of American civil religion have been disproportionately Durkheimian. As early as 1953, W. Lloyd Warner described the religious properties of our Memorial Day observances from the social-anthropological perspective he shared with Durkheim.[4] Others have described the consensual residue of our Judeo-Christian heritage, including Will Herberg in his description of our much-diluted "religion in general."[5] But surely the most provocative analysis of American civil religion

2. Emile Durkheim, *The Elementary Forms of the Religious Life* (New York: Free Press, 1912), p. 419.

3. Ibid., p. 427.
4. W. Lloyd Warner, *American Life: Dream and Reality* (Chicago: University of Chicago Press, 1953).
5. Will Herberg, *Protestant, Catholic, Jew* (Garden City, NY: Doubleday, 1955).

came from Robert Bellah in 1967.[6] Bellah's seminal article has spawned a considerable literature of debate, extension, and reconsideration.

Richey and Jones examined this literature and extracted five major uses or connotations of civil religion.[7] These include folk religion, religious nationalism, democratic faith, Protestant civic piety, and the transcendent universalist religion of nation. While all have a certain validity, the last is the most central. This is the meaning originally stressed by Bellah and then refined in the conceptual reviews of Coleman,[8] Gehrig,[9] and Hammond.[10] It is certainly the

6. Robert N. Bellah, "Civil Religion in America," *Daedalus*, 96:1-21 (Winter 1967), reprinted in R. N. Bellah, *Beyond Belief* (New York: Harper & Row, 1970). By referring to the sociological work on civil religion generally as the work by Bellah, we are masking much variation in the work of several different, creative scholars. In fact, there are several sources devoted to historical and conceptual nuances only briefly mentioned here. See Russell E. Richey and Donald G. Jones, *American Civil Religion* (New York: Harper & Row, 1974); Sidney Mead, *The Nation with the Soul of a Church* (New York: Harper & Row, 1975); and Gail Gehrig, *American Civil Religion: An Assessment*, Society for the Scientific Study of Religion, Monograph Series, no. 3 (Storrs, CT: Society for the Scientific Study of Religion, 1979). Readers interested in subtler shades of meaning are encouraged to consult these sources; we wish to settle on a more or less majority definition and then deal with the substantive issues of civil religion in the current body politic.

7. Richey and Jones, *American Civil Religion*, pp. 4-18.

8. John A. Coleman, "Civil Religion," *Sociological Analysis*, 31(2):67-77 (Summer 1970).

9. Gehrig, *American Civil Religion: An Assessment*, p. 18.

10. Phillip E. Hammond, "The Conditions for Civil Religion: A Comparison of the United States and Mexico," "The Rudimentary Forms of Civil Religion," and "Pluralism and Law in the Formation of American Civil Religion," in *Varieties of Civil Religion*, ed. R. N. Bellah and P. E. Hammond (New York: Harper & Row, 1980).

meaning that is most squarely within the Durkheimian tradition, hence the one to which most sociological allegiance has been pledged.

Bellah's account of civil religion used words that come directly from Durkheim:

What we have, then, from the earliest years of the republic is a *collection of beliefs, symbols, and rituals with respect to sacred things and institutionalized in a collectivity*. This religion—there seems no other word for it—while not antithetical to and indeed sharing much in common with Christianity, was neither sectarian nor in any specific sense Christian.[11]

For Bellah American civil religion is a self-contained religion, with its own set of sacred symbols, distinct from any particular sectarian or churchly meanings. While grounded in the Christian tradition, its symbols and meanings are uniquely American, transcending denominational or religious differences. The churches have helped to bolster civil religion, but they are not the primary guardians of its traditions. Similarly, although government and political acts and rituals are a part of the civil-religious institutional base—for example, presidential addresses, Fourth of July celebrations—the civil religion does not depend on any particular administration or political institution for its support. Bellah is explicit and adamant that American civil religion is not to be confused with national self-worship. Civil religion, being transcendent and universal, is an understanding of America's role in history and each person's role as an American citizen. Certainly it goes beyond mere nationalism by placing the nation before a God who is both Author and Judge. It also goes beyond the various folk religions investigated by

11. Bellah, *Beyond Belief*, p. 175, italics added.

Warner and others, as well as the general way of life embodied in American religion according to Herberg.

Bellah noted more recently that the crux of the civil religion issue is the "religio-political problem."[12] That is, what stance are religion and politics, faith and power, to take toward each other? In contrast to the form of power at the disposal of the state, religion draws upon an authority that transcends worldly matters. To what degree and under what conditions does religion lend an aura of legitimacy to political power, and to what extent can the state enact the shared values and moral order at the religious core?

There is another problem at the heart of civil religion. In addition to Bellah's concern over religion and politics, there is the question of religion and culture. In both cases, there is a danger of assuming relationships that are at best problematic. Indeed, another Durkheimian characteristic of the American civil-religious literature is the tendency to define a phenomenon in terms of its consequences. This often produces a near tautology by limiting analysis to only those cases that fulfill the conditions set. For example, Gehrig draws on Bellah and others in defining our civil religion this way: "American civil religion is the religious symbol system which relates the citizen's role and American society's place in space, time, and history to the conditions of ultimate existence and meaning."[13]

But does American civil religion in fact fulfill these tasks? In seeking an answer to this critical question, we must first establish the independent existence

of a civil religion and then ask how this relates to both politics and culture in the contemporary United States.

EVIDENCES OF AN AMERICAN CIVIL RELIGION

Like any complex social phenomenon, civil religion may exist in different ways at different levels of a society. It may also be sought through different strategies with differing results. So far it has been most commonly cited as a dimension of our national political ceremonies, using evidence that is part historical and part anecdotal. Warner found it in the religious tone of local Memorial Day observances,[14] and Conrad Cherry has identified it in the funerals of political leaders.[15] Others have commented on the invariant references to a general God—but not a sectarian Christ—in presidential addresses, Supreme Court decisions, and legislative declarations. The written words of American statesmen, politicians, and religious leaders often place the nation in a direct relationship with divinity, whether asking for its blessings or calling the body politic back to its founding values. And certainly the elevation of many political leaders to the status of quasi-saints—Washington and Jefferson—or martyrs—Lincoln and John F. Kennedy—has a distinctly religious cast.

As intuitively important as all of this is in establishing the case for an American civil religion, questions remain. One concerns the degree to which civil religion is actually experienced by individual Americans as part of their own lives

12. Bellah and Hammond, *Varieties of Civil Religion,* p. vii.
13. Gehrig, *American Civil Religion: An Assessment,* p. 18.

14. Warner, *American Life.*
15. Conrad Cherry, "American Sacred Ceremonies," in *American Mosaic,* ed. P. E. Hammond and Benton Johnson (New York: Random House, 1970).

and life decisions. Work in the Bellah vein has been criticized for being too elitist and too historical while neglecting the contemporary citizen in the street and suburb. Thus, Bellah analyzes national documents such as the Declaration of Independence and the inaugural addresses of American presidents as well as the writings of various founding ancestors. There is little evidence, however, of the general public's adherence to civil-religious principles; there is no attempt to measure its degree of urgency. Perhaps this is why Bellah discerns the "transcendent universalist" ethos in his civil religion. By focusing on elite political sources, Bellah finds a prophetic theology not uncovered by Warner, Cherry, and others in their ethnographies of small-town America and its folk-religious rituals. Further, Bellah's elite perspective leads him toward a normative stance on civil religion. Rather than determine what people believe and act upon in their daily lives, he discovers what we, as a people, are called to be in the nation's best and brightest historical moments. America ought to have a civil religion of such worth and urgency; indeed, this is Bellah's overriding implication.

But Bellah is by no means alone in the vineyard of civil-religious scholarship. He has stimulated considerable activity in others, including researchers who have used questionnaires and sample surveys to examine the prevalence of civil religion at the individual level. With rare exception,[16] these studies have supported the existence of an American civil religion.[17] Without belaboring the

statistical details or the validity of the various questions developed and combined into summary indexes, several general findings are consistent and significant.

First, people's civil-religious attitudes cling together while standing apart from other church behavior and religious belief factors, indicating a syndrome somewhat distinct from sectarian/denominational religiosity. Second, civil religion does not stand so far apart as to be disqualified as a truly religious phenomenon. People who score high in other aspects of religiosity, such as church attendance and religious belief, also tend to score high here. In fact, the more conservative persons are in churchly religion, the more likely they are to score high on civil religion. While this last finding should give pause to those who identify civil religion with the liberal prophetic thrust in American history, the overall pattern is encouraging. Civil religion emerges from survey data as a genuine religious dimension, distinct from but related to traditional and conservative religious outlooks.

The relationship between civil religion and what can be called creedal or sectarian religion is critical. The case for civil religion would be damaged if either no relationship at all emerged or if the relationship was so close as to suggest that the two are one and the same. Here is a rare case in which a theory can be sustained by ambiguity, and surely there

16. Michael C. Thomas and Charles C. Flippen, "American Civil Religion: An Empirical Study," Social Forces, 51(2):218-25 (Dec. 1972).

17. See Ronald C. Wimberley et al., "The Civil Religious Dimension: Is It There?" Social Forces, 54(4):890-900 (June 1976); William A. Cole and P. E. Hammond, "Religious Pluralism, Legal Development and Societal Complexity," Journal for the Scientific Study of Religion, 13(2):177-89 (June 1974); James A. Christenson and R. C. Wimberley, "Who Is Civil Religious?" Sociological Analysis, 39(1):77-83 (Spring 1978); and R. C. Wimberley, "Civil Religion and the Choice for President: Nixon in '72," Social Forces, 59(1):44-61 (Sept. 1980).

is more than enough ambiguity to suffice in the results we have summarized. But there is another problem lurking here. Any long-term cultural motif or ideology must have an institutional base to provide organized and ritualized reinforcement. If civil religion's base is not creedal religion, what is it? There are various possibilities. For example, Hammond sought to uncover the institutional roots of American civil religion in the courts and the universalistic ethos of American law. As he put it, "If civil religious ideologies are thought of as balloons I am asking who is able and willing to hold the balloon strings."[18] Alas, Hammond's data suggest that Americans do not regard the law and the courts in the way he hypothesized. Whatever the potential of the legal system to be the "churches of the civil religion," it does not now function in that capacity. Meanwhile, another possible institutional base is the American political system.

POLITICS AND
CIVIL RELIGION:
WHO'S USING WHOM?

Like its relationship with creedal religion, civil religion's relationship with politics and government must tread a narrow line. Too distant and it is only a marginal irrelevancy; too close and it becomes an idolatrous cloak of transcendental rhetoric tossed over the pursuit of momentary ends. Bellah insisted that America's civil religion was not mere national self-worship. However, as civil religion seeks political succor, it is vulnerable to being co-opted altogether. It is important to distinguish between civil religion as discourse and as determinant. Various groups may use the

18. Hammond, "Conditions for Civil Religion," p. 44.

discourse as a way of articulating their special values and agendas. Few may be truly impelled by its deeper claims.

America is often understood not as striving to understand and follow God's will, but as the very embodiment of that will. It is no accident that the original prophetic quotation "My country, right or wrong; when right to be kept right, when wrong to be put right" was popularly shortened to only the self-congratulatory first phrase. The message was clear: my country is always right. The transcendent universalist aspect may be too challenging and too subtle to survive the bumper-sticker world of political rhetoric. Still, after originating in the Puritan vision of a moral covenant between God and civil society, it remains a latent strain in American religiopolitical legitimation that surfaces in the midst of crisis and charisma. Martin Luther King, Jr.'s ringing words—"thank God Almighty I'm free at last"—united the message of black evangelical Protestantism with a vision of a socially and politically integrated nation; Jesse Jackson built a presidential campaign on the civil-religious values of democratic inclusion and just retribution, all in the rhythmic cadences of the pulpit; Jerry Falwell has delineated a plan of political action that assumes an omnipotent God seated in judgment over the nation. The fact that both Left and Right use a civil-religious discourse to frame their political visions may suggest universality. On the other hand, it may also mean the civil religion has become a sophisticated gloss.

Civil-religious language has long enabled Americans to use religion in defining themselves politically. It was, and is, a language decidedly Christian in tone and assumptions, but cleansed of references that are too specific or narrow. It was a way of certifying political morality without violating the separation of church and state and the etiquette of nonsectarian pluralism, whatever the sectarian power configuration might be. Indeed, civil-religious discourse produced a particularly American response to the religiopolitical problem: a culturally legitimate religion of the nation that transcended sectarian differences while justifying a social order at least partially based on those differences. The civil religion never became the civil church. But several developments have pushed the nation past the conditions that allow a truly unifying civil religion. Politically there has been an over-heralded but nonetheless real de-alignment of traditional parties and coalitions. There has occurred a growing issue awareness and group consciousness as various constituencies have begun to refashion their political identity in terms of ethnicity, race, gender, and/or a single salient issue.

In all of this, the relationship between politics and religion has taken a paradoxical turn. Richard Neuhaus has recently deplored the "naked public square" or the absence of true religious sensibilities in political decisions of moment.[19] At first blush the charge seems peculiar and perhaps self-serving. Neuhaus laments the lack of input from his own former religious allegiance— liberal Protestantism—as a way of justifying the influence of his current religious community—the new conservatism. Surely few national political campaigns in recent history have been more "religionized" than those of Ronald Reagan. And yet the religious significance of the Reagan campaigns is deceptive.

19. Richard John Neuhaus, *The Naked Public Square* (Grand Rapids, MI: William B. Eerdsmans, 1984).

Of course, to many it seems strange that religion should have played any role at all in the Reagan-Mondale contest. After all, were church and state not formally separated nearly 200 years ago? And for at least the last 100 years, has the trend not been one of increasing secularization, a process by which traditional religion of all sorts loses public power and private urgency?

One could understand Reagan's campaign if it were in the great tradition of American third-party politics—fascinating but losing appeals to small constituencies out of step with the larger electorate. But Reagan is anything but a loser. Political analysts continue to disagree on how much the Moral Majority factor contributed to his win in 1980. Meanwhile, he ran even stronger while using religion all the more in 1984. The reason may be less apparent than has met the ear.

Reagan's rhetoric has undeniable appeal for evangelicals, fundamentalists, and others whose religious commitment is the pivotal point in their lives. But these remain a minority of the electorate, and many are traditional Democrats. More critical and more surprising is Reagan's appeal to those caught up in the currents of secularization, those whose ties to religious tradition are uncomfortably weak and generally not as strong as their forebears'. This larger voting bloc is confused about the relationships between religion, morality, and politics in both their personal lives and the public arena. And who can blame them?

Issues such as prayer in the public schools, aid to parochial education, and cooperation between state and church in matters such as welfare and refugee services have bedeviled the nation's finest legal minds for years. Recent statements of church leaders may have muddied more than clarified the waters, especially when the Catholic bishops move simultaneously to the right on abortion and to the left on nuclear freeze. In truth, church and state have never been fully separate in this country, nor have religion and politics. While there are certainly differences between Reagan's views of their inseparability and those of, say Khomeini, Kahane, or Cotton Mather, the distinctions are elusive.

In addition to confusion, secularization produces guilt. Religion is not easily neglected or shucked off in a country that has long prided itself on the paradox of great religious freedom combined with strong religious observance. There remains something primordial about religion in American culture. Even where religion has lost its compelling salience, we tend to hang on to the form if not the function. Indeed, this is partly a matter of good form, as well as continuity with generations past and a hedge against future crises not yet imaginable. In all of this, secularization breeds uneasiness and a guilt that requires expiation. Here Reagan performs a special service.

In many ways, Reagan is a prototype of the secularizing—although not fully secularized—person. With only vague denominational ties, his own religious practices are unclear and unintimidating. Some on the religious Right are unsure if he is born again. According to others, he may be the least personally religious president in recent memory, and one for whom religion could be almost entirely a matter of form without function. Of course, such things are hard to know, especially since, in Peter Berger's terms, private religious virtues are often lost amid public religious rhet-

oric.[20] Meanwhile Reagan's statements on religion, morality, and politics imply a syllogism that is difficult to rebut without being cast as anti-Christ. Thus: (1) religion and morality are inseparable; (2) the government—especially its current administration—is nothing if not moral; hence (3) there must be religion in government. If morality and religion are inextricable, we can demonstrate our morality by supporting religion. Conversely, a vote against religion is a sign of immorality itself.

Of course, all of these linkages are forced to the point of spuriousness. Like many political bubbles, they burst when analyzed closely. Nevertheless they add to the confusion and guilt. Even among the 60 percent of the nation who do not attend religious services regularly, there are many to whom religious rhetoric sounds reassuring, as do pro-family and other traditionalist values. Somehow symbols become more important than substance, and Reagan himself may be the very best symbol available. He won considerable support from those who disagreed with him on specific issues—for example, from the substantial numbers of young Catholic women who are pro-choice on abortion. In a secularizing America, a vote for Reagan may have become the political equivalent of attending church only on Christmas and Easter. And politicians are less likely than clergy to look gift parishioners in the mouth.

The point is not that recent presidential elections have hung in the religious balance. However affected by the religious rhetoric—either "vague beliefs firmly held" or "firm beliefs vaguely acknowledged," according to Kenneth

20. Peter L. Berger, *The Heretical Imperative* (Garden City, NY: Anchor/Doubleday, 1979).

Woodward[21]—most voters have responded more to their perceived self-interest as reflected in the consumer price index. This itself is a commentary on the decline of civil religion as a mobilizing force. Indeed, all of this suggests a quite different interpretation of politics, religion, and civil religion than has been common in the literature to date. Insofar as religion's influence is due to secularization rather than the sustained traditions of the sacred, civil religion seems to be losing both emotional depth and historical continuity.

It may help to explain why the language and discourse of civil religion have become more of a portable facade than the surface reflection of a core commitment. Without arguing that this interpretation is either definitive or exhaustive, it is worth noting that it would lead us away from Durkheim and back in the direction of Rousseau. Such movement, however, requires an examination of still one more critical relationship—namely, that between American civil religion and American culture.

CIVIL RELIGION AND A CULTURAL CENTER NOT HOLDING

One of the dangers of working in the wake of Durkheim is the tendency to blur the differences between simple societies such as his Arunta and complex societies such as our own. Thus, there has been a persistent strain toward unity and consensus in the theory of civil religion. The literature is pervaded by a tendency to assume that all cultural elements, including civil religion, are bound together; that any value that has a wide resonance in the

culture at large is part of our civil-religious heritage; and that civil religion both stems from and shores up a cultural consensus and moral unity that society requires for its very existence. But it is doubtful whether America ever existed as an ideological whole; it is implausible that any religion can now provide our secularizing society with the moral integration necessary to make civil religion a compelling national creed. Indeed, as Richard Fenn has pointed out so trenchantly, not all societies may require a religiously grounded cultural consensus at their core.[22] Assuming so risks explaining too little by attempting too much. An adequate theory of civil religion must allow enough latitude and offer us enough analytic tools to make useful distinctions between, say, the Arunta, seventeenth-century New England, and twentieth-century United States.

Many proponents of a civil religion have recalled the social cohesion of Puritan New England. Although the covenanted character of these early communities is itself being called into question,[23] it is clear that greater dissensus and conflict have emerged with greater complexity over time. From the seventeenth century to the current threshold of the twenty-first, America may have come full circle from a congeries of small communities through a more or less integrated society and now back toward an uneasy coexistence of splintered groups differing as to race, ethni-

21. Kenneth L. Woodward, "Faith, Hope and Votes," *Newsweek,* 17 Sept. 1984, p. 34.

22. Richard K. Fenn, *Toward a Theory of Secularization,* Society for the Scientific Study of Religion, Monograph Series, no. 1 (Storrs, CT: Society for the Scientific Study of Religion, 1978).

23. Stephen Innes, *Labor in a New Land: Economy and Society in Seventeenth Century Springfield* (Princeton, NJ: Princeton University Press, 1983).

city, gender, economic position, and, of course, religion. These new structural conditions cast severe doubt on the prospects of any single civil religion. American society may be becoming too fragmented, polarized, and secular for a substantive consensus to remain at its core. In Richard Merelman's terms, American culture has become too "loosely bounded" to support a coherant canopy of meaning.[24] It is in this sense that the center may be giving way.

Of course, such changes have accelerated since World War II. Within the sphere of religion alone, the most significant religious development may be the rise and mainstreaming of American Catholics. In addition, there have arisen new religious movements with both Western and Eastern roots, a resurgent fundamentalism, a tendency toward religious privatization, and a variety of humanistic options. All of these have challenged the cultural dominance of a white Anglo-Saxon Protestant elite. Consensual religiopolitical norms legitimizing one and only one civil religion have become progressively more hollow.

Ironically, the same ferment of the 1960s that created a need for a reassuring and reunifying civil religion also eroded the conditions for its existence. Broad coalitions dissolved; interest-group and issue politics emerged; many centers replaced the center. Pluralism became contested, and the American mosaic began to resemble the fractured vision of cubist art. While civil-religious discourse continued to use the culturally resonant language of cohesion, it seemed increasingly a rhetoric without a reality.

Indeed, cynics began to envision such fragmentation that even the concept of America itself was becoming an abstract fantasy insofar as it referred to a unity beyond the superficial boundaries of the state. Perhaps the most saddened and disappointed of all was Robert Bellah himself. Once a source of buoyant hope, only eight years later he was lamenting our "broken covenant."[25]

Of course, the nation has not dissolved. Indeed, when compared to such truly splintered societies as Northern Ireland or Lebanon, the United States has remained firmly united. But deepening structural and cultural divisions suggest that our recent political displays of patriotism and national pride are a form of bravado from a confused body politic rather than a true reaffirmation of civil religion itself.

The liberal political and social agendas of the 1960s were fueled by a rapidly expanding economy. Economic contraction has led to the politics of scarcity. The prophetic civil-religious currents of the civil rights movement now confront such intractable issues as affirmative action and comparable worth. Reagan himself has legitimated a me-first survival ethos while tying it to older traditional values associated with religion, the family, and economic entrepreneurship. As the white upper-middle classes have reasserted their hold on American politics and economics, the dominant discourse of civil religion has also changed. Jesse Jackson notwithstanding, it has become again a religious nationalism, justifying and legitimating the status quo. Conservative Protestantism has articulated its political demands in nationalist terms, linking the a priori

24. Richard M. Merelman, *Making Something of Ourselves: On Culture and Politics in the United States* (Berkeley: University of California Press, 1984).

25. Robert N. Bellah, *The Broken Covenant* (New York: Seabury Press, 1975).

approval of the Almighty with the actions of the American body politic. It is worth repeating how ironic it is that this most sectarian of religious communities has chosen for its political standard-bearer one of the most generically religious presidents in U.S. history. Yet, such is the potential of civil-religious discourse, regardless of the reality behind its symbols.

Once again it appears that the American tradition of civil-religious analysis may have taken the wrong French fork in moving more in the direction of Durkheim than Rousseau. Rousseau's view of a civil religion imposed from the top as a way of manipulating public loyalties may have more validity than Durkheim's more trenchant conception of a culturally grounded civil religion, tied to a deep and underlying set of shared values and moral commitments. And yet Durkheim was aware that no complex society could constantly experience the sort of perfervid civic faith that has been so often idealized. Indeed, he commented this way on the France—and Europe—of the early 1900s:

We are going through a stage of transition and moral mediocrity. The great things of the past which filled our fathers with enthusiasm do not excite the same ardour in us, either because they have come into common usage to such an extent that we are unconscious of them, or else because they no longer answer to our actual aspirations; but as yet there is nothing to replace them. . . . In a word, the old gods are growing old or already dead, and others are not yet born. . . . This is what rendered vain the attempt of Comte with the old historic souvenirs artificially revived; it is life itself, and not a dead past which can produce a living cult. The day will come when our societies will know again those hours of creative effervescence, in the course of which new ideas and new formulae

are found which serve for a while as a guide to humanity.[26]

Perhaps our own day of "creative effervescence" will also come again. However, any reversal of our recent pattern of differentiation and dissensus is more likely to come about through calamity than through any collective act of spiritual will. There is nothing like disaster to temporarily breach divergence. Hence the wag's remark that an unpopular president up for reelection must be watched very carefully lest war break out with Canada.

CONCLUSION

In his thoughtful book on the social history of Western and moral philosophy, *After Virtue,* Alasdair MacIntyre argues that breakdown of the consensual *polis* as the main unit of social and cultural life has produced a fragmentation of meanings attached to moral concepts.[27] Moral arguments now often speak past each other because the participants are using different discourses rooted in different notions of the moral society. Moral philosophy must therefore examine the context and uses of moral concepts in political debate; the search for invariant meanings is fruitless.

So it is with civil religion. The breakdown of eighteenth-century Puritan religious consensus in the United States has been followed by a breakdown of the moral and cultural consensus that it left as legacy. As a result, discussion of the universal meanings of civil-religious tenets has become an enterprise in scho-

26. Durkheim, *Elementary Forms of the Religious Life,* pp. 425-28.
27. Alasdair MacIntyre, *After Virtue: A Study in Moral Theory,* 2nd ed. (Notre Dame, IN: University of Notre Dame Press, 1984).

lasticism. Instead, analysis should focus on the contexts and uses of civil-religious language and symbols, noting how specific groups and subcultures use versions of the civil religion to frame, articulate, and legitimate their own particular political and moral visions. As Samuel Huntington points out in his work on the "American Creed" and its political passions, Americanism is not a logically consistent intellectual ideology.[28] It is an emotive, affective, normative vision; it reflects both the consensus and dissensus on key values that define the nation. It can live with logical inconsistencies because at base it is illogical. In Richard Fenn's evocative terms, there has been a "trend toward abstractness" in our definitions of national purpose.[29] This is the result of an increasing disjunction between our culture and our structure, between our traditional systems of meaning and the existential reality of our current lives.

And yet it is not surprising that, in Phillip Hammond's phrase, "civil religions are found where they are sought."[30] This is not just a matter of analytic wish-fulfillment. The symbols, language, and forms do remain. As the cultural center dissolves, however, its expressions are increasingly adopted by those on the flanks who find them useful for legitimizing programs of reform or retrenchment. As Huntington notes, the gap between the political ideals of the American creed and political reality is a readily available weapon to those who challenge the status quo. This is not to say that the use of civil-religious symbolism by social movements is necessarily cynical or hypocritical. Movements must interpret and legitimate themselves to their own members, as much as to the cultural mainstream. People must be motivated to act politically; the resonant symbolism of civil religion helps serve that purpose by placing the movement's goals within the frame of legitimate political discourse. Ideally this may motivate members, neutralize opponents, and co-opt the sympathies of neutral onlookers. The forms of cultural consensus again mask the structural divergence in group and issue politics.

The relationships among civil religion, creedal religions, and culture have changed significantly in the 200 years of American national life. Rather than try to resurrect a moral and cultural cohesion as an act of faith, we need to examine it anew as an act of scholarship. The debate over whether there is any longer a civil religion is to some degree superficial. The more basic question is whether the United States is any longer a civil society. From Durkheim's standpoint, a society that is not bound by a single civil culture is not a single society at all. Perhaps we are becoming not only the United States of America but the United Societies of America, in quite a different sense.

28. Samuel P. Huntington, *American Politics: The Promise of Disharmony* (Cambridge, MA: Belknap Press, 1981).

29. Richard K. Fenn, "Bellah and the New Orthodoxy," *Sociological Analysis,* 37(2):160-66 (Summer 1976).

30. Phillip E. Hammond, "The Sociology of American Civil Religion: A Bibliographic Essay," *Sociological Analysis,* 37(2):179 (Summer 1976).

Religion in America

By GEORGE GALLUP, Jr.

ABSTRACT: This article reviews recent survey indicators on religious life in America. Generally the surveys reveal a rising tide of religious interest. The "highly spiritually committed" are more satisfied with their lives, more tolerant of others, and more concerned with the betterment of society. Despite the high interest in religion, there are glaring inconsistencies: levels of morality and ethics remain low, hunger is a reality for many Americans, and levels of self-esteem are low for many persons.

George Gallup, Jr., is vice-chairman of the Gallup Organization, Inc., and director of the Princeton Religion Research Center.

PROBABLY no more difficult task faces the survey practitioner than that of measuring the religious mood of the nation. First of all, religious beliefs are varied and subtle and do not yield easily to categorization. Second, no consensus is found among researchers on what can be considered the key elements of a vital religious faith. The result is that we do not have, as yet, a set of leading spiritual indicators in which we can place full confidence.

At the same time, however, the steadily increasing output of survey statistics on religion is helping to fill some of the gaps in our knowledge. The following survey findings—these from recent surveys conducted by the Gallup Organization and the Princeton Religion Research Center (PRRC)—offer important clues, I believe, to the state of religion in the United States.

A majority of Americans—8 of 10—say they are Christians, but only half that number know who delivered the Sermon on the Mount. Most Americans think the Ten Commandments are valid rules for living, but many have a tough time recalling exactly what those rules are. Among teenagers, 3 in 10 do not know the significance of Easter for Christians; among teenagers who attend church regularly, 2 in 10 do not know it. Of unchurched Americans, two-thirds believe in the divinity of Jesus Christ and that he was resurrected from the dead. The belief that Jesus will return to earth someday is held by 62 percent of all Americans. Of the total American adult population, nearly half believe in creationism—that is, that all living creatures were brought into being within the last 10,000 years—and 37 percent believe the Bible to be the actual word of God, to be taken literally, word for word.

One-third of church members believe that a homosexual cannot be a good Christian or Jew. Two-thirds of all Americans think their chances of going to heaven are "good."

Americans have a variety of other beliefs in the otherworldly. A large portion of teenagers—69 percent—believe in angels; 24 percent believe in Big Foot. Astrology has a significant following: 23 percent of adults, many of whom regularly attend religious services, and 55 percent of teenagers. Reincarnation has a smaller following: the same percentage of adults—23—but the share of teenagers drops to 27 percent.

Some of the survey results indicate religious behavior. For instance, nearly as high a proportion of unchurched Americans as churched say they attended Sunday school or the equivalent when they were growing up. Despite lack of affiliation with a religious institution, three-quarters of the unchurched pray and want their children to have religious training. Watching religious television shows does not drain people or money from local churches. A large majority of college students—93 percent—say there is "no chance" that they would join a cult, such as "the Moonies."

With respect to people's lives in general—that is, not restricted to the religious sphere—the strength of religion's impact varies. Half of the unchurched feel that organized religion is not effective in helping people find meaning in life; 39 percent of those going to church agree. Despite these figures, one person in three has had a dramatic life-changing religious experience—a proportion that has changed little over the last quarter century. Religious "fundamentalists," compared to others, are not so well tolerated by better-educated Americans. Greeted with more tolerance by these Americans are persons of different nationalities, races, and life-styles; the less education Americans have, the less tolerant they are of these different groups. We also find that for teenagers, of the greatest persons in history, Jesus ranks fifth.

Church attendance makes little difference in people's ethical views and behavior with respect to lying, cheating, pilferage, and not reporting theft. For example, equal proportions of churched and unchurched admit to overstating deductions or understating income on their tax forms.

Despite the considerable attention given the issue of religion and politics, relatively few Americans—4 percent—report that the clergy of the church or synagogue they attend urged them to vote for a particular presidential candidate or a particular political party during the 1984 presidential campaign. Still, 51 percent of Americans would not vote for an atheist for president. Concerning the place of religion in society, nearly half of all Americans think this statement—"This state shall be separate from the church and the church from the school"—is found in the U.S. Constitution. In fact, these Americans are mistaken; the statement is from the constitution of the Soviet Union.

Now, these disparate survey items are not only interesting in themselves—and perhaps, in some cases, shocking—but they also shed light, I believe, on the complex picture of religion in America today:

—the widespread appeal or popularity of religion;
—the glaring lack of knowledge;
—the inconsistencies in belief;

—the superficiality of faith; and
—in part, the failure of organized religion in some respects to make a difference in our society.

THE REASON FOR RESEARCH

These survey findings may be intriguing and help shed light on the spiritual condition of Americans, but we should ask the question, Is research on religion really necessary, or is this pursuit of academic interest only?

I believe there are three important reasons for probing the religious and spiritual lives of people in the United States and around the world.

First of all, there are sociological reasons. Our survey evidence suggests that the spiritual dynamic in American life often has more to do with how we think and behave in society than do the more traditional background characteristics such as age, level of education, and political affiliation.

Let's examine this assertion. Those in our surveys who fit our category of "highly spiritually committed" appear to be a breed apart from the rest of the populace in at least four key respects. For one thing, they are more satisfied with their lot in life than are those who are less spiritually committed—and far happier. A total of 68 percent of the highly spiritually committed say they are "very happy," compared to 46 percent of the moderately spiritually committed, 39 percent of the moderately uncommitted, and 30 percent of the highly uncommitted. Second, they tend to place greater importance on family life than do persons in less spiritually committed categories. Third, they tend to be more tolerant of persons of different races and religions than are those who are less spiritually committed. Finally, they do not turn inward; rather, they are vitally concerned about the betterment of society. They are, for example, far more involved in charitable activities than are their counterparts. A total of 46 percent of the highly spiritually committed say they are presently working among the poor, the infirm, and the elderly, compared to 36 percent of the moderately committed, 28 percent of the moderately uncommitted, and 22 percent of the highly uncommitted.

What makes these findings even more remarkable is the fact that these persons tend to belong to lower socioeconomic groups than the population as a whole, and surveys have shown that these groups tend to be less happy and less satisfied with their lot in life than are higher socioeconomic groups, less tolerant of persons of different races and religions, and, finally, less involved in charitable activities. So despite enormous pressures, economic and otherwise, these people appear to be living their faith to a remarkable extent.

This set of findings, and others, suggests that any exploration of the nature and direction of U.S. society would be woefully incomplete without a knowledge of the role that religious convictions play in shaping our opinions and behavior.

In addition to the sociological, there are practical reasons for undertaking religious research. Bluntly stated, churches in the United States have a marketing problem. Good communication involves listening as well as talking. Before a church can plan for its future and operate on the basis of facts—not assumptions—it should seek answers to certain basic questions:

1. What are the current levels of religious belief, practice, and knowledge, spiritual commitment, and stewardship among the people of the church?

2. To what extent do people of the church put their faith into practice?

3. What are the spiritual and physical needs of the people that the church is supposed to serve?

4. What is bringing people to a given church—and what is keeping them away?

It is my belief that every church in America ought to conduct a survey. Too many churches—even strong ones—are drifting without an understanding of their strengths and weaknesses, without clear goals, and without a plan to achieve them. Incidentally, the PRRC, in conjunction with Continental Research Associates, will soon publish a survey manual kit to shed light on the four basic questions. The manual will provide step-by-step guidance on how volunteers can conduct a survey of church members— and even of the broader community where their church is located.

Finally, there are compelling religious reasons for conducting survey research into people's spiritual lives. If, as the vast majority of people of the Free World believe, there is a God who is interested in humanity, then it becomes our urgent duty to examine the relationship of human beings to God with all the skill we can muster.

In this respect, we are fortunate to have at our disposal an efficient and accurate way to explore people's religious beliefs—the scientific sample survey, which along with the printing press, the computer, and television must be regarded as one of those scientific discoveries of modern history that has had, and will continue to have, the greatest impact on the religious lives of mankind.

*Some of the
surveys conducted*

Survey research in the area of religion has lagged far behind survey research in virtually every other field—politics, consumer behavior, and many other fields. There are a variety of reasons for this lag, including the belief that it was inappropriate or impossible to probe spiritual feeling. Church leaders, furthermore, were unsophisticated about polling, thinking it would be enormously expensive and difficult.

At any rate, it was not until fairly recently that survey research in the field of religion began in earnest. A growing number of denominations, for example, are now involved in the study of religious phenomena, particularly those relating to institutional religion.

Furthermore, we have seen the emergence of independent research organizations concerned with religion, including the PRRC, which was founded in 1977 to gain a better understanding, through scientifically conducted surveys, of the nature and depth of religious commitment in the United States and abroad.

Since 1977 the Gallup Organization, often in conjunction with the PRRC, has conducted a number of national surveys on religion for a wide variety of clients. The following are just a few of them:

—the first global survey—covering 70 nations—dealing with religious beliefs and practices;[1]
—the most comprehensive attempt to explore the life-style, attitude, and belief differences between churched and unchurched Americans;[2]
—the first major survey of the religious beliefs and practices of Hispanic Catholics in the United States;[3]
—the first major survey of the religious beliefs and practices of the Greek Orthodox population in the United States;[4]
—the most comprehensive survey of evangelical Christian laity and clergy in the United States;[5]
—a comprehensive national survey designed to explore the core of the faith of Christians and the role of Jesus Christ in the lives of Americans;[6]
—a survey, believed to be the first of its kind, to determine the impact of the electronic church on the beliefs, attitudes, and life-styles of the American people;[7] and
—an exploration of the factors that separate the Left from the Right, in terms of religious beliefs, and the steps that can be taken to bring them together.[8]

In 1982, the Gallup Organization conducted an intensive survey for the Robert H. Schuller Ministries. The sur-

1. Conducted by the Princeton Religion Research Center, Princeton, NJ, and the Gallup Organization, Princeton, NJ, for the Charles F. Kettering Foundation, 1977.
2. Conducted for a coalition of 31 faiths and denominations, 1978.
3. Conducted for *Our Sunday Visitor,* 1978.
4. Conducted for the Greek Orthodox Archdiocese of North and South America, 1980.
5. Conducted for *Christianity Today,* 1978.
6. Conducted for the Robert H. Schuller Ministries, 1983.
7. Undertaken by the University of Pennsylvania Annenberg School of Communications, Philadelphia, PA, and the Gallup Organization, and initiated by the National Council of Churches, the United States Catholic Conference, and National Religious Broadcasters, 1983.
8. Completed in 1984, this survey was undertaken for the Robert H. Schuller Ministries.

vey was designed to measure the relationship among levels of self-esteem, life-style factors, and religious beliefs. It examined various components of what may be described as one's self-concept or image. Three key measures were employed. First, a standardized measure of self-esteem was used. It was originally developed by Dr. Morris Rosenberg, a sociologist who has conducted a number of studies in the area of self-esteem. The Rosenberg self-esteem scale may be described as a measure of one's attitude toward self, or one's self-worth. Second, a scale was developed especially for this survey that attempts to measure one's self-concept with respect to personal qualities such as leadership ability and perseverance. Finally, a scale developed for the study was used to measure one's self-concept with respect to personal qualities such as dependability, generosity, and friendliness.

Recently the Gallup Organization has been exploring the development of faith in the adult age cycle.[9] Preliminary findings from this survey indicate that, despite the common belief that faith is something given, constant, and unchanging, people go through the same kind of passages in their religious lives as they do in other forms of personal development.

*Increased interest
  in surveys*

Why has interest in survey research in the field of religion grown so markedly

9. Part of a larger study undertaken for Faith Development in the Adult Life Cycle, a research project of the Religious Education Association of the United States and Canada in cooperation with the Center for Religious Education, College of St. Thomas, St. Paul, MN, 1982-85.

in recent years? A number of key reasons, some noted earlier, can be offered.

One is a growing awareness of the need to probe beneath the level of religious involvement to the bedrock of spiritual commitment. The most important statistic for churches is, in the last analysis, not the proportion of people who are members of churches or who attend regularly—although these are vital survival statistics—but the proportion who could be classified as "highly spiritually committed"—truly devout, if you will. In addition, surveys are attracting more and more attention as a practical, efficient, and relatively inexpensive way to find out key information regarding a local church—for example, levels of religious belief, practice, and knowledge, as well as stewardship potential. Surveys can also help address a widespread concern of a very practical nature: that the decline in the number of church members in many denominations draws moneys away from churches.

Among religious bodies, there is a growing interest in evangelization—reaching out to the nominally religious or the nonreligious. Churches are becoming more willing to listen to the laity. And there is an increased willingness among various churches to tackle mutual problems together, in the spirit of ecumenism. Surveys can assist in these efforts.

From a sociological perspective, the importance of examining religious beliefs and practices is receiving increased recognition. Recent surveys give still further evidence of the importance of the religious dynamic in determining the overall attitudes and behavior of a populace.

And then, of course, there are strictly religious reasons for a growing interest in survey research in the effort to shed light on vital questions: What do people believe about God? How strongly do they hold these beliefs? What differences do strongly held beliefs make in terms of the life of the individual and in terms of society as a whole? How is a strong faith developed?

WHAT SURVEYS REVEAL

What are our surveys telling us about the contemporary religious scene?

There would appear to be, in America today, a rising tide of interest in religion. A majority of Americans, for example, say they are more interested in religious and spiritual matters than they were five years ago. New religious ferment is noted on the college campuses of the nation, with a marked increase in the last five years in the number of students who say religion is important in their lives and who attend church regularly.

It seems that the people of this nation are coming increasingly to believe that the problems of the world will not be solved through people's efforts alone but through a change of heart and a turning to God—not simply through social engineering but through social engineering energized and uplifted by spiritual renewal.

Americans today appear to be searching with a new intensity for spiritual moorings. What is prompting this search? One of the key factors is a need for hope in these troubled times of nuclear threat. Accompanying this need, a note of desperation is sometimes found in the comments of survey respondents: "Where else but to God does one turn in times like these?" Another factor is a gnawing loneliness among Americans— greater loneliness, we find in surveys,

than is found in many other nations— which is causing Americans urgently to seek supportive and dependable fellowship. One of the greatest problems of our times is that of strained relationships. Third, we find a disenchantment with modern life-styles and with what is perceived to be a lack of rules and an anything-goes philosophy in society.

Americans express a high level of confidence in our local and national religious leaders. This is coupled with a high level of religiousness among the American people: 9 in 10 Americans state a religious preference; 8 in 10 say religion is important in their lives. Even a high proportion of the unchurched can be classified as believers. Most of us pray and believe in the power of prayer. We want our faith to grow and we want religion to play a greater role in society.

Given the high level of public confidence in our churches and clergy, and the fact that Americans are essentially a religious people who want to deepen their faith, organized religion would seem to have enormous opportunities in the immediate years ahead.

But if the opportunities are great, so are the challenges. Among these are the following three, which will set much of the agenda for the churches in the 1980s and 1990s.

The first challenge is to raise the level of ethics and morality in the United States. A large majority of Americans, we discovered in a recent *Wall Street Journal*/Gallup survey, believe that the level of ethics among the public has declined over the last decade, and additional findings on behavior from the same survey show that this belief is well founded. Columnist Michael McManus questions the impact of religion in our society and makes this observation: "If religion does not produce a more ethical, loving society, something is fundamentally wrong with the way that religion is being practiced."[10]

The second challenge is dealing with hunger and deprivation in the United States. In a recent Gallup poll, one-fifth of the U.S. population claimed that there were times during the preceding 12 months when they did not have enough money to buy the food, clothing, or medical supplies their families needed. Among blacks, close to half reported these conditions.

The last challenge is to raise the level of self-esteem or self-worth among the American people. In a survey we conducted for the Robert H. Schuller Ministries, we discovered that 3 in 10 Americans have a low sense of self-worth. Low self-esteem is considered by many experts to be the number one psychological problem in America today.

It will be the ongoing task of survey researchers in the field of religion in the years ahead to measure the success of churches in meeting challenges such as these, as well as exploring the quality of people's religious lives. And, in view of the fact that we live in a world that has become increasingly violent—at the beginning of 1985 there were 40 major or minor wars in the world, with religious factors sometimes exacerbating the situation—perhaps the most important role of religious research in the decades ahead will be to shed light on ways that will help people and nations see more clearly not that which divides them but that which unites them.

Yet there would seem to be ample survey evidence to support the views of Colton, who wrote: "Men will wrangle for religion; write for it; fight for it; die for it; anything but *live* for it."

And quoting Jonathan Swift: "We have just enough religion to make us hate. But not enough to make us love one another."

10. Michael McManus's nationally syndicated column, "Religion and Ethics."

Book Department

INTERNATIONAL RELATIONS AND POLITICS

BERTRAM, CHRISTOPH, ed. *Defense and Consensus: The Domestic Aspects of Western Security.* Pp. 136. New York: St. Martin's Press, 1984. $25.00.

NURICK, ROBERT, ed. *Nuclear Weapons and European Security.* Pp. ix, 142. New York: St. Martin's Press, 1984. $22.50.

SIGAL, LEON V. *Nuclear Forces in Europe: Enduring Dilemmas, Present Prospects.* Pp. x, 181. Washington, DC: Brookings Institution, 1984. $22.95. Paperbound, $8.95.

The 14 papers that constitute *Defense and Consensus* were first presented at the twenty-fourth annual conference of the International Institute of Strategic Studies in September 1982. The conference was devoted to a most elusive aspect of NATO's security policy: how domestic political factors influence NATO defense policies.

The authors, all notable journalists, professors, or domestic defense officials, did agree on at least one point. A domestic consensus no longer exists within individual countries represented in NATO. This statement establishes a common point of departure for each author to provide the reader with explanations for the reasons for the lack of consensus and the how-to of reestablishing it.

In summary, the lack is attributed to several circumstances. Societies have become more skeptical of NATO's worth and thus question domestic expenditures and policies vis-à-vis NATO. Affluent times have passed, and domestic economic considerations are therefore given priority over NATO's military needs. Automatic trust in political and military institutions has eroded. Finally, governments are no longer willing to incur large deficits in public expenditures that they accepted in the past as a price of security.

The authors' proposals to reestablish a consensus are not as well stated. Of the 14 papers, I found the 3 written by Messrs. Fromm, Ruehl, and Nishihara to be quite profound. Each examines the role of the media and their influence on defense policy. All three reach the same conclusion: the impact of the press on defense policymaking is marginal at best. Joseph Fromm characterizes the press in the United States as a "conveyor belt" for government; Lothan Ruehl and Masashi Nishihara claim that the press in Europe and in Japan, respectively, "follow the fashions." Except for the neutron bomb debates of a few years ago, no single decision on defense policy seems to have been taken or not taken because of press reporting.

In searching for a way to reestablish the public consensus, one solution is proposed. Both NATO nuclear and nonnuclear defense spending must be put into a "context of expectations." That is to say, only a consensus on the substantive problem of what Western policy should be toward the Soviet Union will establish a context that will make the specific military efforts acceptable and reassuring.

In conclusion, the solution becomes clear: consensus must be built by the positive leadership of Western governments. *Defense and Consensus* makes this quite plain, and for this reason is recommended reading.

In *Nuclear Weapons and European Security,* the articles are given focus by an interesting opening conundrum, "Would the United States risk Chicago for the sake of Hamburg?" Having said this, editor Robert Nurick attempts to answer his own question with five excellent articles whose primary thrust is to probe the credibility of the U.S. threat to employ its nuclear weapons in defense of Europe. Certainly the answer to this determines how other NATO members will plan their doctrines of flexible response.

Although unknowingly reiterating the central message in *Defense and Consensus,* Nurick believes that while NATO's nuclear posture may be adequate to deter the Soviets, it no longer reassures Western publics. A key to the focus in all five essays is the dilemma of NATO's nuclear doctrine since its inception in the 1950s: NATO must have the capability to deter and yet it must also accommodate both the European concern about becoming the central battleground and the equally understandable American desire that any nuclear guarantee should not automatically entail its own devastation.

The United Kingdom's nuclear doctrine vis-à-vis NATO should remain, as noted by Peter Nailor and Jonathan Alford, tied to a larger NATO strategy, but it should also be an independent force so as to add to the Soviets' uncertainty about the former's capabilities. Anthony Cordesman, in "Deterrence in the 1980s," seems to understand the

problem only too well. Any doctrine must focus on the central premise: the risk of any escalation of a European war must be limited enough to avoid unacceptable damage to the United States. This would, at least on paper, give the United States a counterforce capability to retaliate against the Soviets.

Two other articles, by Gregory Treverton and Christopher Makins, call for a more realistic approach to a viable nuclear doctrine. Nuclear policy is seen here as a political problem that cannot be solved at one time but only made, through incremental change, more politically manageable.

In conclusion, a point is made by Makin that I believe puts the entire NATO doctrine in a proper perspective: the uncertainties surrounding the use of nuclear weapons work both ways. If the West cannot eliminate its own uncertainties, it can, at least, make sure that Soviet uncertainties persist as well.

Having addressed the necessity of reestablishing domestic consensus and the need for credibility, I enjoin the reader to complete this trilogy by reading *Nuclear Forces in Europe.*

To Leon Sigal, author of *Nuclear Forces,* December 1979 was a watershed for the NATO alliance. On that date, the USSR began to deploy new theater nuclear missiles within range of Europe. NATO reaction was twofold: to deploy new U.S. ballistic and cruise missiles in Europe capable of striking deep into the USSR, and to announce its intention to pursue arms control negotiations with the Soviets. Sigal is probably close to the truth when he states that no decision regarding NATO nuclear policy has so divided Western European public opinion and engendered deeper fears among European publics that new deployments might increase the chance of nuclear war.

Against this backdrop, Sigal examines the dilemmas created by the 1979 decision. He covers the entire gamut of the rationales, deployments, politics, and negotiations that have become NATO nuclear doctrine.

I have not found a better or more concise book on the subject. Sigal's conclusion is ominous: the precarious stability that existed between the United States and the Soviet Union for two decades in Europe is being negated by the deployment of the Pershing II missile. The point of no return is being reached. To this I say, "Amen."

RICHARD E. JOHE

Winston-Salem
North Carolina

CORDESMAN, ANTHONY H. *The Gulf and the Search for Strategic Stability: Saudi Arabia, the Military Balance in the Gulf, and Trends in the Arab-Israeli Military Balance.* Pp. xxiii, 1041. Boulder, CO: Westview Press, 1984. $45.00.

Claiming that the Persian Gulf "has become an area whose strategic importance to the United States rivals that of Western Europe or Japan," Cordesman presents us with almost a thousand tightly packed pages on the eight oil-producing states of the Gulf, threats to the supply of their oil to the West, and U.S. strategic options in the Gulf given the Arab-Israeli conflict. Although much of the content is highly technical, the book still reads well. Over 150 maps, charts, and tables accompany the text. Surprising in a book so long, there are few editorial and factual mistakes, such as the substitution of "White Russians" for "Great Russians" when mentioning dominant ethnic groups in Soviet society.

Cordesman, who has many years of experience in the Departments of Defense, Energy, and State and is international policy editor of the *Armed Forces Journal,* devotes about a third of the book to U.S. military involvement with Saudi Arabia, "the key to securing the West's energy supplies" in the Gulf area where "55% of the world's proved oil reserves" are located. Attention is also given to the small, but friendly, conservative oil-producers: Kuwait, Bahrain, Qatar, Oman, and the United Arab Emirates, as well as to the present conflict between Iran and Iraq. Cordesman sees the current oil glut as a temporary phenomenon with surging demand in the 1990s pushing prices "more than 50% above their level in 1980 dollars." The Soviet Union, tied down in Afghanistan and Eastern Europe, is not considered a direct threat to the Gulf but will play a spoiler role, assisting radicals in their attempts to subvert the conservative Gulf states internally or perhaps rearming the Iranian giant of the region to provide a direct military threat.

At present, Cordesman sees Saudi Arabia and the small Gulf states as "acutely vulnerable to attacks on [their] oil facilities." But in his concluding chapter, he is optimistic that an "informal strategic partnership" with the United States can be forged that will guarantee the security of the Gulf states without threatening their internal stability.

The only fly in the ointment is Israel. Cordesman does not want to back away from the U.S. role of "ultimate guarantor of Israel's security." But U.S. partnership with the friendly Gulf states demands that Israel and its U.S. supporters not oppose Saudi purchases of more advanced combat fighters and armored vehicles, as the sale of the AWACs was almost defeated in 1981. Cordesman constructs elaborate arguments to demonstrate why such weapons in the Gulf pose no military threat to Israel. What is a threat, he maintains, is the increasing capabilities of Syria and other hard-line Arab states to overwhelm Israel in the late 1980s and 1990s with massive amounts of manpower and equipment—a threat that can be removed only by an Arab-Israeli settlement of the Palestinian issue.

The United States, therefore, must prod Israel toward a settlement. It must "put tighter controls on the arms it sells Israel [and] cannot continue to accept actions like Begin's annexation of the Golan . . . or Israel's invasion of Lebanon." It must also "oppose Israel at least to the point at which the U.S. continues to support a peace settlement acceptable to the Palestinians living on the West Bank and in Gaza."

Elsewhere in the book Cordesman writes of the Iraq-Iran conflict that "any cease-fire or 'peace' will be no more than the prelude to rearmament or revenge... hatreds have been built up that will explode periodically into war even if one side does achieve 'victory.'" Considering that he correctly perceives here the fragility of any lasting settlements in this most volatile area of the globe and documents the intensity of Arab feeling about Israel—"the Palestinian issue has become the Arab equivalent of the American morality play"—one might question Cordesman's advice. He puts little emphasis on energy conservation despite the fact that U.S. per capita energy consumption is almost twice that of West Germany, an industrial country with a similar standard of living. Reducing dependence on Gulf oil might be a less expensive way to protect U.S. interests in the Middle East—one that, in addition, would not jeopardize the security position of Israel, our only truly dependable ally there.

RICHARD J. WILLEY

Vassar College
Poughkeepsie
New York

KWITNY, JONATHAN. *Endless Enemies: The Making of an Unfriendly World.* Pp. xi, 435. New York: Congdon & Weed, 1984. $19.95.

Jonathan Kwitny's major argument is that the United States has, since the end of World War II, behaved in ways that have been detrimental to the interests of client states, third parties, and even Americans themselves. He also argues that such behaviors have been committed in the name of national security.

Kwitny's book is no mere restatement of the revisionist thesis that the United States is responsible for all the ills in the world. He is neither anti-American nor pro-Soviet, anti-capitalist nor pro-Marxist, neutralist nor pacifist. He is proud of the principles underlying the founding of the United States, but feels that those principles no longer guide U.S. foreign policy, that they have in fact been betrayed. And there is an empirical record that supports Kwitny in this regard.

But why have U.S. policymakers behaved in ways contrary to those principles? Quite simply, to combat and contain the Great Satan—international communism—plus to ensure that U.S. commercial interests prevail around the globe. And if this leads to actions that might otherwise be defined as unethical or immoral, we must bite the bullet because, as so-called realists would tell us, international relations occur in a milieu where traditional considerations of morality are null and void. And in any case, if it all works, why bother? It is just a necessary evil.

But does it all work? A retired U.S. foreign service officer once confided to me that he was not at all surprised that people in Central America were seeking assistance from the USSR. "After all, they perceive, and rightly so, that the governments that are oppressing them are supported by the U.S." So they go to the only other superpower around, to "avoid American imperialism" and to be sustained by an ideology that effectively explains "their colonial oppression."

Accordingly, U.S. foreign policy, whether expressed through trade, aid, the International Monetary Fund, or covert operations, has in many cases proven to be counterproductive and self-defeating. The United States—and the rest of the world—are less, rather than more, secure as a consequence of these actions, actions that are due in part to the tendency of U.S. policymakers to "reduce the world's problems to simplicities."

Although the book has clearly been written for the nonspecialist, I would have preferred some attempt at rigorous demonstration of causal connections between U.S. policies and subsequent developments; more references, plus some sense of how representative Kwitny's sample is of U.S. policy or international relations in general. I would have preferred to see Frantz Fanon listed correctly as a French West Indian who, although extremely partial to the Algerian cause during the French-Algerian war, was surely not "an Algerian." And I would have liked to see some recommendations as to how the United States and other countries might pursue less confrontational, less dysfunctional policies.

But none of this should be allowed to detract from Kwitny's message—that the greatest power in the history of the world may be going astray, and without many of us realizing it!

DENNIS J. D. SANDOLE
George Mason University
Fairfax
Virginia

SEMMEL, BERNARD. *John Stuart Mill and the Pursuit of Virtue.* Pp. xi, 212. New Haven, CT: Yale University Press, 1984. $17.50.

Because there are many liberalisms—who since the French Revolution is not to be counted as a liberal of some kind or another?—there are many John Stuart Mills. Mill's liberalism has been seen in terms of anti-statist minimalism and proto-socialism; in terms of Benthamite utilitarianism properly understood and romantic intuitionism liberally construed; in terms of negative liberty and the protection of the individual from public and political encroachment; as well as in terms of positive liberty and the capacity for self-realization nourished by education and culture.

None of these contradictory interpretations is inconsistent with Mill as a liberal, but only because Mill's liberalism is deeply paradoxical if not outright contradictory. Depending on whether he is associating himself with utility, community, the heroic self, the self-interested client, or the noble aristocrat, Mill's defense of liberty may mean many different things. Bernard Semmel's new monograph on Mill and virtue takes its cue from the epigraph to *On Liberty,* a citation from Wilhelm von Humboldt that reads, "The grand, leading principle, towards which every argument unfolded in these pages directly converges, is the absolute and essential importance of human development in its richest diversity."

For Semmel, Mill is less the child of his zealous utilitarian father and the early behavior modification schemes of Jeremy Bentham than of the romanticism of intuitionists such as Coleridge to which he was driven in his late adolescence. His first concern is not with radical anomic freedom as the liberty of the isolated individual from all external constraint; rather it is with the pursuit of virtue and excellence—a pursuit conditioned by, but not limited to, liberty in and of itself. As Semmel sums it up at the end of his book:

The story of the choice of Hercules [between sensual pleasure and virtue] was Mill's personal myth. He sought to make its lesson the public morality of all of society. Like the ancient philosophers whom he admired, and their Christian-Stoic disciples of the Renaissance, as well as the moral philosophers of the Scottish Enlightenment and the humanists Carlyle and Matthew Arnold, Mill understood that a good society could not long survive the eclipse of a freely chosen virtue.

Semmel supports his argument with a careful scrutiny of familiar texts reinterpreted through the perspective of rather less familiar relationships. Mill and the Unitarians, Mill and Carlyle, Mill and Arnold, Mill and Coleridge, Mill and Toqueville, as well as the better known Mill and Comte and Mill and Harriet Taylor are examined along with relevant texts. The method is that of the intellectual historian—which is to say, Semmel takes for granted conceptual polarities like negative and positive freedom or utilitarianism and intuitionism and focuses instead on the intellectual camps into which the protagonists of his story were thrust by their various allegiences. He is not engaged in theorizing liberalism as a philosophy so much as in seizing up liberal theory as an ideology. In situating Mill among his contemporaries—some luminaries, others merely journeymen—Semmel develops a convincing case for Mill as a champion of virtue first of all, and liberty only afterward, as virtue's instrument and emblem.

Yet intellectual biography has its limits, and Semmel's little book—although written with a straightforward and attractive style—

suffers from the defects of the genre. By declining to examine critically the categories by which Mill is politically and ideologically classified, and by neglecting the paradox and ambivalence that—as with every truly great theorist—are central to Mill's work, Semmel draws a much more orderly picture of Mill's conceptual world than the richly jumbled reality of his thought ought to allow. Mill may have used Coleridge to exorcise the demons of his father and Bentham, but the demons played on, and utility never ceased to condition all of his thinking. He may have yearned for a notion of the individual rich with self-development, but his tract on liberty became a beacon for radical individualists who feared and despised public culture and community. Mill's career was spent bridging rather than taking sides. His liberalism has come to mean so many things to so many people because it reaches out to encompass and overcome the dichotomies by which lesser philosophers identify themselves.

To a certain degree, this is the essence of Mill's greatness, of the greatness of every philosopher in the great tradition. Locke is no more an unvarnished defender of property and commerce than Rousseau is an unmitigated collectivist. Like them, Mill is deeper and broader than his interpreters, which is why there are so many of them but only one of him.

Nonetheless, among the many, Semmel writes thoughtful prose and portrays history with a careful eye and a stylish pen. Although the tree of liberalism does not grow under his ministrations—that is not his intention—certain of its roots are skillfully unearthed and exposed; for this, students of English liberalism have reason to be grateful.

BENJAMIN R. BARBER

Rutgers University
New Brunswick
New Jersey

*AFRICA, ASIA, AND
LATIN AMERICA*

COHEN, PAUL A. *Discovering History in China: American Historical Writing on the Recent Chinese Past.* Pp. xviii, 243. New York: Columbia University Press, 1984. $25.00.

Prior to World War II, American historians with a serious interest in modern China could be counted on the fingers of one hand. Books dealing with the subject, even the best of them, tended to be based on foreign-language sources, dealt primarily with China's relations with the West, and were usually written by missionaries, diplomats, and journalists. Beginning with the 1950s, this situation changed quickly as result of the increased importance of China in America's view of the world. Since then there has emerged a constant stream of works by professional historians, well trained in the language and the skills necessary to make use of the increasing amounts of source materials available. It is not surprising that in the process of this development, some attempts should be made to survey the field, but, to my mind, no one has done it with such intellectual depth and integrity as Paul Cohen in his new book, *Discovering History in China.*

Cohen begins his book by pointing out that

the supreme problem for American students of Chinese history, particularly in its post-Western impact phase, has been one of ethnocentric distortion. One source of this problem is the obvious fact that the West—our West—has played a direct and vitally important part in recent Chinese history. Another source, somewhat less obvious, is that the Chinese themselves, both Marxist and non-Marxist, in reconstructing their own history have depended heavily on vocabulary, concepts, and analytical frameworks borrowed from the West, thus depriving Western historians of compelling insider-produced alternatives to our own outsider perspectives. These perspectives have, until very recently, tended to distort Chinese history either by exaggerating the role of the West or, more subtly, by misconstruing this role.

He then proceeds to deal with three concepts that have tended to produce these distortions. The first is the view that modern Chinese history has been dominated by China's efforts to respond to the challenge posed by the West. As Cohen points out, this view is not entirely wrong, but by placing such emphasis on impact and response, disproportionate attention is paid to West-related facets of the history, internal factors are overinterpreted as responses to foreign impact, and China's unresponsiveness to the foreign challenge is characterized as resulting from a remarkable inertia in China's state, society, economy, and thought.

The second concept is a natural extension of the challenge-response approach, but stresses the contradictions of tradition and modernity. In its crudest form the tradition-modernity concept is reduced to labels: backward-uncivilized-bad as opposed to modern-civilized-good. Chinese society prior to the arrival of the West is simplistically viewed as remaining unchanged since the third century B.C., and little recognition is given to the fact that change can be both constructive and destructive or that the results of modernization can be used for both constructive and destructive purposes. In the hands of such historians as Joseph Levenson, however, the approach becomes much more complex. To Levenson the central question for Chinese intellectuals was how to be both Chinese and modern. This led him to overemphasize the impact of the West both in terms of its effect in bringing about a crisis in Chinese civilization and the amount of attention paid to the West by Chinese intellectuals, particularly during the nineteenth century.

The third concept dealt with by Cohen is the argument over imperialism—what was it, and was it good or bad for China in the process of modernization? Again Cohen points out that these approaches tend to distort both our concept of the impact of the West and understanding of the internal changes taking place in the Chinese economy.

In his final chapter Cohen discusses a more recent approach that he describes as being a China-centered history of China. The chief identifying feature of this China-centered approach, which has been gaining ground since the 1970s, is that it begins with Chinese problems set in a Chinese context. These problems may be influenced, even generated, by the West, or have no connection with the West at all, but either way they are Chinese problems, experienced in China by Chinese, and their historical importance is measured in Chinese rather than Western terms. Thus internal factors such as factionalism within the governing elite, the changing role of the Chinese gentry, the nature of regionalism, and the struggle between urban and rural constituencies have received much more attention from our historians, and this, in turn, has led to the development of provincial and even county-based studies, as well as studies that have adopted a vertical approach recognizing the wide range of social strata within Chinese society and the wide range of regional differences within these strata. Ths new approach has also broadened its grasp of China-centered problems by adopting theories, methodologies, and techniques from the other social sciences. One major consequence of the new approach is the abandonment, by most historians, of 1840 as a general time marker for modern Chinese history and the realization that the entire period from the 1550s to the 1930s constitutes a coherent whole.

Discovering History in China is an excellent survey of the field and should be required reading for any serious student of modern China, historian or otherwise. Its chief defect is that it does not go the extra mile by criticizing the present results of the new approach or attempting to suggest where we should go from here.

W. ALLYN RICKETT

University of Pennsylvania
Philadelphia

KRAUSS, ELLIS S., THOMAS P. ROHLEN, and PATRICIA G. STEINHOFF, eds. *Conflict in Japan.* Pp. viii, 417. Honolulu: University of Hawaii Press, 1984. $24.95. Paperbound, $9.95.

The editors of *Conflict in Japan* have assembled essays on topics ranging from interpersonal relations and village dynamics to labor relations, women's rights, educational power struggles, parliamentary and intragovernmental political machinations, and even the price of rice. Each of these essays is clearly presented and informative, and a few, such as Steinhoff's saga of student radicals, tell stories of conflict in modern Japan that are gripping.

The editors' goal is to provide an alternative to the harmony paradigm that they argue dominates Western views of Japan—and Japanese views of themselves. The alternative offered is the conflict model, with an emphasis more on Simmel, Coser, and Dahrendorf than on Marx.

For a book that promises to do battle with an old paradigm and put forward a radical perspective, *Conflict in Japan* is curiously conservative in approach. Many of the essays read like textbook chapters—albeit good ones—less a presentation of new material than an overview and summary of existing wisdom on postwar Japanese society. Several of the essays seem to be less new approaches than old approaches wrapped up in a fancy new package, with the addition of references to Dahrendorf and the substitution of the term "conflict management" for "harmony." For better or worse, this is the rarest of recent books on power and conflict: there is nary a mention of Foucault, of semiology, or of the politics of discourse.

A weakness of this book is that there is too narrow a historical perspective. As the editors point out, conflict theory allows for a focus on change, for a diachronic appreciation of social phenomena. Several of the essays in *Conflict in Japan* do take a historical perspective, but none goes back before World War II. The result is that the book as a whole leaves the unintended impression that conflict in contemporary Japan is largely the result of the American occupation introducing alien institutions and values—including democracy; women's, workers', and students' rights; and educational liberalism—into a previously harmonious culture. An essay or two on conflict in prewar Japan would have been a welcome addition.

Yet, despite these words of criticism, I strongly recommend *Conflict in Japan* both to Japan specialists and to readers interested in learning about how familiar social and political issues are played out in a non-Western setting. *Conflict in Japan* would make a fine text for a course in contemporary Japanese society.

JOSEPH J. TOBIN

East-West Center
Honolulu
Hawaii

PRATT, JOHN CLARK, comp. *Vietnam Voices: Perspectives on the War Years, 1941-1982.* Pp. iii, 706. New York: Viking Penguin, 1984. Paperbound, $12.95.

Vietnam Voices is poetic history in the tradition of Aeschylus. Yes, it is another one of those Vietnam books, but this one is different: it is fun. While most such books tend to promulgate a particular perspective on the war, Pratt's volume is distinguished by an ecumenical outlook. A compilation of documents authored by people ranging from the humblest Vietnamese peasant to the president of the United States, the book is an intermingling of excerpts, taken from a variety of sources—from novels; policy statements; antiwar poems; Vietcong, Pathet Lao, and Khmer Rouge tracts; field action reports; memos; speeches; letters; diplomatic cables; and the like. As such, the book easily could have turned into an incoherent mass. Pratt avoids this pitfall, weaving a narrative that transports the reader through 40 years of the Vietnam experience from U.S. intelligence operations in Indochina in 1941 to

U.S. support for the founding of the Cambodian anti-Vietnamese rebel alliance in 1982.

Pratt opens with quotes from a 1982 news conference at which President Reagan incorrectly declared, among other things, that "the first moves toward combat moves in Vietnam" occurred when "John F. Kennedy authorized the sending in of a division of marines." Pratt's message is clear: Americans can hardly be expected to draw constructive lessons from the Vietnam experience when they have precious little idea of what actually happened there. Pratt aims to "provide a comprehensive introduction to a search for understanding" of the Southeast Asian wars. It is an ambitious goal, and one largely achieved.

There are, however, some minor flaws. In places, the narrative is frustratingly discontinuous, and slightly episodic, with some apparent non sequiturs. Many documents reprinted here have been heavily edited, and in places this has a disconcerting and possibly distorting effect. For example, one key speech partially reprinted is President Nixon's 30 April 1970 address on the Cambodian incursion. That address was probably one of the most intense of Nixon's entire career and unquestionably one of the most significant public statements by U.S. officials over the course of the entire Indochinese conflict. To edit it is a shame and smacks of pop history. One is left with the sense that this book should be redone as a four-volume series, restoring 2000 or so of the pages slashed from the original manuscript.

On balance, much of this editing was no doubt judicious and necessary. The justaposition of choice quotes often lies just this side of an inspired sense of counterpoint and irony. This book will enlighten anyone wishing to hear more clearly the voices calling from our past and warning about our future.

CRAIG ETCHESON

University of Southern California
Los Angeles

RABINOVICH, ITAMAR. *The War for Lebanon, 1970-1983.* Pp. 243. Ithaca, NY: Cornell University Press, 1984. $19.95.

This book is a study of the modern history of Lebanon, particularly the critical period since the 1975-76 civil war. The author, Itamar Rabinovich, is a well-known scholar and currently head of the Dayan Center and Shiloah Institute for Middle Eastern and African Studies at Tel Aviv University.

The book describes the political actors in the Lebanese arena, both domestic and international, and the interaction among them. Rabinovich acknowledges the complexity of the Lebanese struggle as one involving different sects, political parties, and regions. However, he sees the war as resulting, in part, from a coalescence of these groups into two political camps: the one, "largely Christian," interested in maintaining the political status quo in Lebanon; the other, "largely Muslim," desirous of changing it. In this struggle, nothing less than the identity of the Lebanese state was at stake.

"In the twentieth century," Rabinovich claims, "conflict over Lebanon has revolved around four rival concepts of the Lebanese state: a small Christian Lebanon; a greater Christian Lebanon; a greater pluralistic Lebanon, and an Arab Lebanon." The struggle for power in Lebanon has led to two civil wars: the 1958 civil war, and the longer and far bloodier war of 1975-76 with its far-reaching consequences for regional and international politics.

The book studies these consequences, including the Syrian intervention in Lebanon; the presence of pro-Khomeini Iranian elements in the country; the Israeli invasion of 1982 and the following war with Syria; the role played by foreign powers; and the important Palestinian question.

In all this Rabinovich emphasizes the political side of the story, tending to downplay economic factors and their relation to the Lebanese state and the current crisis. In fact, he underestimates the role played by the maldistribution of wealth and privilege in

Lebanon between the wealthy Maronite north and the poor Shiite south, an important factor in understanding the current explosive situation in the country.

The book concludes with an assessment of the situation in Lebanon after the Israeli invasion of that country, planned by Ariel Sharon. According to Rabinovich, the invasion achieved only one of its major objectives—the eviction of the PLO from southern Lebanon. Other aims, such as "the reconstruction of the Lebanese state," a Syrian "loss of position in Lebanon," and the achievement of "normal open relations" with Lebanon, failed. Rabinovich concludes that the war "did not break the deadlock" in Lebanon "and seemed, in fact, to have in some ways compounded it."

While there is a need for works attempting to elucidate the Lebanese situation, the themes in this book are not entirely new. One of the most interesting exceptions is the material on the secret contacts between the Maronites and the Israelis, not only during the 1970s, but reaching back to Zionist leaders like Weizmann in the 1940s. Rabinovich is in a good position to know of these as he has been a consultant to both the Likud and Labor governments.

LOUAY BAHRY

The University of Tennessee
Knoxville

EUROPE

BESSEL, RICHARD. *Political Violence and the Rise of Nazism: The Storm Troopers in Eastern Germany in 1925-1934.* Pp. xii, 215. New Haven, CT: Yale University Press, 1984. $20.00.

Richard Bessel has done thorough and detailed research on the documentary material available in West and East Germany and Poland on the rise of the Nazi Brown Shirts (SA) in what was, until World War II, eastern Germany. Bessel is a lecturer in history at the Open University in Britain. His factual statements are supported by footnotes that, on occasion, cite two, three, or even four different sources. The political, socioeconomic, cultural, and psychological aspects are all given due weight, presented clearly and fully, and related to each other. His final conclusions are set forth succinctly in an "Epilogue" and "Conclusions."

The use of violence to achieve political ends is certainly nothing new. It has been going on for millennia. However, our twentieth century has surely set a record in this regard. Wars, purges, efforts to destroy entire social classes or races, air bombardments of civilian populations—including the use of atomic bombs—assassinations, and terrorist activities of many kinds—who knows the grisly total thus destroyed? It is possible that, because of the larger populations and much more destructive means, more human beings have been violently destroyed in our century than in the entire period from the death of Christ—himself a victim of political violence—until 1914.

World War I gave millions of men first-hand experience in the use of violence. Most were repelled, but after the war some of the front-line fighters banded together to continue playing cops and robbers with a vengeance. There appeared the Red Guards of Lenin, the IRA in Ireland, the Fascists in Italy, and, in Germany, first the *Freikorps* and then the storm troops, both brown and red. These and similar groups elsewhere used violence regularly and systematically to advance their aims. They preached and practiced a veritable cult of violence.

Adolf Hitler, with his deep instinctive feeling for the subconscious forces at work in human beings, understood that violence actually attracts many persons. One has only to watch the faces of the audience at a bull-fight or boxing match to comprehend what is involved. Hitler therefore consciously glorified and urged the use of violence by his SA. The SA became the pseudomilitary arm of the party to protect, as it were, its meetings and activities and to stage aggressive propaganda marches.

At the *Machtübernahme* the SA was well on the way to becoming a *Volksarmee*. The SA comprised close to a million men, and

yet, 18 months later, Röhm and many of his
lieutenants were dead by order of their
beloved *Führer*. The Night of the Long
Knives, 30 June 1934, meant the beginning
of the end for the SA. Their numbers shrank
as the SS grew and more than replaced them
and their role in party and state.

Bessel shows clearly why Hitler decided
to render the SA impotent after he attained
power. He no longer needed it, and much of
its "illegal" violence was damaging his
movement in the eyes of the law-and-order-
loving middle class who loomed so large in
his following. Moreover, the *Reichswehr* did
not take kindly to the idea of a *Volksarmee*.

Furthermore, much of the SA had responded strongly and favorably to the
Socialist emphasis in National Socialism.
They came to believe that a second revolution more extreme than that of January 1933
was needed. These tendencies had appeared
even earlier. As a joke current in the Weimar
Republic ran, "Why is the SA like roast
beef?" Answer: "Because it's brown on the
outside and red on the inside."

The SS, which purged the SA and succeeded to its role, emphasized the word
"national" in the party name in an intensely
racist manner. Although it was to use violence on a much larger scale than had the SA,
the SS did so in a much more efficient, disciplined, and orderly manner, which was what
Hitler wanted. The concentration and exter-
mination camps of the SS were run according to the legal procedures of the Third
Reich, and with due regard for the bureaucratic forms and papers that had to be filled
out and filed in the required number of
copies.

This work is instructive reading for
anyone who is concerned about the political
violence that continues to buffet humanity in
our own day, whether this violence is through
the state itself or private volunteer armies or
by terrorist groups or individual assassins.

H. F. MACKENSEN
Fairleigh Dickinson University
Teaneck
New Jersey

GABRIEL, RICHARD S. *The Antagonists: A
Comparative Assessment of the Soviet
and American Soldier*. Contributions in
Military History no. 34. Pp. xii, 208.
Westport, CT: Greenwood Press, 1984.
$29.95.

This careful, possibly misleading, and
perhaps useful book could have been written
by a well-informed intelligence officer about
French, Russian, and German soldiers in
July 1914. As a contribution to military
sociology or anthropology rather than history, it will supply congressional committee
war-gamers with abundant material on a
conventional conflict on the traditional battlefields of central Europe. It is full of interesting information on "sixty characteristics
deemed important to military effectiveness."
These are then plotted on a U model to show
the "comparative degree of advantage or dis-
advantage" that each army has over its
adversaries. It does give a clear picture of the
kinds of problems each military establishment is worried about. So long as the reader
realizes that quantification of these worries
produces a piece of science fiction, the book
will do no positive harm, and may be helpful
to policymakers.

Its basic methodological flaw is that we
can learn from the Soviet military press, or,
indeed, from our army's survey materials,
how drug or alcohol abuse would affect their
combat performances. That they get +4 to
our –3 for drugs and –3 to our +2 on alcohol
does show that heroin and vodka are dangerous substances. So they get –4 for assaults
on officers or other authorities, while we get
+4 for nonviolence. Perhaps two-thirds of
Gabriel's mathematical guesses are very
shaky. Those on active and reserve manpower, hours under control, numbers of
tanks, and so forth are obviously sounder.
The problem is their linkage to unit esprit,
soldier motivation, and alienation in combat.

We all know that our volunteers are less
qualified than their conscripts (–1 to +5), and
less representative of our total population
(–1 to +6). We also know that we spend less
time on military ambience, a bit more than
spit and polish, and related to the time spent

in field training (−4 to +4). But we are substituting high-tech machines for labor, as we cannot force our citizens to put their bodies on the line but can and are willing to pay for expensive gadgets. Indirectly, then, this book raises profound questions about our army's readiness for the least likely of wars. When it is used to point out known weaknesses in its training and motivation, it is a valuable book—but only for those who know enough about military intelligence to know that estimates about intangibles are only educated guesses. In August 1914, in less tightly controlled societies, everyone was well informed about the opponent's equipment, men, and commanders. Who would have guessed that the Russians, French, Belgians, or British would have fought as well as they did against such odds? We are now as far from the last Great War as they were from 1874. That men fight well when they, and in our case, their families, are in the same boat is one of the factors that military anthropology cannot quantify.

THEODORE ROPP

Duke University
Durham
North Carolina

KOSS, STEPHEN. *The Rise and Fall of the Political Press in Britain.* Vol. 2. Pp. x, 718. Chapel Hill: University of North Carolina Press, 1984. $34.00.

The history of interconnections between leading and aspiring political figures in Great Britain and publishers, editors, and writers of that nation's newspapers presents a fascinating mosaic. It is one the late Stephen Koss captures splendidly in this depiction of intricate road maps of British twentieth-century political realignments.

Relying upon a vast store of archival materials, including many personal memoirs and reports of three Royal Commissions on the Press, Koss has written a lucid narrative. The foremost theme of Volume 2 is the prolonged decline during the twentieth century of the prior enmeshment of political party leaders and the political press. In unraveling details of the theme, a cast of seeming thousands is introduced. Many of the major figures, or their families, provide sundry linkages to varying, shifting political issues and to the fortunes of specific contenders for political power over the decades.

The range of such issues of contention for both parties and the press naturally is extensive, including subjects as diverse as the Boer War, free trade, Ireland, the great depression and appeasement of Germany, and post-World War II developments. Considering the nature and vast variety of the topics discussed, perhaps it is a minor criticism that there is occasional difficulty following such matters as election results or party and parliamentary leadership turnovers in the context of the narrative. Nor does it particularly detract from the main theme that post-World War II events are not covered as thoroughly as previous epochs. This latter section primarily highlights the accomplished fact of political independence of the press from political parties.

The work contains many important, even enlightening, discussions surrounding its major theme. Included among these are the following: early party subsidies and investments in the press; editors as party representatives; early press "trustification" culminating in spreading corporate ownership in the 1970s; the never-ending Byzantine world of fighting between press barons and leaders of cabinets and party factions; the decline of the Liberal party and the growth of the Labor party; the frequency of cabinet coalitions of questionable bedfellows and the attempts of certain press leaders to destroy coalitions and reinvigorate partisan party politics; the press typically thwarting attempts at government regulation while still entering gentlemen's agreements throttling news stories; and machinations of segments of the press to involve Winston Churchill in a war cabinet in 1939. The list is nearly endless. Volume 2, as well as Volume 1, is a tribute to solid scholarship; a much appreciated amount of dry wit, depicted in excellent cartoons; and a detailed mastery of subject matter.

CHARLES A. JOINER

Temple University
Philadelphia
Pennsylvania

NYE, JOSEPH S., Jr., ed. *The Making of America's Soviet Policy*. Pp. ix, 369. New Haven, CT: Yale University Press, 1984. $27.50.

KILLEN, LINDA. *The Russian Bureau—A Case Study in Wilsonian Diplomacy*. Pp. xii, 202. Lexington: University Press of Kentucky, 1983. $22.00.

The Making of America's Soviet Policy is a noteworthy exception to the rhetorical flotsam that accumulates during a presidential election. Judicious in tone and comprehensive in scope, this publication of the Council on Foreign Relations probably influenced few ballots. But Mr. Reagan's advisors as well as concerned citizens would do well to carefully read the conclusions of Joseph S. Nye and his colleagues.

Their book is about the principal strategic challenge to the United States: how to deal with the Soviet Union. Successive presidential administrations have subscribed to a foreign policy strategy designed to contain the expansion of Soviet power and to influence the constellation of political forces within the Soviet state. Like his predecessors, Ronald Reagan shaped containment to fit his own world view. The result has been a policy of containment by confrontation. An American arms buildup was orchestrated to reestablish U.S. military superiority and to bleed the Soviet economy into submission. Not to mention the fact that President Reagan has seemed to cherish every opportunity to take the Soviet regime to the dock of world opinion.

The Nye volume seeks to present a reasonable alternative to Mr. Reagan's brand of diplomacy without raising false hopes. The strategy is variously described as "containment with communications and negotiations" or as a "managed-balance-of-power" approach to the Soviet problem. This, according to the authors, demands acceptance of the fact that rivalry is at the heart of all relations between Washington and Moscow. A Soviet-American condominium is as unrealistic a choice for the United States as the dream of a fortress America. The United States, they argue, can ill afford a dominant Soviet role in world affairs. Nor can U.S. national security be enhanced by isolating the Soviets. Their remedy rests on the twin goals of military strength and peaceful engagement. Moderation is their answer to America's Soviet dilemma.

How the United States can achieve the dual objectives of peace and strength is the unifying theme of this book. The least original of the book's recommendations are proposed by those contributors who grapple with the policymaking process itself. Of greater value to the reader are three superb essays on the historical record of Soviet-American relations. Ernest May turns his attention to the early years of the cold war in order to discern the reasons for a presidential penchant to exaggerate the Soviet threat for immediate domestic dividends. Stanley Hoffman examines the causes for detente's failure to meet the expectations of its architects, and Samuel Huntington looks at the downturn in Soviet-American relations that followed the 1972 SALT I accords. Huntington also takes the opportunity to venture an informed guess about the future state of affairs and suggests that Ronald Reagan's strident anti-Communist reputation may allow him to act the way Jimmy Carter wanted to act but could not. Herein lies the difficulty that is given only a passing nod by the Nye volume. President Reagan's success as a peacemaker will depend no less on his willingness to treat the Soviet Union as an equal and legitimate partner in negotiations instead of as an international outlaw. Woodrow Wilson, the first president to face the Soviets, learned this lesson at a cost.

Linda Killen has written an informative account of an organization that otherwise may have gone unnoticed except by the diplomatic historian—the Russian Bureau of the U.S. War Trade Board. The bureau existed for a little less than one year from October 1918 to July 1919 as a go-between for American business and the Russian consumer. The bureau earned a minor profit from its activities but failed to make Russia a "fit partner" for Wilson's "league of honor." The failure was caused in no small way by the collapse of the Russian currency and transportation system, and the absence of law and order. The more basic cause, according to Killen, was Wilson's own stubborn effort to try to deal with Russia in spite of the Bolsheviks. American aid was targeted toward Siberia and Northern Russia, areas where White forces with the assistance of the Entente Powers had temporarily held Lenin's Red Army at bay.

Killen writes with authority about the bureaucratic strife in Washington as Wilson attempted to defeat Germany and cope with the Russian Revolution. The conflict between the Departments of State and Commerce over U.S. foreign policy toward Russia and Colonel House's efforts to place the White House staff at the policy helm are only too reminiscent of the political clashes of recent years in official Washington. Killen's description of the tensions between the United States and its allies during their abortive foray into Russia are equally instructive. At one point, Wilson's cabinet even considered the possibility of a full-scale war with Japan over Japanese involvement in Cossack attacks against American troops guarding the Trans-Siberian Railroad. More to the point is her conclusion that Wilson's refusal to recognize Soviet Russia precluded American efforts to modify the very ideology it feared.

PAUL MICHAEL KOZAR

Falls Church
Virginia

TERRY, SARAH MEIKLEJOHN, ed. *Soviet Policy in Eastern Europe.* Pp. xv, 375. New Haven, CT: Yale University Press, 1984. $27.50.

This collection of essays provides a comprehensive survey of the USSR's policies toward its Eastern European allies in the years since the Polish and Hungarian revolutions of the 1950s. The volume includes both historical surveys of the USSR's policies toward individual countries and essays focusing on particular regional problems. In general, the historical surveys seem to be far less successful in broadening our understanding of Soviet policy than the discussions of particular problems. A few of the historical surveys seem to be reworkings of materials published elsewhere while others attempt to cover so much ground that they seem quite superficial. Some of the historical surveys devote so much attention to domestic developments within the East European states that the USSR's own policies are given little attention. Moreover, the attempt to cover a wide range of political, economic, and military developments within the confines of a single essay often leads to an overreliance on secondary sources and clouds the originality of the authors' own contributions. Finally, the efforts to predict future developments in the region are not particularly enlightening.

In contrast, the essays that focus on particular problems, such as developments in political economy, energy policy, theoretical discussions of socialist development, and the Warsaw Pact, generally prove to be the more successful contributions to this volume. These essays seem far less dependent on secondary sources than do many of the historical surveys—although there are exceptions—and therefore present the authors' own conclusions with far greater clarity. Most important, the focus on a particular problem provides an effective framework for a detailed discussion of Soviet policy per se and for comprehensive comparisons of the USSR's policies toward the different states in the region.

Despite the immense variation in the quality of these essays, the collection as a whole does reveal some general characteristics of the USSR's policies in Eastern Europe. The volume clearly demonstrates that the Soviet leadership is perplexed and confused about developments within Eastern Europe, has no fresh or imaginative ideas to deal with the problems of the region, and is evidently unwilling or unable to do more than muddle through from crisis to crisis.

JONATHAN HARRIS
University of Pittsburgh
Pennsylvania

UNITED STATES

CORNEBISE, ALFRED E. *The Stars and Stripes: Doughboy Journalism in World War I.* Pp. xiii, 221. Westport, CT: Greenwood Press, 1984. $29.95.

The *Stars and Stripes* is probably the most famous army newspaper of all time. The eight-page weekly was published in Paris, under the auspices of the General Staff of the American Expeditionary Forces in Europe, from 8 February 1918 until 13 June 1919. Inaugurated primarily as a vehicle for improving morale among the widely scattered American troops, the *Stars and Stripes* quickly established itself as a popular and significant channel of communication. At the height of its popularity the paper had a weekly circulation of 526,000 copies.

Despite the brevity of its format, the *Stars and Stripes* was a diverse publication that offered its readers a regular source of news from home and from the battlefront, an editorial page, cartoons, artwork, paid advertising, and an extensive selection of poetry and letters to the editor.

Alfred Cornebise invites readers to consider the *Stars and Stripes* as a cultural artifact of World War I and as a potentially valuable source of data for the social and cultural historian. "The paper is a prism," he writes, "providing us with useful and fascinating glimpses and insights, often presented in an amusing fashion, into the life of

Americans soldiering in Europe, far from familiar scenes, under the conditions of a great war."

Cornebise emphasizes reportage, rather than analysis, in his survey of the *Stars and Stripes.* The book is intended to be "a sampler of AEF life" and makes liberal use of direct quotations and poems to convey the essential character and flavor of the newspaper. An introductory chapter details the paper's origins, personnel, and operations. The next eight chapters survey a number of themes that recur throughout the 71 issues of the *Stars and Stripes*: advertising; army mess and uniforms; military hierarchy; medical topics, religious faith, and death; morale and esprit; images of the Allies and the enemy; sports and entertainment; and education. The final chapter assesses the paper's accomplishments and its significance.

Cornebise has done an exemplary job of balancing the conflicting demands of accessibility and scholarly documentation. Casual readers will find a lively description of an interesting journalistic enterprise. Scholars wishing to explore some topic in depth will find the 23 pages of notes and the 3-page bibliographical essay invaluable.

JAMES TODD HAYES
St. Peter
Minnesota

COUVARES, FRANCIS G. *The Remaking of Pittsburgh: Class and Culture in an Industrializing City, 1877-1919.* Pp. viii, 187. Albany: State University of New York Press, 1984. $33.50. Paperbound, $10.95.

Two decades ago most historians conceived of the history of the American city in preindustrial and industrial terms. This simple dichotomy crumbled under the detailed and comparative research of the "new social history" that emerged in the 1960s. Magnification of the urban world revealed a complex evolution of social and economic phenomena. While most historians today recognize the dominance of commerce or long-distance trade for the aspirations and institutions of the early nineteenth-century city, few have agreed upon the character of the urban experience that existed between the commercial era and the industrial metropolis of the early twentieth century. In *The Remaking of Pittsburgh* Francis G. Couvares vigorously advances an argument for viewing the years of industrial transition as ones in which workers achieved their greatest sense of belonging, prestige, and even power. Couvares calls this city the plebian city.

The study unfolds from a central observation. "How did the city that embraced the labor struggle of 1877 [the railroad strike] turn into the city which so fiercely repudiated the labor struggle of 1919 [the steel strike]?" Adopting the community approach of recent scholars of the working class, Couvares examines the social and political dimensions of workers' lives along with the power of skilled craftsmen in the growing iron and glass industries of post-Civil War Pittsburgh, their solidarity with other workers despite ethnic divisions, and the success of trade union organization. He emphasizes the plebeian culture by which energetic popular entertainment, amateur sports, local neighborhood social organizations, and public civic rituals integrated workers into the community, giving them a sense of full participation and citizenship.

In the 1880s, however, new forces emerged and began to unravel the workers' position in the plebeian city. Technological innovation and work reorganization diminished the importance of skilled workers in the production of steel at the same time that the widespread use of eastern and southern European immigrants in unskilled laboring jobs severed formerly fragile worker loyalties. Symbolized by defeat in the Homestead Strike of 1892, the trade unions' power in the work place faded, while competitive activities of the new boss-ruled political organization challenged labor's role in the community. As the suburbs lured middle-class persons away from the older residential city,

workers became increasingly segregated in specific neighborhoods. New cosmopolitan forms of middle-class entertainment blossomed in counterpoint to plebeian activities, and progressives bombarded the beleaguered working classes with uplifting social reforms and paternalistic programs. Embattled at the work place and segregated in the urban community, workers turned to new mass entertainment activities for leisure in the early twentieth century. The plebeian culture, which by integrating work, leisure, and residence had positioned workers in the community, gave way to a mass of workers separate from other social groups of the city.

Couvares's contribution to understanding the American city lies in his integrating concept of the plebeian city, within which leisure activities command a central position. Although his description of leisure in turn-of-the-century Pittsburgh is also well done, the analysis of the industrial metropolis raises little new information. Rather, Couvares may have oversimplified the examination of workers and middle-class Pittsburghers, leaving important questions to be answered. The progressives' targets were the new immigrants; what were the attitudes and activities of the older workers and their children who slowly experienced social and economic mobility? Pittsburghers of Irish, British, and German heritage were neither simply the downtrodden proletariat nor the new middle class. Their positions in the community must be part of the interpretation of early twentieth-century Pittsburgh. Concise, well-written, and imaginatively conceptualized, *The Remaking of Pittsburgh* improves our understanding of the city during the years of industrial transition and advances several interpretations concerning the subsequent industrial metropolis, which should stimulate closer examination.

EDWARD K. MULLER
University of Pittsburgh
Pennsylvania

JOHANNES, JOHN R. *To Serve the People: Congress and Constituency Service.* Pp. xv, 294. Lincoln: University of Nebraska Press, 1984. $19.95. Paperbound, $10.95.

The 1984 election is over. Not only did President Reagan easily win a second term, but the power of incumbency once again proved so strong that voters returned to office virtually all veteran House and Senate candidates.

Most members of Congress believe, and conventional wisdom reinforces the view, that service to constituents—or "casework"—contributes measurably to the likelihood of a successful campaign. In fact, in perhaps the most revealing portion of *To Serve the People*, author John R. Johannes concludes that "casework per se . . . does not seem to provide any particularly strong electoral advantage."

Johannes arrives at this conclusion after reviewing the casework process in great detail. He begins with the assumption that "a veritable revolution of casework in Congress" has occurred since the 1960s and proceeds to examine the causes and consequences of the so-called ombudsman role. He describes the nature of the system and who is involved, and he attempts to measure and analyze the casework burden. He scrutinizes the interaction between congressional and executive agency staff, their rules and norms of behavior; he assesses the equity of the prevailing system and its value to the more visible legislative oversight function of the Congress.

Not surprisingly, Johannes discovered that the sudden enthusiasm for government programs in the 1960s led to more laws, more regulations, more paperwork, and more constituent problems that in turn generated "an independent, largely bureaucratized semi-institutionalized" casework system. The processing of inquiries is highly routinized and nondiscriminatory. What seems to count is the merit of the case. Political clout certainly exists, but, as Johannes states, "it is neither widely spread nor frequently involved." Although casework does not offer the opportunity for systematic oversight of a program's management or effectiveness, it does provide low-cost, generally accurate intelligence that can under certain circumstances lead to proposed legislation or changes in agency regulations.

Johannes presents a number of suggestions for improving the current system, ranging from radical straw men such as a national ombudsman or a centralized congressional committee to incremental reforms that include better training for casework staff and more integration of casework with other congressional activities, especially legislative and oversight duties. While he believes that the results would be worth the effort, Johannes recognizes the existence of a number of institutional barriers to change that will likely inhibit progress.

To Serve the People is a thorough, even meticulous description of congressional constituency service. Johannes asks the right questions and organizes material well. Unfortunately, the data available are from the mid- to late 1970s and the conclusions they allow are often tentative at best. Moreover, Johannes uses jargon that I found unnecessarily arcane and includes in the text explanations of regression analysis that might better have been relegated to the notes.

All of this is to say that a well-conceived project that includes extensive analysis has raised more questions than it has answered. As a result, *To Serve the People* should be of interest to scholars whose specialty is the study of Congress, but it should have less appeal to the general reader.

JOSEPH ANTHONY IMLER
Arlington
Virginia

KELLERMAN, BARBARA. *The Political Presidency: Practice of Leadership from Kennedy to Reagan.* Pp. xii, 300. New York: Oxford University Press, 1984. $22.50.

Barbara Kellerman has written a book on the presidency that will interest a wide-ranging audience. Her basic thesis is that Americans historically have been hostile toward authority and that this cultural phenomenon creates difficulties for leaders wishing to exercise power. In this situation, presidents have to rely not on naked power but on their powers of persuasion. Presidents are effective mainly when they elicit the cooperation of other elites within government, such as legislators and bureaucrats. While not a new point, Kellerman makes the case that this idea often is unappreciated, both by presidents and by outside observers.

Perhaps the most interesting part of this book is Kellerman's case studies of the six presidents from Kennedy to Reagan. Some of these men were able to rise above cultural constraints and leave their mark on national policy. The key, she says, lies in the personal qualities of these individuals—having a vision and understanding that leadership is a political process, that is, one that requires careful attention to other leaders and the "nature of the times." She cites Johnson's handling of the War on Poverty and Reagan's leadership with respect to the 1981 budget cuts as success stories, while Carter's push for an energy program ranks much lower on the effectiveness scale.

This book is a very accessible bit of research. Lay readers will find it a pleasure to read. It is well organized and quite enjoyable. It reviews the scope of postwar presidencies and draws interesting contrasts. It also tries to put the case studies into a broader, more theoretical framework.

Ultimately, however, the book is somewhat unsatisfying. It gives observers the impression that presidents succeed or fail because of their approach to the office. In reality, presidents often succeed less because of their own efforts and more because they are the beneficiaries of outside events. For example, Reagan has been praised for having a vision and being a "great communicator." But these qualities did not save his party from major losses in the 1982 midterms or from achieving only minor congressional gains in the 1984 elections. The role of leadership obviously is important, but it

should not completely distract people from the ups and downs of any administration or from the external social and economic events that affect perceptions of leadership qualities.

DARRELL M. WEST
Brown University
Providence
Rhode Island

SOWELL, THOMAS. *Civil Rights: Rhetoric or Reality*. Pp. 164. New York: William Morrow, 1984. $11.95.

A senior fellow at the Hoover Institution, Stanford University, Thomas Sowell is a black, conservative economist who has provocatively challenged the basic tenets of American liberal thought of the past 20 years.

In his newest book, Sowell makes a strong case that contemporary civil rights activism is concerned more with theory and symbolism than with hard reality. He attacks the liberal beliefs that discrimination against American minorities is always the root cause of poverty and that political action is the most effective way to end poverty. Many ethnic groups have suffered discrimination in American history, he argues. Yet, they have survived and prevailed. How? By concentrating on economic solutions to their problems, not on political or governmental action.

More and more, Sowell believes, civil rights activists are ignoring essentials. He says the early stages of the civil rights movement constituted a necessary first step for blacks and other minorities because this phase helped open the doors for economic equal opportunity. But equal opportunity for jobs has given way to affirmative action; the struggle to provide adequate resources in American schools for black children has given way to busing.

Civil Rights: Rhetoric or Reality is an important book, one that will no doubt arouse controversy. There are moments when Sowell abandons pure scholarship for advocacy, and he often fails in his analysis to give sufficient weight to the effect of the psychological burden of generations of discrimination in America against blacks and other minorities. Generally, however, his observations are perceptive and may inspire some needed reevaluation of contemporary social action programs.

FRED ROTONDARO
National Italian American
    Foundation
Washington, D.C.

SOCIOLOGY

CSIKSZENTMIHALYI, MIHALY and REED LARSON. *Being Adolescent: Conflict and Growth in the Teenage Years.* Pp. xvi, 332. New York: Basic Books, 1984. $21.95.

Researchers and practitioners who specialize in adolescent behavior will welcome Csikszentmihalyi and Larson's contribution to our limited store of knowledge about the adolescent experience. The book is a sensitive portrait of teenagers' daily lives that derives from an innovative study the authors conducted in 1977. Seventy-five Chicago-area teenagers agreed to wear electronic beepers for one week and to report their activities and moods when signaled by the researchers at random intervals each day. Report forms asked the participants what they were doing when signaled, and with whom and where, and self-ratings were solicited on scales measuring feelings of concentration and mastery, desires to be doing something else, and various mood states—for example, alert, happy, irritable, strong, angry, and so forth. This experience sampling method (ESM), an increasingly popular research tool among social scientists, permitted a detailed recording of the teenagers' interactions and emotional states as they occurred, and as the teenagers perceived them.

Perhaps the most difficult task facing researchers who employ the ESM is processing the wealth of information they obtain about unique individual experiences in a way that permits general statements about patterns of thought and behavior. Csikszentmihalyi and Larson share some of their participants' 4489 reports with the reader through discussions and copies of particular reports and graphic summaries of the activities and moods of selected individuals, and these presentations highlight the difficulties the authors must have encountered in attempting to arrive at general conclusions about the adolescent experience. What is immediately apparent from these presentations is that similar stimuli evoke quite different responses from different teenagers. While this observation may be less than profound, Csikszentmihalyi and Larson document it well and entertain the reader in the process.

Had Csikszentmihalyi and Larson not exposed the reader to the individual reports, some of their general findings might be considered mundane. For example, the authors found that teenagers' moods change dramatically within short periods of time and that they feel best when they are with friends and worst in the classroom. Neither will surprise most readers. What might surprise the reader is that unstructured and, perhaps, deviant activities are not the most enjoyable for teenagers. Instead, they appear to derive their greatest joy from activities that involve high levels of concentration, rules of interaction, feedback, suspension of self-consciousness and a sense of belonging to something larger than themselves. These "flow experiences" stem from such seemingly disparate events as rock concerts, family outings, organized sports, music or dance performances, and excursions with friends; the pattern suggests that teenagers enjoy challenge and structure provided that the activities are meaningful and they are proficient at them.

The chapter devoted to flow experiences is most insightful and will inspire those of us who teach adolescents toward reworking our methods. Those of us who do research on adolescent attitudes and behavior will long for more such conclusions from these data and will hope for further reports from Csikszentmihalyi and Larson. Taken as a whole, the book is worthwhile reading for educators, parents, counselors, and researchers whose primary interest is the adolescent experience.

JAN F. BRAZZELL
Louisiana State University
Baton Rouge

MATTHIESSEN, PETER. *Indian Country.* Pp. xii, 338. New York: Viking Press, 1984. $17.95.

Peter Matthiessen is, above all else, a master craftsman with a talent for creating word pictures that are vivid, angry, biased, and, alas, one-dimensional. As I was carried along by the flow of Matthiessen's narrative, I kept wishing that the writer's call for an immediate retreat to the past were possible, and that doing so would benefit Native Americans, whose exploitation has been ceaseless since the intrusion of unwanted Europeans so long ago. The hero of the saga is traditionalism, and Matthiessen takes, or makes, every opportunity possible to vilify all else, especially Indians, suggesting that some accommodation with whites, the late twentieth century, and progress—whatever that means—is still a real option for consideration. For example, he maintains that all Hopi must shun electricity because it would serve as "an inducement to buy . . . expensive appliances," which would lead to "increasing dependence on the white man for goods and services." Like Borland's *When the Legends Die*, Matthiessen pleads for a total rejection of whites and their technology— the twin enemies of all who accept the Creator and traditional values—and their bribed full- and mixed-blood toadies who have grasped the brass ring of American progress and fear letting go lest Native Americans lose the will to fight and allow

white capitalists to carry the day uncontested.

Can Native Americans return successfully to their traditional ways of life? Is it necessary to do so without accommodation? If not, what might the bits and pieces of accommodation be? One will not find the answers to these and myriad other questions in this volume. What is found is an essay similar, in part, to William Least Heat Moon's philosophical travelogue, *Blue Highways*, which offers anger without options, total resistance and not a national policy crafted by Indians, and leaders who are called to reject future coexistence instead of leaders trained to meet the enemy on philosophical and judicial battlefields that are not, and never have been, black and white. Retreat is the hero; thoughtful readers will question that fact. But, if they wish to do philosophical battle with this writer, they need to be warned that Matthiessen writes with clarity, style, and persuasiveness; he has fought vehemently against white encroachment, as this volume's essays suggest, and he presents here a belief that is gaining acceptance these days. Despite the difficulty readers may have with this thesis, he will leave them ashamed, angry, and confused about where to go from here. The volume should be read and answered. I guarantee that the former will be easier to do than the latter.

ARTHUR H. DEROSIER, Jr.
The College of Idaho
Caldwell

NELKIN, DOROTHY and MICHAEL S. BROWN. *Workers at Risk: Views from the Workplace.* Pp. xvii, 220. Chicago: University of Chicago Press, 1984. $20.00.

This book assesses the "perceptions and concerns of workers" who are exposed to chemicals in their occupational environments. The approach attempts to describe the significance of subjective experiences and their relationships to workers' behavior.

The study is based upon open-ended interviews with 75 employees in a variety of occupations in which there is exposure to chemicals. "Twenty-nine work as chemical operators, maintenance workers, and technicians in large chemical, pharmaceutical, food processing or industrial plants. Four workers are maintenance or technical workers in small production firms." Sixteen of the informants are laboratory technicians and maintenance workers in universities, agencies, or research institutes; there are also four fire fighters, four railroad workers, three health care workers, four artists, and three gardeners.

Technical background interview support was provided by interviews with industrialists, government agencies, universities, and union leaders.

Work risk is considered a social concept, and definitions of dangerous occupational conditions therefore "take place in a nexus of social, political and economic conditions."

Accurate data on the human and economic costs of chemical hazards to exposed workers are unfortunately unavailable; mention is made of the institutional and methodological obstacles to obtaining such information. It is known that there are 63,000 commercial chemicals being used in American industrial enterprises.

Labor and industry have taken different positions on work risks, health, and job safety. Since the late 1960s, the arguments and public discussions about environmental affairs have sharpened, and certain issues have come to be seen as the responsibility of management. Some large industrial enterprises have accepted the responsibility by taking strong measures in support of health and safety programs, but the incentives have tended to be related to insurance costs and productivity on the plant floor and assembly lines.

Worker and management explanations about what is to blame for occupational risks indicate a wide range of perceptions. The laboratory technician says the fans do not work, and management replies that the engineers are studying the problem, to which the worker replies, "We'll all be dead before the study is finished." A photo-lab processor complains about poor ventilation in the darkroom plus inadequate exits in case of fire. The employer claims that the building design makes impossible any changes for safety's sake.

A common thread appears in the workers' responses: management is either ignorant of or apathetic about potentially harmful working conditions, and supervisory negligence is symbolic of the perceived employer indifference. "If you come down with a rash or even if 10 come down with a rash, the company says it's all your individual problem."

There are protection controls, but the informants have little faith in their effectiveness; this is especially so with those who have to work with poorly designed equipment. If it is poorly designed, yet essential to production, management has employees work with it as is.

During the Carter administration, there was faith in the Occupational Safety and Health Administration (OSHA). By 1984, however, that agency placed greater emphasis on "personal protective equipment and [on workers' bearing] primary responsibility for safety on the job."

Why do workers accept and adapt to recognized job dangers? The study concludes that "most people accept risks because they need a job." The acceptance may be buttressed by rationalizations: "all work has a certain amount of risk involved"; "it's a normal part of the job"; "we'd never get any work done if we had to wait around to find out if things are safe."

The employee voices are not strident. Some are satisfied but not happy with their work. Some activists blame the system and want political intervention. Some indicate helplessness.

Nelkin and Brown are commended for listening, for their understanding and obvious sympathy. They tell us that more has to be known, and that labor and industry must accept mutual responsibility for correcting dangerous work places.

GEORGE H. HUGANIR
Temple University
Philadelphia
Pennsylvania

NEWMAN, EVELYN S., DONALD J. NEW-MAN, and MINDY L. GEWIRTZ. *Elderly Criminals*. Pp. xxvi, 252. Cambridge, MA: Oelgeschlager, Gunn & Hain, 1984. $25.00.

Written by 18 contributors, this book deals, basically, with two issues. First, it describes crimes committed by the elderly. Second, it describes and evaluates the society's response to these crimes.

The description of elderly crime matches our commonsense expectations. We are told that the incidence of crime among the old is rare, and that the old commit predominantly crimes that require little physical fitness and energy. Thus, they shoplift rather than steal cars or commit rape, and they tend to be white-collar cheaters or tax evaders rather than robbers or hitmen. All this is hardly surprising and contributes little to our knowledge. The basics of gerontology account well enough for the gradual disappearance of all kinds of energy-consuming activities, criminal or not, in the course of aging.

The second theme of the book—how elderly criminals are and should be dealt with—constitutes a genuine problem, especially in a society where the proportion of the population that is old is growing. In particular, are and should they be punished or helped, and, if punishment is the response, how harsh is it and how harsh should it be? Several contributors address these questions. They present the bits of accumulated knowledge about elderly criminals in the hands of police, in courts, jails, and prisons, and in social work programs. They discuss a wide range of options, some of them rational, others not: establishment of geriatric

courts, treating the old as basically insane or childlike; profuse application of fines and probation to keep the old out of confinement; preventive and rehabilitative services; and so forth.

Various contributors advocate punishment of the elderly if guilty, but they have in mind a rather mild punishment. What are their reasons for the recommended leniency? One reason seems to be sympathy for the old—which largely reduces to sympathy for the weak. Another one is that the majority of elderly offenders are not dangerous. Still another reason—the idea of justice—has been, despite its importance, overlooked in this book. The older elderly convicts are, the more they suffer in confinement. Their anxieties and helplessness exceed those of the general population, they are particularly vulnerable to harassment by younger inmates, and, owing to their limited life expectancy, a few years in confinement acquire an ominous meaning. There is a basic principle of justice—treat like cases alike—but identical penalties bring about more suffering when imposed on the old. Is this not an important enough reason for punishing the old somewhat more leniently than their younger counterparts for identical offenses?

The book constitutes a collection of articles rather than a rounded whole. Consequently, repetitions occur. Ambiguities include the meaning of the title; for some contributors the criminal is "elderly" at 55, for others at 60 or even 65. The book focuses on first-time elderly offenders—shoplifters, drunk drivers, child molesters—with long, crimeless lives behind them. Some chapters, however—for example, the otherwise very thoughtful contribution by D. I. Rubenstein—also deal, confusingly, with a very different kind of offender—the inmates who, following most serious crimes, have aged in prison after decades of confinement.

Many of the contributions are interesting and would make valuable articles. It is dubious, however, whether the entire product is sufficiently rich in content to make a book. The desire to produce a book resulted in too extensive and sometimes insignificant descriptions of elderly crime. And the chapters on elderly criminals in the arms of the law and of other agencies bring about many questions, but a very limited body of well-established knowledge and few publicly convincing policy recommendations.

JAN GORECKI

University of Illinois
Urbana-Champaign

REX, JOHN and SALLY TOMLINSON with the assistance of DAVID HEARNDEN and PETER RATCLIFFE. *Colonial Immigrants in a British Society: A Class Analysis.* Pp. xv, 357. London: Routledge & Kegan Paul, 1983. Paperbound, $10.95.

Race relations vis-à-vis two immigrant communities, West Indians and South Asians, and their British hosts is brought into sharp analytical focus in this study of Handsworth, "a particular 'inner-city' area of Birmingham." Chapter 1 is a theoretical introduction on the appropriate subject of "class analysis and colonial immigrants." The last three chapters seek to draw the inevitable conclusions from a microstudy: Chapter 7 on "From Immigrants to Ethnic Minority"; Chapter 8 on "Race, Community, and Conflict"; and the ninth and last chapter, which brings out conclusive findings on "Working Class, Underclass, and Third World Revolution."

Chapter 2 is interesting for its layout of British political ideologies and the race question. It is interesting to be told that Enoch Powell represents not just a transient idea but a basic ideology of British politics. Powell, the authors observe, "became the most charismatic figure in British politics, at least for a while, and one who might in suitable circumstances even be able to break the grip which the Conservative and Labour Parties had on political power."

Chapters 3, "Handsworth—The Population and Social Structure of a Multi-racial Area"; 4, "Black Immigrants at Work"; 5,

"Black Immigrants and the Housing System"; and 6, "Black Immigrants, Schools, and the Class Structure," form the core of the book. Work, houses, schools, and class are what matter in a sociological probe. But we must ask ourselves whether this probing is adequately representative of the triangle of human consciousness—Britishers, West Indians, and Asians—that is being examined. One example is a simple attempt of the authors to group South Asians and West Indians as blacks. My experience in Britain and North America has been that Black Power feels badly that it has not had the cooperation of the browns in their political struggle. The blacks of North America feel the same way. The Asians, especially the South Asians, prefer to fit into the system. The blacks want to fight the system and win their rights.

The story is related very meticulously and is well documented on the three vital questions of work, houses, and education. In all this the immigrants find themselves an underclass. But a relevant question keeps coming up all the while in this otherwise brillant exposé. Have enough samples of similarly underprivileged whites been asked for their opinions and their reasons for holding them? There is some evidence of such questioning but to me, enough of a balance has to be struck to arrive at the facts. In other words, are underprivileged whites no worse off than underprivileged blacks?

Chapter 8 ends with the gloomy prognostication that it now looks as if electoral advantage is to be gained by the political parties by their opposing the black population.

The last chapter is telling in its conclusion. There is little future for the black population in lining up with Labour or even Trotskyism. There is a polarization between blacks and whites. There is patent discrimination against blacks. The authors regretfully note that "nearly half the West Indians and two-thirds of the Asians thought the races got on well," while approximately 60 percent of whites envisioned the problems in the area as due to the presence of the colored people or the deterioration of the area that inevitably arises from the physical presence of colored people. Again we ask the question, Is this a superficial answer by the whites of the particular area or can there be deeper underlying reasons? It was for the authors to find out the answers. The book ends with a terrible indictment: "the choice is really between effective political organization on their own behalf and mindless violence and despair." In our view, must Britain go through the racial violence that the United States did to evolve a civil model, or is Britain really feeling that its treatment of immigrants is no different from the way in which the French and the West Germans treat theirs?

A. JEYARATNAM WILSON
University of New Brunswick
Fredericton
Canada

SCHWARTZ, JOEL. *The Sexual Politics of Jean-Jacques Rousseau.* Pp. xi, 196. Chicago: University of Chicago Press, 1984. $17.00.

Joel Schwartz examines the writings of political philosopher Jean-Jacques Rousseau in order to explain his contradictory and complex views of sexuality and politics. Schwartz believes it impossible to understand the political contentions of Rousseau without incorporating his conception of sexuality. The focus of this work is on Rousseau's basic assumptions regarding male-female differentiation, sexual desire and romantic love, and the impact of the institution of the family.

The assumptions constituting the foundation of Rousseau's philosophy are that in a primitive state, humans are isolated, independent individuals. Sexuality is the link that moves us from individual self-sufficiency to political dependence. Because of sex, we must depend on another person, and this is the beginning of an interdependence that requires people to act less selfishly in society. Sex teaches dependency and co-

operation without exploitation, a relationship that then generalizes to the political sphere. Sexual relationships are exercises in mutual domination, and politics is the arena in which we strive for domination over others. Sexuality is in fact a manifestation of the desire to rule, and the sexual relationship is a political relationship because men and women alternate in it as ruler and ruled.

Differentiation of males and females requires mutual dependence that eventuates in political betterment. Rousseau contends that women are more social than men because they are weaker and must depend on men. When a man senses the relative weakness of the women who are dependent on him, he becomes a more effective provider and defender. As a relationship equalizer, women induce men to depend on them also. Male dependence is beneficial to the group because a man who recognizes his dependence on women will also be the citizen who recognizes his dependence on society.

To overcome the fact that men have a weaker desire for sex than women, men attempt to increase psychologically their feelings of physical strength by boosting their self-esteem. The result is expressed by Rousseau as "he desires to be desired more than he truly desires." Women attempt to increase male desire by withholding sexual favors on the theory that what is reluctantly given is desired more. At the same time, women attempt to temper their own desire through "female modesty." Otherwise their desire would be insatiable and potentially fatal to the men who might attempt to satisfy them. Sexual enslavement of women through female modesty, public opinion, and authority is necessary both for the protection of men and for the required assurance to husbands that they are the biological fathers of the children they support; this point is made by M. J. Sherfey in *The Nature and Evolution of Female Sexuality* (1972). Rousseau goes on to say that women must make men dependent in order to enslave men sexually and equalize the balance of power.

The emergence of permanent dwellings led to the institution of the family, which put an end to the possibility of individual freedom and independence while introducing a definite division of labor. Rousseau maintains that stable habitation leads to family, which leads to the development of agriculture, which encourages the claiming of private property, which results in the establishment of government and a political community.

Schwartz discusses the relevance of the sexual politics of Rousseau as they apply today, incorporating technological considerations and current research on sex and gender differentiation. At times, Schwartz protests too much that Rousseau is innocent of misogyny. Schwartz succeeds at the difficult task of explaining the contradictory philosophies of Rousseau while identifying the link between sexuality and politics and delineating the resulting implications for individuals and society. The excellent notes and author-subject index are an added plus of this work.

L. L. HOYT CROFT
Arizona State University
Phoenix

ECONOMICS

ALPEROVITZ, GAR and JEFF FAUX. *Rebuilding America*. Pp. xi, 321. New York: Pantheon Books, 1984. Paperbound, $10.95.

RIVLIN, ALICE M., ed. *Economic Choices 1984*. pp. xii, 171. Washington, DC: Brookings Institution, 1984. $22.95. Paperbound, $8.95.

In their challenging and thoughtful book, *Rebuilding America*, Gar Alperovitz and Jeff Faux probe deeply into the current politicoeconomic state of American society. What they find is a controlling coalition of big business and big government, whose actions are characterized within the ideological framework of free enterprise but whose *modus operandi* consists of business

dependence on government as achieved through political influence. The term "Broker State" is used to depict this institutional arrangement, which has been demonstrated by the economic rescue of business giants such as Penn Central, Lockheed, and Chrysler as well as by the upward-income-redistribution policies of the Reagan economic program.

The economic problems of the nation are further linked to the failure of both the free-market and Keynesian schools of economic thought to recognize that it is possible to simultaneously contol inflation without creating unemployment. This failure of recognition results in a scenario that is aptly described as the "economics of decline." Alperovitz and Faux offer a policy prescription, based upon the concept of democratic planning, for improving the performance of the American economy. The planning would build upon the conservative premise of economic freedom as well as the liberal premise of economic justice. Planning, of sorts, is said to exist already in the ongoing interaction between big business and big government. It is argued that such planning should be rationalized, so as to represent equally all economic segments of American society.

The thrust of the new policy would pursue a full production—full employment—economy in which all Americans could consume adequate quantities of such necessity goods as food, energy, housing, and health services. A mix of policies, inclusive of an income policy related to the planning effort, would help to attain simultaneously both full employment and stable prices. Emphasis would be placed upon the goal of community full employment at the subnational government level, in coordination with both private-sector and federal government decision-making inputs. This democratically derived planning, based on both individual and community values, would be strategically pinpointed, so as to exert maximum favorable influence without necessitating detailed planning for every segment of the economy. Economically depressed communities would be saved, if feasible, via the in-migration of growth industries.

In *Economic Choices 1984*, edited by Alice Rivlin, the focus is upon the specific problem of large federal structural budget deficits. The book provides a clear analysis of various components of the Reagan economics program, which have resulted in these deficits (Chapter 2). In classifying the deficits as a serious long-run problem, the authors associate themselves with the majority opinion among economists of both conservative and liberal persuasions.

The book, with its 11 contributors—all except one of whom are members of the Brookings Institution staff—offers a credible set of proposals to deal with the structural deficit problem. These encompass a multifaceted set of spending-reduction and tax-increase recommendations, which is appropriate in light of the fact that the problem itself has multiple causes. Moreover, the deficit-reduction decisions are viewed as opportune times to reconsider overall budgetary priorities.

Domestic spending would be constrained, but without further cuts in poverty-relief programs (Chapter 3). Defense spending would also be constrained, but without encroachment upon national security capabilities (Chapter 4). Taxes would be increased through the adoption of a new cash-flow tax on personal and corporate incomes—thus replacing the present allocationally inefficient and distributionally inequitable income tax structure (Chapter 5). The role of the United States in the international economy, as related to the problems of both growing and declining industries, is considered and policies are suggested to assist dislocated workers as well as to facilitate industrial change (Chapter 6). Finally, the growing problem of poverty is assessed, along with proposals to reverse this trend (Chapter 7).

A comparison of the two books reveals both important similarities and differences.

Both books consider current economic problems and provide explicit policy solutions. Both are analytically strong, well documented, and well written. However, the scope and depth of problem analysis is much greater in the Alperovitz-Faux volume. It not only considers the federal structural deficit problem, the exclusive focus of the Rivlin book, but it also takes a close look at the overall institutional process by which economic outcomes are determined in American society. In addition, a major point of contention with contemporary economics is raised when it is argued that "economics *cannot* be value-free."

Finally, the question may be asked whether the recommendations of either book are likely to be adopted. The odds would appear to be especially strong against implementation of the major institutional changes required by the Alperovitz-Faux proposals, despite the relative optimism displayed by the authors. The same politico-economic forces that have allowed the Broker State to thrive are still very much in place. Why should these forces now relinquish their self-rewarding political influence? It would seem that even the much more modest recommendations of the Rivlin book would face major obstacles to adoption. Can it really be expected that advantageous tax loopholes and spending benefits would be voluntarily sacrificed in order to eliminate federal structural deficits? Indeed, a considerable difference exists between policies that might be adopted under a favorable set of political parameters and the policies that will actually be adopted under the existing parameters.

Accordingly, the Broker State seems destined to continue. Moreover, the embedded federal structural deficits will be difficult to reduce.

BERNARD P. HERBER
University of Arizona
Tucson

CORTES, MARILUZ and PETER BOCOCK. *North-South Technology Transfer: A Case Study of Petrochemicals in Latin America.* Pp. viii, 176. Baltimore, MD: Johns Hopkins University Press, 1984. $25.00.

The economics and politics of technology transfer are increasingly at the center of relations between advanced industrialized countries and the developing nations of the Third World. Regrettably, much of the scholarly work on the subject has remained on the surface and has failed to explore the complexities of the process. Economic liberals have assumed that transfers are generally benign and thus have ignored the consequences of economic dependence and the dimensions of political control. Radical writers have often ignored the leverage that receiving countries have in striking technology deals and have viewed northern control over technology as simply a new form of Third World exploitation. Few studies have looked closely at the process of technology transfer in particular industrial sectors in order to assess the motives of suppliers and recipients and to sort out the benefits and costs, both economic and political, on each side.

Mariluz Cortes and Peter Bocock seek this deeper understanding in their case study of technology transfer in the Latin American petrochemical industry. Using data generated by 1976 surveys of 280 plants located in seven Latin American countries, they first sort out the component parts of the successful transfer—planning and design, detailed and basic engineering, procurement and construction, staff training and maintenance services—and review the variety of forms by which technology can be purchased, ranging from highly packaged turnkeys to joint ventures to foreign-owned subsidiaries. Second, they explore the interests and motives of technology suppliers, their most important distinction being between those who provide technology and also produce petrochemicals from those who do not produce chemicals but are licensed to export the hardware and know-how. The data reveal that nonproducers are most active in the export of technology for the production of basic petrochemicals and some intermediates while the chemical producers export technology for final and specialized products as well as some intermediates. The contractual terms preferred by suppliers also vary. Nonproducers prefer turnkey or packaged transfers with little interest in ongoing participation in the foreign enterprise. Producers are less disposed to packaged transfer and frequently seek to participate in foreign production through joint ventures or outright ownership of foreign subsidiaries. The interest of other suppliers such as engineering contractors, equipment suppliers, and financing agencies are also treated.

Attention is then directed to recipient countries. Based on the seven-country sample, it is argued that the interests and leverage of such countries vary widely and are determined by such factors as the history of chemical production in the country, the size of the domestic market, the availability of raw materials, export opportunities, the domestic regulatory framework, the role of public enterprises, and local technological capabilities. Brazil and Mexico, blessed with an abundance of favorable attributes, appear to be best positioned to negotiate favorable terms of transfer, while Chile and Peru are likely to have the greatest difficulty. Argentina, Venezuela, and Colombia occupy the middle ground.

While Cortes and Bocock shy away from decisive conclusions, they do argue that the character of technology agreements in petrochemicals is affected most by the type of product transferred—basic, intermediate, or final—and by circumstances in the recipient country. For this industry, they provide evidence that product maturity is seldom a crucial determinant in the character of contractual agreements, countering the broader claims of product-cycle adherents. They also argue that suppliers show considerable flexibility in meeting recipient-country needs and demands and that such suppliers have become more flexible over time.

This is an important case study that ably provides a much-needed journey through the intricacies and complexities of the technology-transfer process. Two minor reservations should be noted. First, while one applauds Cortes and Bocock's empirical efforts, relying on data compiled almost a decade ago raises questions about trends in the late 1970s and early 1980s. These were years of excess capacity and restructuring in global petrochemical markets that one might expect to have had some impact on the terms and conditions of technology transfer. No effort is made to update the data and address these changes. Second, as frequently happens with case studies, Cortes and Bocock regularly define their analytical objectives too narrowly. At many points, the text serves to do little more than interpret what is contained in the many charts and figures, resulting in rather dry reading. Missing is an effort to place the lessons of this study among broader issues raised by technology transfer, which Cortes and Bocock's careful empirical work certainly entitles them to do.

THOMAS L. ILGEN

Brandeis University
Waltham
Massachusetts

OSBERG, LARS. *Economic Inequality in the United States.* Pp. ix, 307. Armonk, NY: M. E. Sharpe, 1984. $25.00. Paperbound, $13.95.

This book provides a good overview of the issues involved in the study of economic inequality. It is not a book intended for the expert but rather for the interested layperson or student. With its broad-brush approach, it is well suited for use as a text or as supplementary reading for courses dealing with the distribution of income and wealth.

The initial chapters are descriptive, seeking to quantify the degree of economic inequality that exists now and its trends over time. Osberg emphasizes here that choice of definitions and means of measurement may materially affect any conclusions drawn. He looks at a variety of the factors involved, both theoretical and practical, ranging from the inclusiveness of the definition of income, to deficiencies in available data, to the period of time over which economic resources should be measured. Notably, he succeeds in ridding the statistical formulas used to measure inequality of their mystery and demonstrates that no one formula is unequivocally the right one.

Osberg turns from a description of the extent of inequality to a discussion of the theories that attempt to explain its existence. He provides clear exposition of the theories, rendering them accessible to the student, and smoothly integrates the results of empirical efforts in this field into the theoretical discussions.

Osberg looks briefly at the division of income among factor shares, but for the most part he takes the return on capital as given and examines theories that address the determination of labor earnings. He attempts to give various schools of thought a fair hearing; and where he concentrates on one more than another, he acknowledges the fact. Frequent citations and an extensive bibliography provide the reader the means to pursue further a particular interest.

The human capital school of the determination of earnings is one of the most developed, and gets the longest look by Osberg. Here the individual—or the individual's parents—makes decisions on investment in education and training. The rational individual weighs the costs and benefits of the investment: will the return, in terms of increased earnings in the future, be high enough to justify the expense and time spent now? Turning to a structuralist interpretation of earnings determination, Osberg notes that the emphasis here is not on the choices open to the individual but on the constraints he or she faces. The workings of the labor market are seen to be in large part the result of historical and social forces; wage and employment policy are set administratively within the firm and past policies tend to continue; specialization renders on-the-job training more important than more general education, and this is controlled by the firm, not the individual. The labor market may be viewed as segmented: many individuals can gain employment only in the secondary labor market, which employs unskilled labor and where wages are low, nonwage benefits nonexistent, employment unsteady, and working conditions less pleasant than those of the primary market. The segmentation becomes self-enforcing as workers in this secondary market have no incentive or opportunity to develop the traits necessary to gain access to the primary market. Depending on how radical one's view, this segmentation may be seen as the result of technology—the division between capital-intensive and labor-intensive production—or of class conflict.

In Osberg's discussion of the theories, the issue of measurement again comes to the fore. Theories cannot be tested without means of valid measurement. But even more fundamental, he emphasizes, is the explicit recognition of one's theoretical perspective, because the policy prescriptions engendered by different views of the world will also differ. From the structuralist viewpoint, for example, mandated affirmative action may be seen as necessary to break down institutionally set barriers. From the neoclassical, efforts should be directed toward ensuring competition among employers because over time market forces should result in a decrease in discrimination in hiring and promotion. One's perspective affects not only the answers arrived at but also the questions asked.

Some of the students who use this book will go on to be policymakers and analysts. If they retain the lessons Osberg presents—that definition, measurement, and perspective may well have enormous influence on conclusions drawn—the quality of policy analysis and of policy decision making should be improved.

DEBORAH LAREN
University of Michigan
Ann Arbor

WENDLING, WAYNE R. *The Plant Closure Policy Dilemma: Labor, Law and Bargaining.* Pp. xvi, 166. Kalamazoo, MI: W. E. Upjohn Institute for Employment Research, 1984. $16.95. Paperbound, $11.95.

KOCHAN, THOMAS A., HARRY C. KATZ, and NANCY R. MOWER. *Worker Participation and American Unions: Threat or Opportunity?* Pp. viii, 202. Kalamazoo, MI: W. E. Upjohn Institute for Employment Research, 1984. $17.95. Paperbound, $12.95.

In the most recently concluded economic slowdown, the term "concession bargaining" became the euphemism for "givebacks." In that environment, some employers merely dictated terms, unions grew intransigent, and many individuals on both sides suffered. Two recent books deal with the potential effect of collective bargaining on cushioning the impact of economic retrenchment. *The Plant Closure Policy Dilemma* takes a hard, close look at one solution to this retrenchment, while *Worker Participation and American Unions* examines the broader ramifications of using the collective bargaining system as a means to forge the cooperative effort needed to streamline and improve American business.

Wayne R. Wendling, a senior research economist, suggests that collective bargaining may be the most appropriate institution for solving plant closure problems. His essential premise is that the most commonly cited reasons for plant closings—low productivity, high wages, and inflexible work rules—are issues that have been or could be handled through the bargaining process.

The conundrum surrounding the employer's duty to bargain over plant closings is accurately traced from the U.S. Supreme Court's decisions in *Fibreboard Paper Products Corp.* v. *NLRB* through *First National Maintenance Corp.* v. *NLRB*, with proper weight given to dicta and subsequent decisions by the National Labor Relations Board and the federal courts. A review of the case law, according to Wendling, indicates that it may be possible to fashion a per se rule to assign rights in a way that will maximize the production of goods and services and accommodate the social costs of this maximal production. Wendling discusses the most prominent proposals that could be adopted as a per se rule: the Employment-Substitution Rule; the Seven-Point Criteria on Whether Bargaining over Closure Is Mandatory; the Brockway Motors Three-Part Test; and the Rebuttable Presumption Rule. Finding that each requires the cumbersome use of a case-by-case analysis, Wendling proposes his own per se rule: "there is a mandatory duty to bargain over the decision to close a plant or relocate its operation. The key consideration is expeditiously determining when additional bargaining is warranted."

As employers must bargain over the effects of plant closure, Wendling correctly points out, the uncertainties arise in attempting to predict whether alternatives to closing are feasible. If the employer is required to bargain over the decision to close, he reasons, then the union will receive timely notice of the decision and will have an opportunity to explore with the employer all alternatives to closing. This "information" bargaining will ultimately disclose whether "additional bargaining is warranted," according to Wendling. He emphasizes the balance that must be struck between maximizing the production of goods and accommodating the social costs of this production. Where a plant loses its access to a vital natural resource, for example, there would be no likelihood that additional bargaining could alter the facts or produce a socially more productive solution to closing. Wendling proposes a seven-part procedure for determining whether this additional bargaining is warranted. The procedure envisions a bifurcated process: after initial bargaining has occurred, the progress will be reviewed to determine if a solution is likely. If none is likely, further bargaining will not be required in order to meet a good-faith requirement.

Although Wendling's proposal would require an amendment to the National Labor Relations Act and is itself unwieldy, there is much to be said in favor of the substantive provisions concerning timing and injection of the NLRB into the process as a mediator-arbitrator. *Plant Closure* is a well-written, well-researched, and well-executed book. The author, an economist by trade, has subtly, and perhaps inadvertently, encouraged a philosophy that may one day replace the historical role of adversaries in labor relations: the cooperative effort. There is much to commend in this book, not the least of which is its call for cooperation in resolving the plant closure dilemma.

The most obvious, if not most successful, embodiment of this cooperative effort may very well be the quality-of-work-life programs (QWL) that have emerged in recent years. In *Worker Participation and American Unions*, Kochan, Katz, and Mower examine the causes and effects of worker participation programs such as those at Xerox Corporation, Packard Electric, and other companies. The authors' central premise is that "worker participation processes move through several stages of evolution as they unfold." To test the stability of these worker participation experiments, they trace programs through the contract cycle—that is, from the initiation of the experiment to at least one follow-up negotiation of the bargaining contract. Their examination extends to the views of union members and management officials as to the validity of the programs, and whether and how they could be improved.

Five case studies produced mixed reactions to the worker participation program devised at each plant. The authors concede that the existing adversarial relationship probably was the biggest single factor in the way the parties accepted the program:

Each type of experiment is likely to go through periods of enthusiasm followed by skepticism and perhaps even disillusionment and decline. What appears to separate out those cases that survive is an awareness of the need to negotiate a way through problems and conflicts without destroying trust.

Unfortunately, implicit in this statement is that trust exists between the parties. This is not always the case. Furthermore, as a vehicle for establishing trust, the worker participation experiment appears to be an adjunct, rather than a primary tool. In the context of the embattled steel and auto industries, the authors acknowledge that the employers' need for increased productivity and the workers' need for job security have blurred the line between the new experiment and historical collective bargaining. The worker participation programs demand great flexibility on the part of both top management and top union officials, the authors note, and there are few leaders ready to accept the needed changes.

Although worker participation programs have the potential to contribute significantly to the work place, both for employers and employees, the most successful programs involve unions as full partners in the decision-making process, according to the authors. But the bottom line, they advise, is that union leaders need to think strategically about the conditions that must exist for worker participation to be in the interests of their members and the steps needed to link these processes to the union's broader strategies for improving the effectiveness of its bargaining relationship.

Worker Participation is a sober, objective presentation of an idea propounded in *Plant Closure*: cooperative efforts for the benefit of both union and management. Logically, the more desperate the parties, the more limited the options, and the greater is the possibility of cooperation for mutual survival, for example, the avoidance of plant closure. But the broader application of this principle of cooperation—in less desperate situations—makes the parties more suspicious of disrupting the status quo. If *Worker Participation* helps to convince a few people that cooperation can work better than confrontation, then it has served a valuable purpose. Both books are well worth the price of admission.

JOSEPH E. KALET
The Bureau of National Affairs, Inc.
Washington, D.C.

OTHER BOOKS

ABERNATHY, M. GLENN, DILYS M. HILL, and PHIL WILLIAMS. *The Carter Years: The President and Policy Making.* Pp. vii, 227. New York: St. Martin's Press, 1984. $22.50.

BANKS, MICHAEL, ed. *Conflict in World Society: A New Perspective on International Relations.* Pp. xx, 234. New York: St. Martin's Press, 1984. $27.50.

BEICHMAN, ARNOLD. *Herman Wouk: The Novelist as Social Historian.* Pp. 100. New Brunswick, NJ: Transaction Books, 1984. $14.95.

BERGQUIST, CHARLES, ed. *Labor in the Capitalist World-Economy.* Pp. 312. Beverly Hills, CA: Sage Publications, 1984. $28.00. Paperbound, $14.00.

BROWN, HAROLD and LYNN E. DAVIS. *Nuclear Arms Control Choices.* Pp. ix, 55. Boulder, CO: Westview Press, 1984. Paperbound, $8.95.

CHERNENKO, K. U. *K. U. Chernenko: Speeches and Writings.* Pp. xiii, 256. New York: Pergamon Press, 1984. $25.00.

COOK, BLANCHE WIESEN. *The Declassified Eisenhower: A Startling Reappraisal of the Eisenhower Presidency.* Pp. xxx, 432. New York: Viking Penguin, 1984. Paperbound, $8.95.

DAVIDOW, JEFFREY. *A Peace in Southern Africa: The Lancaster House Conference on Rhodesia, 1979.* Pp. 143. Boulder, CO: Westview Press, 1984. $16.75.

DRAGUNSKY, DAVID. *A Soldier's Memoirs.* Pp. 296. Moscow: Progress, 1984. Distributed by Import Publications, Chicago, IL. Paperbound, $4.95.

FALBO, TONI, ed. *The Single-Child Family.* Pp. xv, 304. New York: Guilford Press, 1984. $27.50.

FORSYTHE, DAVID P., ed. *American Foreign Policy in an Uncertain World.* Pp. 575. Lincoln: University of Nebraska Press, 1984. $16.95. Paperbound, $9.95.

FOWKES, BEN. *Communism in Germany under the Weimar Republic.* Pp. xiii, 246.

New York: St. Martin's Press, 1984. $25.50.

FREDERIKSE, JULIE. *None but Ourselves: Masses vs. Media in the Making of Zimbabwe.* Pp. viii, 368. New York: Viking Penguin, 1984. Paperbound, $16.95.

FREY, LINDA, MARSHA FREY, and JOANNE SCHNEIDER, eds. *Women in Western European History.* Pp. lxvi, 1088. Westport, CT: Greenwood Press, 1984. $55.00.

GERZON, MARK. *A Choice of Heroes: The Changing Face of American Manhood.* Pp. viii, 279. Boston: Houghton Mifflin, 1984. Paperbound, $6.95.

GRAEBNER, WILLIAM. *A History of Retirement: The Meaning and Function of an American Institution, 1885-1978.* Pp. x, 293. New Haven, CT: Yale University Press, 1984. Paperbound, $9.95.

GRUBEL, HERBERT G. *The International Monetary System.* Pp. 214. New York: Viking Penguin, 1984. No price.

GUZZETTA, CHARLES, ARTHUR J. KATZ, and RICHARD A. ENGLISH, eds. *Education for Social Work Practice: Selected International Models.* Pp. v, 118. New York: Council on Social Work Education, 1984. No price.

HARDING, HARRY, ed. *China's Foreign Relations in the 1980s.* Pp. xv, 240. New Haven, CT: Yale University Press, 1984. $18.50.

HAYNES, KINGSLEY E. *Gravity and Spatial Interaction Models.* Pp. 88. Beverly Hills, CA: Sage Publications, 1984. Paperbound, $6.50.

HEUSSLER, ROBERT. *Completing a Stewardship: The Malayan Civil Service, 1942-1957.* Pp. xvii, 240. Westport, CT: Greenwood Press, 1983. $37.50.

HILLS, JILL. *Information Technology and Industrial Policy.* Pp. 291. Dover, NH: Croom Helm, 1984. $30.00.

HOLMES, STEPHEN. *Benjamin Constant and the Making of Modern Liberalism.* Pp. vii, 337. New Haven, CT: Yale University Press, 1984. $27.50.

HOLZER, MARC and STUART S. NAGEL, eds. *Productivity and Public Policy.* Pp. 296. Beverly Hills, CA: Sage Publications, 1984. $28.00. Paperbound, $14.00.

HUMANA, CHARLES. *World Human Rights Guide.* Pp. 224. New York: Universe Books, 1984. $20.00.

INTERNATIONAL MONETARY FUND. *Exchange Rate Volatility and World Trade.* Pp. vii, 62. Washington, DC: International Monetary Fund, 1984. Paperbound, $7.50.

JOHNSTON, R. J. and P. CLAVAL, eds. *Geography since the Second World War: An International Survey.* Pp. 290. Totowa, NJ: Barnes & Noble Books, 1984. $27.50.

KEDDIE, NIKKI R., ed. *Religion and Politics in Iran.* Pp. x, 258. New Haven, CT: Yale University Press, 1984. $27.50. Paperbound, $8.95.

KING, LESLIE J. *Central Place Theory.* Pp. 96. Beverly Hills, CA: Sage Publications, 1984. Paperbound, $6.50.

KIRALY, BELA K. *War and Society in East Central Europe.* Vol. 4. Pp. xvii, 651. New York: Brooklyn College Press, 1984. $40.00.

KRIEGEL, ROBERT and MARILYN HARRIS KRIEGEL. *The C Zone: Peak Performance Under Pressure.* Pp. xxi, 142. New York: Doubleday, 1984. $11.95.

LENDER, MARK EDWARD. *Dictionary of American Temperance Biography.* Pp. xiv, 572. Westport, CT: Greenwood Press, 1984. $45.00.

LINDEMANN, ALBERT S. *A History of European Socialism.* Pp. xxi, 385. New Haven, CT: Yale University Press, 1984. $30.00. Paperbound, $12.95.

LITVINOFF, BARNET, ed. *The Letters and Papers of Chaim Weizmann.* Vol. 2. Pp. xxii, 750. New Brunswick, NJ: Transaction Books, 1983. $39.95.

MANDEL, DAVID. *The Petrograd Workers and the Soviet Seizure of Power.* Pp. xv, 447. New York: St. Martin's Press, 1984. $25.00.

MANSFIELD, HARVEY, Jr. *Selected Letters of Edmund Burke.* Pp. ix, 497. Chicago: University of Chicago, 1984. $27.50.

MEMMI, ALBERT. *Dependence.* Pp. viii, 185. Boston: Beacon Press, 1984. $17.95.

MORTIMER, ROBERT A. *The Third World Coalition in International Politics.* 2nd ed. Pp. xii, 194. Boulder, CO: Westview Press, 1984. $22.00. Paperbound, $9.95.

NORE, ELLEN. *Charles A. Beard: An Intellectual Biography.* Pp. xii, 322. Carbondale: Southern Illinois University Press, 1983. $24.95.

OLSON, GARY L. *How the World Works: A Critical Introduction to International Relations.* Pp. vii, 360. Glenview, IL: Scott, Foresman, 1984. Paperbound, $9.95.

PANKOV, YURI, ed. *Political Terrorism: An Indictment of Imperialism.* Pp. 279. Moscow: Progress, 1984. Distributed by Import Publications, Chicago, IL. Paperbound, $3.95.

PEARTON, MAURICE. *Diplomacy, War and Technology since 1830.* Pp. 287. Lawrence: University Press of Kansas, 1984. Paperbound, $9.95.

PLATO and ARISTOPHANES. *Four Texts on Socrates.* Translated by Thomas G. West and Grace Starry West. Pp. 186. Ithaca, NY: Cornell University Press, 1984. $27.50. Paperbound, $4.95.

PRESSMAN, JEFFREY L. and AARON WILDAVSKY. *Implementation.* Pp. xxvi, 281. Berkeley: University of California Press, 1984. $28.50. Paperbound, $6.95.

PURVIS, HOYT and STEVEN J. BAKER, eds. *Legislating Foreign Policy.* Pp. x, 229. Boulder, CO: Westview Press, 1984. $22.00.

RAKOWSKA-HARMSTONE, TERESA, ed. *Communism in Eastern Europe.* Pp. viii, 391. Bloomington: Indiana University Press, 1984. $25.00. Paperbound, $8.95.

ROBSON, R. THAYNE, ed. *Employment and Training R and D: Lessons Learned and Future Directions.* Pp. xxi, 133. Kalamazoo, MI: W. E. Upjohn Institute, 1984. $16.95. Paperbound, $11.95.

ROTH, GUENTHER and WOLFGANG SCHLUCHTER. *Max Weber's Vision of History: Ethics and Methods.* Pp. xii, 211. Berkeley: University of California Press, 1984. Paperbound, $6.95.

SCHEFF, THOMAS J. *Being Mentally Ill: A Sociological Theory.* Pp. xii, 244. Hawthorne, NY: Aldine Publishing, 1984. $24.95. Paperbound, $12.95.

SCHUCK, PETER H. *Suing Government: Citizen Remedies for Official Wrongs.* Pp. xxi, 262. New Haven, CT: Yale University Press, 1984. $30.00. Paperbound, $9.95.

SHAW, MARTIN, ed. *War, State and Society.* Pp. viii, 266. New York: St. Martin's Press, 1984. $25.95.

SMITH, MICHAEL P., ed. *Cities in Transformation: Class, Capital, and the State.* Pp. 263. Beverly Hills, CA: Sage Publications, 1984. $28.00. Paperbound, $14.00.

SOBEL, ROBERT. *The Age of Giant Corporations.* Pp. xiii, 291. Westport, CT: Greenwood Press, 1984. $29.95. Paperbound, $9.95.

STAN, PAUL. *The Social Transformation of American Medicine.* Pp. xiv, 514. New York: Basic Books, 1982. Paperbound, $11.95.

TARCOV, NATHAN. *Locke's Education for Liberty.* Pp. viii, 272. Chicago: University of Chicago Press, 1984. $22.00.

THOMPSON, W.D.J. CARGILL. *The Political Thought of Martin Luther.* Pp. xi, 187. Totowa, NJ: Barnes & Noble Books, 1984. $26.50.

TILL, GEOFFREY. *Maritime Strategy and the Nuclear Age.* 3rd ed. Pp. x, 295. New York: St. Martin's Press, 1984. $30.00. Paperbound, $15.95.

WALKER, R.B.J., ed. *Culture, Ideology, and World Order.* Pp. xii, 365. Boulder, CO: Westview Press, 1984. $25.00. Paperbound, $11.95.

WARREN, SCOTT. *The Emergence of Dialectical Theory: Philosophy and Political Inquiry.* Pp. ix, 262. Chicago: University of Chicago Press, 1984. $26.00. Paperbound, $12.95.

YORK, PHYLLIS, DAVID YORK, and TED WACHTEL. *Toughlove Solutions.* Pp. 216. Garden City, NY: Doubleday, 1984. $13.95.

INDEX

Of Special Interest

CHILDREN AND RACE

by DAVID MILNER, *Social Psychology,*
Polytechnic of Central London

*"The room was all dressed in white. . . . Under the snow-white coverlet,
upon the snow-white pillow lay the most beautiful little girl that Tom
had ever seen. Her cheeks were almost as white as the pillow and her
hair was like threads of gold spread all about the bed. . . . [Tom] stood
staring at her as if she had been an angel out of heaven. . . . Looking
around, he suddenly saw standing close to him a little ugly, black,
ragged figure with bleared eyes and grinning white teeth. He turned on it
angrily. What did such a black ape want in that sweet young lady's
room? It was himself reflected in the great mirror."*

—Charles Kingsley, **The Water Babies**

From classics of English literature and the latest comics, in school and
through contact with their parents before they enter school, children
absorb different messages about their identities and their expectations. In this exceptionally perceptive synthesis of contemporary
research, Milner clarifies how discriminatory attitudes develop during childhood—and the effects of discrimination on Black children.
He describes how racial awareness is instilled in children by differing
home environments, social experiences, and cultural influences such
as books and television. Examining the attitudes, mental welfare, and
education of Black children, he shows how discrimination and prejudice can stunt a child's development . . . and indicates areas where
change is needed to avoid the worst consequences of racial bias.

"A solid, broad, and well-reasoned overview of this critical topic."

—Thomas F. Pettigrew,
University of California, Santa Cruz

CONTENTS: Introduction / 1. Prejudice: A Pre-History / 2. Psychology and
Prejudice / 3. The Socialization of Attitudes and Identity / 4. Culture and
Prejudice / 5. Children's Racial Attitudes / 6. Race and the Black Child / 7. Race
and Education / 8. Education for Equality / Appendix / References / Index

1983 / 264 pages / $20.00 (h) / $9.95 (p)

SAGE PUBLICATIONS, INC.
275 South Beverly Drive
Beverly Hills, California 90212

SAGE PUBLICATIONS LTD
28 Banner Street
London EC1Y 8QE, England

HOOVER INSTITUTION PRESS—SPRING-SUMMER 1985

Afghanistan: The Soviet Invasion in Perspective, revised edition

by Anthony Arnold

First published in 1981, *Afghanistan: The Soviet Invasion in Perspective* traces the pattern of Soviet policies toward its small neighbor since 1919, with emphasis on the events leading up to the 1979 invasion. Alvin Z. Rubenstein said of the first edition, "Excellent . . . the best account," in *Soviet Studies*.

$10.95. August 1 1985. ca. 168 pp. 0-8179-8212-4 paper

A Documentary History of Indian South Africans, 1869-1982

edited by Surendra Bhana and Bridglal Pachai

This selection of documents represents the major themes in Indian South African history, reflecting their unique problems and the general desire to become South Africans: to enjoy the rights and privileges that all citizens, regardless of race and color, should be accorded.

$19.95. February 15 1985. 306 pp. 0-8179-8102-0 paper.

Financial Reform in the 1980s

by Thomas F. Cargill and Gillian Garcia

Since 1979, the American financial system and the conduct of monetary policy have undergone reforms as sweeping as those of the Great Depression, in their effect on the financial system and in the conduct of monetary policy. These reforms of the 1980s are placed in historical context by reviewing the major objectives of financial regulations; the history of American financial reform, beginning in 1776; and the forces for reform that emerged in the 1960s and 1970s.

$19.95. June 14 1985. 212 pp. 0-8179-8131-4
$10.95. June 14 1985. 212 pp. 0-8179-8132-2 paper.

**HOOVER INSTITUTION PRESS
STANFORD UNIVERSITY
STANFORD, CA 94305
(415) 497-3373**
Chargecard orders accepted by telephone.

The Colonial Office and Nigeria, 1898-1914

by John M. Carland

Conventional scholarly wisdom supports the notion that the British Colonial Office did little more than coordinate and review the proposals of other government bodies during the administrative occupation of Africa. Using Nigeria from 1898 to 1914 as a case study, Professor Carland's revisionist work refutes these interpretations.

$26.95. May 15 1985. 240 pp. 0-8179-8141-1.

The Flat Tax

by Robert E. Hall and Alvin Rabushka

In his 1985 State of the Union Address, President Reagan called for tax simplification, calling it a "giant step toward unleashing the tremendous pent-up power of our economy." The tax simplification plan presented in *The Flat Tax* is "radical, yet thoroughly practicable," according to Nobel Laureate Milton Friedman. The Hall-Rabushka plan has one basic principle: "income should be taxed exactly once, as close as possible to the source of that income"; and a corollary: business and individual income taxes must be integrated.

$7.95. February 1 1985. 134 pp. 0-8179-8222-1 paper

Japan and Korea: The Political Dimension

by Chong-Sik Lee

The modern relationship between Japan and Korea is a paradoxical one. The countries are close both geographically and culturally; yet the Japanese and Koreans consistently list each other among their least-liked countries. *Japan and Korea* analyzes the political, psychological, and economic differences that divide these two neighbors with common geopolitical concerns.

$24.95. September 1 1985. ca. 200 pp. 0-8179-8181-8.

USSR Foreign Policies After Detente

by Richard F. Staar

According to V.V. Zagladin, one of Moscow's leading ideologists, the "historic mission" of the USSR has three aspects: to build communism in the USSR, to assist countries already following the communist path, and to support "social progress" toward communism in *all* other countries. Largely based on primary sources in the Russian language, this volume presents the people, policies, and practices of recent Soviet foreign policies.

$26.95 June 7 1985. 327 pp. 0-8179-8171-3.
$10.95 June 7 1985. 327 pp. 0-8179-8172-1 paper.

Yearbook on International Communist Affairs: 1985.

edited by Richard F. Staar

The *Yearbook,* now in its nineteenth consecutive year, continues its complete, authoritative, and timely coverage of communist parties and international front organizations, providing basic data on membership levels, organization, personalities, and domestic and international policies.

"The information is rich, reliable, and concisely presented. No reference or research library concerned with world affairs can afford to be without a copy"—*Current History*

$49.95. July 1 1985. ca. 600 pp. 0-8179-8271-X.

NEW IN PAPERBACK

BERLIN ALERT: The Memoirs and Reports of Truman Smith

by Robert Hessen

. . . A book that is fascinating in every way."—*The Wall Street Journal.*

In 1940, Truman Smith, along with Charles Lindbergh, was denounced as a Nazi sympathizer. These documents will enable readers to form their own judgment about Smith's patriotism and integrity.

$19.95. 1983. 172 pp. 0-8179-7891-7
$9.95. July 1 1985. 172 pp. 0-8179-7892-4 paper.

NEW from Sage

MARRIAGE AND FAMILY ASSESSMENT
A Sourcebook for Family Therapy

edited by ERIK E. FILSINGER, *Center for Family Studies, Arizona State University*

Here are the leading tools and techniques for marriage assessment from the researchers who developed them. And here's why these techniques are valuable for family practice, where they can be found, and what makes them work . . . and how to interpret the results.

In **Marriage and Family Assessment**, leading researchers compare a wide array of scales, inventories, and other proven assessment techniques. They describe the instruments they're associated with, how they can be used in therapeutic settings, what they're designed to measure, evidence for their accuracy and validity as measurements, and how to utilize them with other techniques. Many measures are given in this volume; clear instructions enable readers to obtain the remaining instruments and scoring sheets. This practical sourcebook—which includes case examples demonstrating a variety of applications—successfully bridges the gap between the latest scientific assessment procedures and family practitioners who can use them to improve their practice.

ABRIDGED CONTENTS: Preface / 1. Assessment: What It Is and Why It Is Important E.E. FILSINGER / 2. The Interview in the Assessment of Marital Distress S.N. HAYNES & R.E. CHAVEZ / 3. Capturing Marital Dynamics: Clinical Use of the Inventory of Marital Conflict A. HUDGENS et al. / 4. The Spouse Observation Checklist R.L. WEISS & B.A. PERRY / 5. Marital Interaction Coding System-III R.L. WEISS & K.J. SUMMERS / 6. Couples Interaction Scoring System C.I. NOTARIUS et al. / 7. Behavioral Assessment for Practitioners R.D. CONGER / 8. The Dyadic Adjustment Scale G.B. SPANIER & E.E. FILSINGER / 9. Clinical and Research Applications of the Marital Satisfaction Inventory D.K. SNYDER / 10. The Marital Communication Inventory W.R. SCHUMM et al. / 11. The Marital Agendas Protocol C.I. NOTARIUS & N.A. VANZETTI / 12. Assessing Marital and Premarital Relationships: The PREPARE-ENRICH Inventories D.G. FOURNIER et al. / 13. Clinical Applications of the Family Environment Scale R.H. MOOS & B.S. MOOS / 14. Stress: The Family Inventory of Life Events and Changes H.I. McCUBBIN & J.M. PATTERSON / 15. Family Adaptability and Cohesion Evaluation Scales D.H. OLSON & J. PORTNER / 16. Other Marriage and Family Questionnaires G. MARGOLIN & V. FERNANDEZ

1983 (Sept./Oct.) / 352 pages (tent.) / $29.95 (h)